MANAGING ARTS PROGRAMS IN HEALTHCARE

A growing body of research demonstrates how the arts – including literary, performing, and visual arts as well as architecture and design – can greatly enhance the experience of healthcare, contributing to improved health outcomes, a better patient experience, and lower healthcare costs. This unique book provides an overview of what the arts in healthcare can achieve and how to implement the arts in the most effective manner.

Exploring possibilities for innovative program design and implementation – from healing gardens through public performances to bedside activities – the text draws on examples from a wide range of arts. The book then goes on to look at how programs can be aimed at specific populations and fields, such as children, palliative care, and caregivers.

This comprehensive reference book is an invaluable resource for all those studying or engaged in creating, designing, managing, and evaluating arts in healthcare programs and initiatives.

Patricia Dewey Lambert, PhD, is Associate Professor and Director of the Arts and Administration Program at the University of Oregon, where she also directs the UO Center for Community Arts and Cultural Policy. Patricia's professional experience in Europe and the United States includes positions as a professional musician, arts administrator, artist manager, foundation programs administrator, English teacher, marketing communications consultant, research fellow, and professor. Her main research areas are international cultural policy, cultural development, arts in healthcare, and arts administration education. She has published articles in *Higher Education*, the *International Journal of Arts Management*, the *International Journal of Cultural Policy*, the *Journal of Arts Management, Law, and Society*, and *Studies in Art Education*. Patricia holds a bachelor's degree in vocal performance from Indiana University, master's degrees in international business and arts management, and a PhD in arts education/arts policy and administration. Patricia currently serves as principal investigator for an interdisciplinary Arts in Healthcare Research Consortium based at the University of Oregon, and she oversees a new master's degree concentration area of study in Arts in Healthcare Management, launched in fall 2012 by the UO Arts and Administration Program. She is also currently training to become a certified therapeutic musician as a student in the International Harp Therapy Program.

MANAGING ARTS PROGRAMS IN HEALTHCARE

Edited by Patricia Dewey Lambert

Routledge
Taylor & Francis Group

LONDON AND NEW YORK

First published 2016
by Routledge
2 Park Square, Milton Park, Abingdon, Oxon OX14 4RN

and by Routledge
711 Third Avenue, New York, NY 10017

Routledge is an imprint of the Taylor & Francis Group, an informa business

© 2016 P. Dewey Lambert

British Library Cataloguing-in-Publication Data
A catalogue record for this book is available from the British Library

Library of Congress Cataloging-in-Publication Data
Managing arts programs in healthcare / edited by Patricia
  Dewey Lambert.
    p. ; cm.
  Includes bibliographical references and index.
  I. Lambert, Patricia Dewey, 1969–, editor.
  [DNLM: 1. Art Therapy. 2. Music Therapy. 3. Behavioral
Medicine—methods. WM 450.5.A8]
  RC489.A7
  616.89′1656—dc23
  2015015926

ISBN: 978-1-138-80210-0 (hbk)
ISBN: 978-1-138-80211-7 (pbk)
ISBN: 978-1-315-75442-0 (ebk)

Typeset in Bembo
by Apex CoVantage, LLC

With heartfelt appreciation
for the first generation of leaders
in the arts in healthcare field,
and the founders of the
Society for the Arts in Healthcare.

CONTENTS

FIGURES

TABLES

BOXES

PREFACE

The integration of arts initiatives, activities, and programs in healthcare facilities of all kinds can be seen everywhere. As a growing body of research demonstrates how the arts contribute to the "triple aim" of improved health outcomes, a better patient experience, and lower healthcare costs, healthcare administrators are both encouraging and financially supporting arts programming in their institutions. And, in an era of turbulent healthcare reform in the United States, hospitals are welcoming the competitive advantage and community engagement opportunities that arts programming and partnerships can provide. These arts-based initiatives manifest as a wide array of aesthetic design choices, healthcare settings that provide a sense of wellbeing, and passive or active encounters with visual and performing artists. As this book illustrates, many extraordinary arts programs exist to benefit patients, patients' families, medical staff, and the community at large.

But with so many healthcare institutions now offering vibrant arts initiatives in their facilities, who is managing these programs, and what do these leaders need to know to effectively and efficiently do their jobs? At present, educational resources for professional managers of the arts in healthcare settings are virtually non-existent. This gap is striking when one considers that about half of America's healthcare institutions report having arts in healthcare programming. There is ever-increasing need for trained specialists to professionally manage organizational policies and practices involving activities such as visual art exhibits, public performances, bedside arts activities, and arts programs for medical staff.

When I started exploring the development of a new graduate-level specialization in Arts in Healthcare Management within a well-established Arts Management program, I knew little of the history, scope, and depth of this field. Over the past five years, it has become increasingly clear to me that the arts in healthcare field is growing dramatically, and urgently requires that entrepreneurial leaders build their capacity to conceptualize, design, implement, and evaluate arts programs in healthcare settings. This book, the first of its kind to focus on professional leadership and management of arts programs in healthcare settings, will hopefully pave the way for additional resources to emerge in the coming years.

In entering this new terrain, I found myself welcomed with open arms by the established leaders in the field, who have gathered annually at meetings of the Society for the Arts in Healthcare since 1991. More recently, this professional association was renamed the Global Alliance for Arts & Health, and then the Arts & Health Alliance, but the organization has retained the same core group of members throughout its life cycle. At the time of this writing, this professional association is once again restructuring. In my view, this represents the transition to young adulthood in the life cycle of this field, as arts programs within healthcare become increasingly mainstreamed and expected as part of patient-centered care and caregiver support services. It is indeed an exciting time to get involved in educating current and future leaders to harness the power of the arts to transform the healthcare experience.

A glance through the list of chapter titles on the contents pages will provide an overview of the scope of the professional field to be discussed throughout the book, and the first chapter presents a concise introduction to the field as a whole. In considering the relationship between arts and health, you will immediately notice a significant gap in this publication: the well-established creative arts therapies are not specifically addressed in any of the chapters. The reason for this is that the creative arts therapies (music therapy, art therapy, drama therapy, and so on) have existed for decades within a highly professionalized system of education, certification, and accreditation. The arts in healthcare side of the field – the focus of this book as introduced in Chapter 1 – encompasses a much broader range of activities, and is in a very early stage of professionalization. Many excellent publications on the creative arts therapies already exist, and this book project is specifically delimited to focus on the "other" areas of engagement in the very large arts and health field.

Another conscious choice for this book project has been to focus solely on the arts in healthcare field in the United States. While the contributing authors sometimes reference international examples, and we are all aware that this field is very active internationally, it made sense for this first book project on this topic to focus only on arts programs within the complexity of the healthcare system in the United States. This provides you with an overview of opportunities for program development within the field as a whole, without shifting the underlying societal and policy framework chapter by chapter to reflect diverse national systems. That said, it would be wonderful to develop international book projects on this topic in the future!

I initiated this book project in fall 2013 to be a "team effort" among leading scholars and practitioners in the arts in healthcare field. Along the way, writing and editing sub-groups were established to provide input to each other in drafting initial chapters, and the contributing authors had the opportunity to provide feedback to each other on all the chapters in winter 2015. The result is a sequence of chapters that complement each other to provide a full overview of the landscape of what's involved in managing arts programs in healthcare.

The concepts, strategies, approaches, tools, and examples offered by the authors provide breadth rather than depth on the topics contained within these pages, but references listed by the authors will point you toward further sources of information. This book offers you an overview of the arts in healthcare field that we hope will stimulate thought, research, and praxis to further propel advancement and professionalization of arts programs in healthcare settings.

Patricia Dewey Lambert

ACKNOWLEDGMENTS

I wish to thank the contributors to this book, both for their pioneering leadership in the arts in healthcare field, and for their willingness to pass on their expertise and knowledge to others. Special appreciation goes to Jill Sonke and Elaine Sims for their assistance in the initial conceptualization of the project and identification of prospective authors, and to Judy Rollins for the extensive writing and editing guidance that she provided to many of the authors.

My faculty, staff, and student colleagues have provided tremendous support in both establishing a new graduate concentration in Arts in Healthcare Management, and in developing related projects, such as this book manuscript. The members of the Oregon Arts in Healthcare Research Consortium (OAHRC) have been wonderful partners in our program and research development initiatives. I am especially indebted to Tina Rinaldi, managing director of the UO Arts and Administration Program and Center for Community Arts and Cultural Policy, for her partnership in exploring, shaping, establishing, and nurturing the new arts in healthcare management field of study. I would also like to express my heartfelt gratitude to Meredith Wong, a graduate fellow who assisted greatly in coordinating the manuscript development in winter and spring 2015, in addition to supporting the work of the OAHRC from fall 2013 through spring 2015. Several additional graduate students played important roles in developing this project: Jaime Galli, Stephanie McCarthy, Brendan Ostlund, Nori Rice, Alex Richardson, Emily Saunders, and Jay Shepherd.

I am sincerely grateful to the funders who have provided support to this book project either directly or indirectly over the past four years: The University of Oregon (UO) Office of Research, Innovation, and Graduate Education "Incubating Interdisciplinary Initiatives" (I3) Award, the UO "Innovations in Graduate Education" Award, a Society for the Arts in Healthcare "ArtHealth Solutions" Consulting Grant, as well as additional support from the UO's Arts and Administration Program, Center for Community Arts and Cultural Policy, and School of Architecture and Allied Arts.

PART 1

Understanding the arts in healthcare field

1

INTRODUCING THE ARTS IN HEALTHCARE FIELD

Patricia Dewey Lambert, Judy Rollins, Jill Sonke, and Randy Cohen

As the field of arts in healthcare expands, there is a growing need for professionalization of arts programs in healthcare settings. Arts in healthcare programs have professionalized to a point where they increasingly require strong leadership and management, and an ever-increasing demand exists for trained specialists to manage organizational policies and practices involving activities such as visual art exhibits, in-hospital performances, bedside art activities, and arts activities for medical staff. In fact, survey findings published several years ago revealed that approximately half of the accredited healthcare institutions in the United States offer arts programs (State of the Field Committee, 2009). In addition, as hospitals and healthcare centers increasingly become engaged in their communities as sites devoted to advancing quality of life, arts programming broadens beyond the immediate institutional walls. It may be inferred that healthcare environments will continue to become part of the fabric of community arts and culture engagement. The demand for professional administrators in the arts in healthcare field will continue to grow, especially as the aging baby boomer population increasingly demands high quality healthcare services. This chapter provides an overview of the arts in healthcare field in the United States, and introduces *Managing Arts Programs in Healthcare.*

According to the *2009 State of the Field Report: Arts in Healthcare:*

> Arts in healthcare is steadily moving forward. Increasingly, healthcare administrators are not only welcoming but also financially supporting arts programming in their institutions. Medical and nursing schools see the value in incorporating arts in healthcare courses or content to help their students develop their observation, communication, and other essential skills. Arts institutions, schools, and colleges are partnering with healthcare organizations to provide arts programming and health promotion experiences in community settings. Architects and designers are creating healthcare

institutions that are not only beautiful, but are also built upon a solid foundation of evidence about what supports safe delivery of care and provides the most positive outcomes for patients, families, and staff.

. . . With the launch of the Society for the Arts in Healthcare's journal, *Arts & Health: An International Journal for Research, Policy and Practice*, a true sense of professionalism is settling in. Professionalism is also reflected by organizations and institutions of higher education's development of coursework to prepare individuals to provide safe and effective arts in healthcare services. Beginnings of certification and accreditation are in the air.

(p. 25)

Professionalization of the arts in healthcare field, however, requires professionalization of artists in healthcare, arts therapists, and administrators to advance the field. While the Creative Arts Therapies have had accreditation and certification mechanisms in place for a long time, the broader arts in healthcare field – which is the focus of this book – is in a very early stage of professionalization.

This chapter introduces the arts in healthcare field by providing an overview of the evolution of the field and discussing the role of the arts in current and emerging healthcare administration trends. The chapter presents the breadth and scope of arts in healthcare programs and initiatives, and provides a typology of these programs. The chapter concludes by introducing the structure and content of this book.

Evolution of the arts in healthcare field in the United States

As argued by Sonke, Rollins, Brandman, and Graham-Pole (2009), "The primary purpose of arts in healthcare is to use creative activities to lessen human suffering and to promote health, in the broadest sense of the word" (p. 107). According to the website of the former Arts & Health Alliance (also formerly known as the Society for the Arts in Healthcare), "Arts in healthcare is a diverse, multidisciplinary field dedicated to transforming the healthcare experience by connecting people with the power of the arts at key moments in their lives. This rapidly growing field integrates the arts, including literary, performing, and visual arts and design, into a wide variety of healthcare and community settings for therapeutic, educational, and expressive purposes." This professional association suggests that the field of arts and health has five areas of focus, comprising patient care, healing environments, caring for caregivers, community wellbeing, and education. It follows that the emerging professional field of arts in healthcare management involves a broad range of institutions, individuals, and activities. Professionals in this field work in settings as diverse as hospitals, hospices, assisted living facilities, long-term care facilities, rehabilitation treatment centers, special needs camps, cancer care programs, VA facilities, military bases, prisons, and community centers.

The history of the relationship between arts and health has existed across cultures from the beginning of recorded time (Sonke-Henderson, 2007). Thousands of years ago, the Greeks anointed Apollo as the god of both music and healing.

Contemporary practice in the creative arts therapies began in the 1940s. The founding of the Society for the Arts in Healthcare (SAH) in 1991 marked the beginnings of formal recognition of the role of the arts in modern healthcare settings. The Society was rebranded as the Global Alliance for Arts and Health in 2012, then again rebranded as the Arts and Health Alliance in 2014. As discussed in Chapter 2 of this book, this professional association was ultimately dissolved in 2014 and, at the time of this writing, transitional steps to a new associational structure are currently underway. In the twenty-three years of its leadership to the field, however, this association and its membership represented significant strides underway in field-building throughout the past quarter century.

With the rise of holistic – or "whole-person" – healthcare in an era of significant healthcare reform, the patient's experience is now of paramount importance. *Holistic healthcare* (sometimes called "integrative medicine") considers the patient's physical, mental, emotional, and spiritual dimensions and needs (Thornton, 2013). In America's state-of-the-art hospitals, design for the patient experience is an articulated priority, and the role of the arts in contributing to a caring environment of healing has begun to change the face of the business of healthcare. Hospital administrators are increasingly seeking to give patients a voice in their healing process, and standardized Press Ganey surveys are used by hospitals to continually assess their competitive advantage in important measures of patient satisfaction with and perceptions of their healthcare experience. As argued by Gerteis, Edgman-Levitan, Daley, and Delbanco (1993), "Quality in health and medical care has two dimensions: one is objective, technical; the other is subjective and qualitative. However dazzling the technological achievements of medical science over the last fifty years, the patient's experience of illness and medical care is at the heart of the first purpose of clinical medicine – to relieve human suffering" (p. 2).

Three significant movements in recent decades of healthcare reform are crucial for arts in healthcare leaders to consider: the rise of healthcare consumerism, increasing public demands for patient-centered care, and the so-called "Triple Aim" of healthcare. Healthcare consumerism has risen rapidly due to readily available information on health-related topics as well as comparative healthcare quality data. In addition, new business models of healthcare require individuals to pay more out of their own pockets, which has increased patients' scrutiny of their healthcare decisions and new demands for improved value and service. Second, today's educated healthcare consumers are driving a patient-centered transformation in healthcare (Frampton, 2009). *Patient-centered care* is essentially "taking an approach to healthcare that consciously adopts the patient's perspective" (Gerteis et al., 1993, p. 5). A model of patient-centered care, exemplified by the Planetree model of healthcare, has led to a mainstream movement of healthcare facilities responding to consumer demands and improving care delivery systems to deliver the most sophisticated technical care in a more personalized, humanized, and demystified manner (Frampton, 2009). The third movement, the Institute for Healthcare Improvement's initiative called the "Triple Aim," is an approach to optimizing health system performance simultaneously along three dimensions: improving the patient experience of care, improving the health of populations, and reducing the per capita cost of healthcare (Berwick, Nolan, & Whittington, 2008; Bisognano & Kenney, 2012).

In light of these movements across the American healthcare system, the arts have an opportunity to increasingly play an important role in meeting new demands of healthcare consumerism, providing patient-centered care, and pursuing the three goals of the Triple Aim. As Susan Perlstein explained as early as 1999, a comprehensive healthcare system must include the arts in order to treat human beings, and not just diseases: "The arts provide preventative and integrative approaches to healthcare, building self-esteem and a sense of identity and belonging, connecting people and celebrating life. All these things are part of an individual's healing process" (p. 2). In 2007, John Graham-Pole suggested that the arts in healthcare field as well as the creative arts therapies were becoming established in three areas of modern Western healthcare: clinical practice, education, and research. Graham-Pole argues that the application of the arts to clinical medicine takes place in two spheres, that of the physical environment of healthcare facilities, and that of the involvement of patients in the creative process. In management of arts in healthcare, these two spheres are identified as the *environmental arts* and as the *participatory arts*. A focus on the healthcare environment includes elements such as architecture, design, visual art collections, and performances in public spaces to improve the experience of being in the healthcare facility. A focus on participatory arts includes active or passive engagement in arts creation by patients, family members, and professional caregivers to enhance emotional wellbeing, self-expression, self-esteem, and autonomy (Graham-Pole, 2007, pp. 7–9).

The arts in healthcare movement (also often termed the arts-for-health movement) has grown dramatically since the late 1990s as information about existing program models, strategies, and approaches has become more accessible. The field continues to expand beyond hospital and hospice settings: "Arts in health models are perhaps equally present in venues outside of hospitals to aid in recovering health on a physical, mental/emotional, and/or spiritual level from a plethora of challenges: substance abuse, disaster relief, preventative programs, arts for disabilities, support for those living with limiting or life-altering conditions, and probably new applications being developed at this instant" (Brandman, 2007, p. 60). As the field continues to grow, new arts management practices will be needed to proactively meet growing demand for these programs. References are beginning to emerge – such as *Transforming the Healthcare Experience through the Arts* by Blair Sadler and Annette Ridenour (2009) – that share model programs and leadership practices in arts in healthcare. However, a dearth of informational resources persists, and an urgent need exists for professional development of those holding the responsibility for conceptualizing, designing, implementing, and evaluating arts programs in healthcare settings.

The organic growth of the arts in healthcare movement

One might envision growth in the arts in healthcare field to be much like a sturdy oak tree (see Figure 1.1). Nourishing the roots of the arts in healthcare movement

FIGURE 1.1 Growth in the Arts in Healthcare Field

Illustration by Stephanie McCarthy

are three proven objectives driving development of successful programs. Janice Palmer (2001) frames these as three simple and basic tenets: *bring beauty into the space around us; celebrate community*; and *touch the spirit*. These three objectives are firmly rooted in fundamental concepts of aesthetics and creativity, and in the goal to promote quality of life. Growing from these three objectives is the trunk of the tree, which can be named "Arts & Health." To take this metaphor a step further, one could imagine some squirrels under the shade of this large, leafy tree – and able to access any of the branches of the tree – as representing diverse arts in healthcare programs' beneficiaries. These squirrels (the beneficiaries of arts in healthcare programs) would be able to gather the "acorns" of arts initiatives and activities to help nourish their health and wellbeing. And taking this metaphor even further, this sturdy tree would need to be consistently "fertilized" by support mechanisms provided through funding, policy, research, advocacy, and education.

The associational infrastructure that provides a "growth medium" for the Arts & Health Tree is discussed in detail in Chapter 2 of this book (see Figure 2.3, in particular).

The first major branch of the tree is that of *creative arts therapies*, which includes the related field of *expressive therapies*. This major branch extends outward to include the distinct professional fields of music therapy, art therapy, drama therapy, dance/movement therapy, and poetry therapy. While the field of arts and health includes the creative art therapies, the focus of this book is on the other three main branches of the tree: *environmental arts*, *participatory arts*, and *arts for caregivers*. Whereas the creative arts therapies are focused on distinct medical outcomes for patients, the purposes of the other areas of arts in healthcare settings aim to assist in promoting the general wellbeing of patients, patients' families and friends, medical staff and other caregivers, and the general public as members of the community.

Internationally, the creative arts therapies (a very closely related field is the *expressive therapies*) have a long and well-documented history. Creative Arts Therapy is defined on the website of the National Coalition of Creative Arts Therapies (NCCTA) as "[the use of] arts modalities and creative processes for the purpose of ameliorating disability and illness and optimizing health and wellness." Establishment of professional associations in music, dance, drama, poetry, and visual arts therapies took place in the second half of the twentieth century. "Each of these disciplines has defined training standards, including credentialing and monitoring, and each shares the goals of integrating psychological, physical, and social functioning and well-being" (Sonke et al., 2009, p. 108). Arts programs in healthcare settings and the creative arts therapies are both important elements of a holistic healthcare field, but it is necessary to understand the distinction between these two professional fields. However, these fields frequently overlap, and programs exist where creative arts therapists and artists in healthcare work together and complement each other. Artists in healthcare "are careful, however, to avoid any claim to formal diagnostic or therapeutic credentialing, but rather seek to offer individual and communal healing in a broadly holistic sense and to create more aesthetic environments for givers and receivers of care" (Sonke et al., 2009, p. 108).

The two professional fields of engagement – creative arts therapy and arts in healthcare – can be grouped together in the overarching field of creative therapy, positioned along a continuum of practice (see Figure 1.2). *Creative therapy* is defined by Warren (2008) as "the use of the arts . . . and other creative processes to promote health and encourage healing. Implied in this working definition is the use of artistic and creative activities to help individuals accommodate to a specific disability; or recover from a specific medical or surgical procedure; or simply improve the quality of an individual's life" (p. 3). While this broad definition of creative therapy may be technically correct, because the term "therapy" is interpreted in a variety of ways, the distinctions and boundaries within the Arts and Health field require more precise terminology.

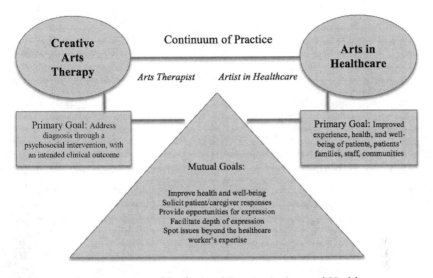

FIGURE 1.2 The Continuum of Professional Practice in Arts and Health

Even in 2008, when he developed the all-encompassing *creative therapy* term, Warren noted that two distinct professional fields exist:

> Over the past 25 years there has been a rise in the use of the arts therapies in healthcare and with it a concomitance to professionalism and organizations to promote it. Parallel to this there has been an upsurge in the role of the arts and artists in healthcare settings and organizations dedicated to their work. . . . Nevertheless, many professional artists and arts therapists not only work amicably shoulder to shoulder in the same healthcare structure, but are also members of organizations representing both approaches to the work.
>
> (p. 4)

The focus of *Managing Arts Programs in Healthcare* is on the "environmental" side of the continuum illustrated in Figure 1.2. Referring back to Figure 1.1, this side of the continuum of professional practice in the field manifests as the main branches of the tree named *environmental arts*, *participatory arts*, and *arts for caregivers*. The practitioner's professional title in the "environmental" side of the field is *artist in healthcare*, *arts/music/drama practitioner in healthcare*, *artist in residence*, or simply *artist*. Only on the Creative Arts Therapy side of the continuum does the professional title *arts/music/drama therapist* exist. A significant challenge in the management of arts programs in healthcare settings is to understand the differences in the professional qualifications of artists working in the facility, in order to most appropriately and effectively allocate personnel resources in implementing arts in healthcare programs.

With reference again to Figure 1.1, the second major branch of the Arts & Health Tree is that of *environmental arts*. This branch includes architecture and design for healthcare facilities, healing gardens, and arts displays. The large field of architecture and design for healthcare environments addresses the interior and exterior of the facility, including many specialization foci such as evidence-based design, patient-centered design of hospital rooms, and wayfinding. All members of the healthcare community benefit from healing gardens that may be located in diverse locations of the facility, such as courtyards, rooftops, and landscaping. In addition to being locations for patients and their caregivers to escape a stressful environment, healing gardens can serve as sites for individual and group arts programs and creative arts therapies. A permanent display of art in a healthcare setting is one of the most common arts in healthcare programs, and often this display includes commissioned paintings or sculptures. Many hospitals also have rotating exhibits of art (professional artists, patients' art, staff art), which can also serve as an exhibit of great interest to community members. Frequently, all members of the healthcare setting's community also have the opportunity to attend performances in lobbies and other public spaces. Many of these performances are instrumental, but performances can also include storytellers, choral performances, theatrical pieces, clowns, and many other types of performing arts. Performances in public spaces can be part of the branches of environmental arts, participatory arts, or arts for caregivers. In fact, there are several hospitals where the staff deliver the arts experience, such as the medical staff who play instruments in the Life Sciences Orchestra of the University of Michigan Health System.

The arts in healthcare *participatory arts* branch focuses on a range of bedside activities, performances in public spaces such as lobbies and waiting rooms, and a wide array of collaborations with the local community. Bedside activities are often a major emphasis of arts programs in healthcare, and many organizations have "art carts" as well as performing artists that make the rounds to patients. Such activities include music (listening and interactive), dance and movement, arts and crafts activities, storytelling and drama, and bedside writing activities for patients and their families. In some healthcare settings, an "art cart" containing poster art is brought to patients so that they may select a visual image to view on their hospital room wall. Interestingly, when offered artwork for their hospital room walls, patients may often decline. Professionals actually see even the act of saying "no" as positive as it is an empowering experience for patients who rarely get the opportunity to say no to anything. In addition to private engagement with art in hospital rooms, patients (and their caregivers) may also engage with visual arts and crafts as well as performances in group settings. In performances and arts activities in public spaces, community collaboration opportunities will likely expand, as potential project partners continue to get involved in the arts in healthcare movement. Key community collaborators in this field can be identified as local artists, local arts organizations, university faculty members, and students.

Numerous arts programs exist that are designed to care for the caregiver. The *arts for caregivers* branch of the field focuses on professional medical staff, paraprofessional caregivers, and informal/family caregivers. A diverse range of arts programs are structured to benefit medical staff members, such as carts with artwork that are brought to staff offices and gathering spaces; staff choirs and orchestras; staff theatre, dance or other performance groups; staff book clubs; as well as creative writing, crafts, or other arts activities for staff. Anecdotal evidence also suggests that staff members often eagerly attend performances in public spaces and greatly enjoy permanent and rotating art displays in the facility. A special emphasis of this branch includes arts programs designed to train medical students and staff.

The need for arts in healthcare management

It is evident from the overview of the arts in healthcare field provided above that professionalization of arts programs, services, and activities provided in healthcare settings involves managerial oversight of many more responsibility areas than may be evident at first glance. Arts in healthcare has grown organically over the years, resulting in a broad range of activities designed to benefit patients, patients' families, medical staff, caregivers, medical and nursing students, and the community. A typology of existing arts programs, services, and activities provided in healthcare settings is provided in Table 1.1. In this chart, one sees major types and subtypes of arts programs in a hospital setting along with an indication of targeted audiences to be served by the program.

From this basic typology of arts in healthcare programs and activities, it is clear that administrators responsible for such programs must possess the ability to work with a wide range of artistic fields, community collaborators, medical personnel, and patients and family members. Arts fields extend from instrumental and vocal music, to visual arts, to creative writing, to dance, to the theatrical arts. In working with healthcare consultants, architects, and designers, arts in healthcare administrators can play a key role in informing the creation of "healing environments." Manifold opportunities exist for partnerships and collaboration with local artists, local arts organizations, university faculty, and university students. In their work, arts in healthcare managers are often the lone pipeline of communication between healthcare facility administration and local arts professionals. And, medical students as well as medical staff are not forgotten in the role of the arts in "caring for the caregiver" – many strong programs connecting the arts with medical personnel already exist.

Overview of this book

Managing Arts Programs in Healthcare is written for anyone interested in creating arts programs in healthcare settings, or improving such programs that already exist. The goal of this book project has been to gather the collective insights and experiences from leading arts in healthcare scholars and practitioners from across the United States in one accessible reference book that will serve to educate university students and healthcare practitioners in this high-growth field. It has

TABLE 1.1 Types of Arts Programs, Services, and Activities in Healthcare

Type	*Sub-type(s)*	*Intended Audience(s)*			
		Patients	*Families*	*Staff*	*Community*
Creative Arts Therapies	Music Therapy Art Therapy Dance/Movement Therapy Drama Therapy Poetry Therapy/Bibliotherapy Intermodal/Other	X	X		X
Art Displays	Permanent displays of art on walls Commissioned artwork Rotating exhibits	X	X	X	X
Performances in Public Spaces	Music performances Storytellers and theatre pieces Other	X	X	X	X
Bedside Activities	Bedside music Bedside arts Bedside dance Bedside drama Bedside writing Carts with poster art Carts with artmaking kits/ projects	X	X		
Healing Gardens	Landscaping Courtyards Rooftops	X	X	X	X
Staff Programs	Carts with artwork (posters) Carts with artmaking kits/ projects Orchestra, chorus, music group Theatre, dance, performance group Book club Creative writing Arts in medicine training programs			X	X

been written to address the needs of professionals in multiple fields, including arts management, healthcare administration, architecture and design, arts therapy, and nursing. Written for a wide audience of students and professionals interested in this field, *Managing Arts Programs in Healthcare* is the first reference book of its kind to focus on professional leadership and management of arts programs and initiatives in healthcare settings. The chapters of this book include a solid theoretical foundation, and also include impressive and inspiring real-world examples and case studies of effective management of arts in healthcare programs. As such, readers will find treatment of the topic of managing arts programs in healthcare to be both conceptual and practical.

For purposes of clearly framing the scope of this book, the authors focus solely on healthcare institutions in the United States. The professional field of arts in healthcare is also large internationally, and it is hoped that an international version of this book will be a future project.

Congruent with the introduction to the arts in healthcare field presented in this first chapter, this book is divided into five parts: (1) Understanding the arts in healthcare field; (2) Managing environmental arts in healthcare programs and initiatives; (3) Managing participatory arts in healthcare programs; (4) Managing arts in healthcare programs for special populations; and (5) Managing arts in healthcare programs for caregivers.

The first part of the book, **Understanding the arts in healthcare field**, provides crucial background information regarding the evolution, scope, scale, structure, and current trends evident in the field as a whole. Building on the foundation provided in this first chapter of the book, Chapter 2 provides a geographic and organizational mapping of the field, and Chapter 3 offers insight into ongoing processes of professionalization currently underway.

In Chapter 2, **Mapping the arts in healthcare field**, Katie White introduces the first comprehensive geographical map of the field in the United States through the PlaceStories online map and community that she has created. The intent in launching this project was to conduct comprehensive research on the arts in healthcare programs and resources in existence throughout the country, provide information on program typology, geographic concentrations, and growth trends, and create an interactive geographical map in an accessible online format that facilitates user contributions and the sharing of information. Her chapter discusses the online map, the data gathered during the mapping process, and the potential for this networking tool to serve as a resource for organizations and practitioners. White also provides a map of the associational infrastructure of the field, focusing on structure, relationships, functions, and outcomes.

In Chapter 3, **Professionalizing the arts in healthcare field**, Jill Sonke discusses how the arts in healthcare field has emerged over the past three decades from its start as a grassroots movement dedicated to humanizing the experience of healthcare to a defined professional field that engages the arts to enhance individual and population health as well as the healthcare system and delivery of care. The arts in healthcare field has grown rapidly, leading to significant challenges today as it approaches the major hurdles of professionalization, including certification and development of a code of ethics and standards of practice. In Chapter 3, Sonke addresses key challenges and opportunities for the field, including its definition and identity, credentialing and certification, training, scope and standards of practice, and employment opportunities. She provides considerable insight into the knowledge areas, skills, and abilities required by professional artists in healthcare, as well as by the professional administrators who manage arts programs in healthcare.

The second part of this book, **Managing environmental arts in health-care programs and initiatives**, addresses program design and implementation of arts programs focused on creating an "environment of healing" in healthcare facilities. The contributing authors in Part 2 illuminate management theories and practices crucial to integrating arts planning into healthcare design, to developing healing gardens, to managing visual art collections in healthcare facilities, and to managing exhibit galleries in healthcare facilities.

In Chapter 4, **Integrating arts planning into healthcare design**, Misty Chambers provides a holistic approach to healthcare design in which the arts are integrated with architecture to address the needs of patients, their families, visitors, and caregivers. She describes key elements that need to be addressed during the design process, including: creating unique visual art opportunities and venues for performing arts, communicating, and coordinating details. Chambers explains that integration of the arts into the planning, design, and construction of a healthcare setting provides the environmental canvas to support healing of the whole person, and it is through this integrated canvas that the built physical environment has the most positive impact.

Annette Ridenour's Chapter 5, titled **Healing gardens**, argues that when art is carefully incorporated into the design of healing gardens, it substantially amplifies the physical, psychological, and spiritual gains for those who use the gardens – patients, visitors, staff, and others. Ridenour suggests that all elements of a garden's design can and should be viewed as art – that walkways, furniture, walls, gates, and other elements are as much part of the art aesthetic of the garden as are such items as sculptures, fountains, and murals. She articulates how successful management of healing-garden art projects requires the establishment of appropriate leadership structures and procedures; effective management of the overall design process; skillful selection, retention, and oversight of artists; wise budgeting; and thoroughgoing evaluation.

Chapter 6, **Managing art collections in healthcare environments**, focuses on how healing art collections (visual arts collections) are defined, built, managed, and funded. Donna Glassford's main argument in this chapter is that a well-structured healing art collection and program can comfort patients, enhance healing, and improve medical outcomes. The major portion of this chapter presents a descriptive, step-by-step guide for establishing and maintaining healing art collections (mission, vision, policy) to managing the collection (funding, art acquisition, curatorial and installation requirements, and care of the collection). Glassford emphasizes planning and practical considerations that are key to achieving the healing benefits of a successful visual arts collection and program.

Closely related to Glassford's chapter is Elaine Sims' contribution on **Exhibit galleries in healthcare facilities**. In Chapter 7, Sims argues that the visual arts have found a receptive home in medical facilities, where they play an important role by enhancing the environment of care in order to help comfort, distract, and normalize what are often experienced as overwhelming and frightening places. In addition to maintaining permanent art collections, some hospital arts programs also include exhibition galleries of rotating art shows. These galleries may augment a permanent collection, or they may provide a more affordable way for a hospital to display art. This chapter provides a comprehensive look at all aspects of running exhibition programs in healthcare today.

Indeed, throughout the world, healthcare facilities of every kind are being transformed by the arts. The field of arts in healthcare is providing new professional opportunities for fine and performing artists, and healthcare settings are, in many areas, becoming community cultural centers of the twenty-first century as they host arts activities and performances. Moving away from a focus on environmental arts in healthcare programs, Part 3 of this book focuses on **Managing participatory arts in healthcare programs**. While there is significant overlap between environmental and participatory arts initiatives and activities, the three chapters included in Part 3 specifically address key management strategies and approaches involved in overseeing performances in public spaces, developing bedside arts activities, and evaluating arts in healthcare programs.

In Chapter 8, **Performances in public spaces**, Jill Sonke discusses how presentation of the performing arts in healthcare settings brings particular challenges and requires a significant level of consideration, planning, and oversight. The chapter presents general concepts that program planners can benefit from understanding, and addresses specific topics, including: developing performance protocols; selecting, preparing, and supporting artists; selecting appropriate venues within healthcare facilities; developing partnerships between performing arts presenters and healthcare organizations; and the importance of artistic excellence in healthcare settings. This chapter focuses solely on overseeing performing arts activities in public settings (such as lobbies and waiting rooms) within the healthcare environment.

In contrast, Chapter 9 provides a comprehensive introduction to designing and implementing **Bedside arts activities**. Judy Rollins notes that many hospital patients cannot or prefer not to leave their hospital room. As a result, today's hospital artists-in-residence (AIRs) are finding that to meet the needs of their patient population, a greater percentage of their time is spent conducting activities directly at the bedside. This chapter discusses the work of bedside artists-in-residence, who they are, and what they do to meet the needs of the lone patient in the single-occupancy room. Rollins also presents considerations for working effectively in this intimate setting.

Evaluation of arts in healthcare programs is imperative, and Chapter 10 of this book provides a useful resource for arts in healthcare program administrators and managers who want to learn how to implement basic program evaluation strategies. In **Evaluating the arts in healthcare program: building a story about the program's activities, paths to improvement, and achievements**, Jana Kay Slater uses a participatory arts-based health education program for patients with dementia and their caregivers as a case study to describe practical strategies for program planning and evaluation. Detailed information is provided about the development of the logic model for the case study, and Slater explains how evaluation findings and recommendations will serve as authentic evidence for justifying program continuation and expansion.

With foundational principles of managing environmental and participatory arts in healthcare programs discussed in parts two and three of this book, parts four and five address program design for several specific population groups. In Part 4, **Managing arts in healthcare programs for special populations**, the contributing authors introduce specific program design for specific populations of military personnel (especially veterans), children, older adults, end-of-life patients and their families, and adults with cancer.

In Chapter 11, titled **How to start an arts program for military populations**, Naj Wikoff explains how many men and women come home spiritually, emotionally, and physically damaged by the experience of serving in the military. This damage can impact their families, loved ones, and community. Wikoff discusses challenges and opportunities for using the arts to strengthen and heal those who have served in the military, and he discusses how to establish partnerships with Veterans Administration (VA) medical centers and local veteran support agencies, as well as work directly with veteran populations. This chapter provides numerous program examples and practical suggestions for designing and implementing an effective arts-based program to help military personnel heal.

Jumping to the world of pediatric care, Chapter 12 provides Judy Rollins' introduction to **The arts in pediatric healthcare settings**. Although a stressful experience for anyone, hospitalization can be especially difficult for children. Hospitals, particularly through Child Life programming, have made great progress to address the psychosocial implications for children, and have learned that with appropriate support, children can weather, and even grow, from the experience. Rollins argues that the arts play a significant role in this support, and maintains that artists working with hospitalized children need special preparation. In this chapter, she describes a four-step process – (1) artist recruitment and selection, (2) artist training, (3) supervised internship, and (4) ongoing education and support – for creating and evaluating a psychosocially sound pediatric arts program.

Shifting from a focus on our youngest citizens to a focus on our senior citizens, Chapter 13 is titled **Arts, health, and aging**. This chapter explores the creative process and its central role in aging, providing a framework for accessing creative potential in later life. Gay Powell Hanna discusses how creativity among older adults can be accessed to contribute to health and wellbeing, lifelong learning, and place-making. Hanna describes examples of effective arts in healthcare programs, including community arts, aging education, and health facilities for older adults across settings, and discusses senior living from independent in-home lifestyles to continuing care communities. In addition, Hanna identifies current research, practices, and policy development that are leading the arts into prominence in terms of actualizing the potential of older people to build social capital, to lower the risk of long-term healthcare, and to improve the quality of life when needed in chronic illness and end-of-life care.

Chapter 14, by Jane Franz and Sandy LaForge, focuses on a specific arts-based intervention called music-thanatology that is being effectively used to support end-of-life patients and their loved ones. Aptly titled **The use of music–thanatology with palliative and end-of-life populations in healthcare settings**, this chapter describes how the trained music-thanatologist delivers live harp and vocal music to the dying patient and family members and friends who may be present. Music is delivered in a prescriptive manner; that is, by assessing the patient and deciding what elements of music may help in relieving pain, reducing agitation, and facilitating relaxation and sleep. Franz and LaForge also offer practical suggestions for establishing a music-thanatology program as a palliative care service in healthcare.

In Chapter 15, titled **Evoking spirit: using the arts with adults with cancer**, Shanti Norris suggests that healing can take place in physical, mental, and emotional realms, and is always possible, even when curing is not. Increasingly, artists are brought into hospital settings to provide psychosocial support for adults with cancer. One such program, the renowned Smith Center for Healing and the Arts, is profiled in detail. Using the Smith Center as a case study, Norris presents ways to create hospital-based arts programs, including working with administrative and clinical staff. This chapter includes strategies and foci for group-based activities, including examples of art techniques for use with adults with cancer.

In Part 5 of this book, **Managing arts in healthcare programs for caregivers**, the focus on designing and implementing programs for specific populations shifts to the needs of medical staff, medical and nursing students, paraprofessional caregivers (such as health aids), and informal caregivers (family, neighbors, and friends). All individuals in this population are classified as *caregivers*, regardless of their status as a highly educated physician, nurse, or other staff member in the healthcare institution (*professional caregivers*), or as a less highly educated healthcare assistant (*paraprofessional caregivers*), or their informal status as a caregiver. The arts can play a role in "caring for the caregiver" with all of these groups.

Chapter 16 focuses on **Using the arts to care for paraprofessional and family caregivers**. Lynn Kable introduces and defines the field of caregiving, providing an overview of what is involved in paraprofessional and informal caregiving, as well as the pressures faced by these groups. She argues how arts programs can contribute to the wellbeing of caregivers through educational and instrumental support; health screening, monitoring, and support; social support; and stress reduction activities. The chapter concludes with four examples of programs in the United States that effectively care for the caregiver.

Complementary to Chapter 16 is Chapter 17, in which Nancy Morgan discusses design and implementation of **Arts programs for medical staff**. Morgan explains that twenty-first century healthcare imposes new burdens on medical staff that impact the wellbeing of patients, organizations, and the professionals themselves. Demand for greater efficiency and cost savings produces inordinate amounts of stress that manifest as burnout, turnover, and medical error. Arts programs for staff have been implemented at major hospitals to alleviate all forms of stress, and the Georgetown University Hospital provides a model of a comprehensive, system-wide arts program for medical and support staff. Morgan refers to the Georgetown case study as a template for recommendations to establish medical staff arts programs.

The final chapter of the book is Chapter 18, titled **Preparing the mind and learning to see: art museums as training grounds for medical students and residents**. While still focused on professional caregivers, the topic of this chapter pertains to the use of arts-based programs in the education of medical students and residents. Indeed, medical schools in the United States and abroad have found that the role of art in their students' training leads to better observation skills, improved critical thinking and empathy, and support improved diagnosing skills and reasoning ability. In this chapter, Lisa Abia-Smith provides examples of successful programs where medical students are required to take a course in visual arts interpretation. Through constructivist approaches, such as VTS (visual thinking strategies), where medical students investigate works of art, keen observational skills are honed and can impact the lives of patients, their families, and the doctors who diagnose them. This chapter serves as a resource for those interested in learning about the relationship between interpretive art experiences and medical training.

Conclusion

Managing Arts Programs in Healthcare comes to print at a time of significant growth in, professionalization of, and restructuring of the arts in healthcare field, as the field becomes increasingly mainstreamed in America's healthcare facilities. The contributing authors represent first- and second-generation leaders drawn from the past three decades of field-building, as well as a few emerging leaders poised to propel further professionalization of the field. The background information, concepts, theoretical frameworks, model programs, strategies, approaches, and tools discussed throughout this book truly represent expertise currently available in the arts in healthcare field. Additional resources and reference lists are provided in the chapters to assist readers with learning more about the topics, and individual contributing authors can be located through reading the biographical information provided at the end of this book. Whereas early founders of the contemporary arts in healthcare field organically developed their work (and often in isolation from others engaged in the field), this book contributes to a growing body of knowledge and praxis that can be readily shared among the increasingly well-networked current and emerging professionals in the field.

This reference book has been written with a broad audience of professionals and students in mind. For readers new to the world of managing arts programs in hospitals, hospices, and other healthcare facilities, this book has been written to provide a comprehensive introduction to the field. For healthcare administrators or medical professionals interested in establishing or expanding arts programs within their institution or practice, this book will serve as a valuable reference. For visual and performing artists, arts organizations, and arts managers seeking new opportunities for collaborative engagement with healthcare institutions in their communities, this book will provide a starting point for learning how to bridge the arts and health fields. For those already engaged as arts in healthcare professional artists or professional administrators, this book will broaden knowledge areas and skill sets, and potentially lead to new ideas for program stabilization and expansion.

Managing Arts Programs in Healthcare synthesizes a quarter century of research and practice into a single resource designed to assist anyone who is interested in transforming the healthcare experience through engaging the visual and performing arts.

References

Berwick, D. M., Nolan, T. W., & Whittington, J. (2008). The triple aim: Care, health, and cost. *Health Affairs, 27*(3), 759–769.

Bisognano, M., & Kenney, C. (2012). *Pursuing the triple aim: Seven innovators show the way to better care, better health, and lower costs.* San Francisco: Jossey-Bass.

Brandman, R. (2007). The development of the contemporary international arts in healthcare field. In J. Sonke-Henderson, R. Brandman, I. Serlin, & J. Graham-Pole (Eds.). *Whole person healthcare: Volume 3: The arts & health* (pp. 43–66). Westport, CT: Praeger.

Frampton, S. B. (2009). Introduction: Patient-centered care moves into the mainstream. In S. B. Frampton & P. Charmel (Eds.), *Putting patients first: Best practices in patient-centered care* (pp. xxvii–xl). San Francisco: Jossey-Bass.

Gerteis, M., Edgman-Levitan, S., Daley, J., & Delbanco, T. L. (1993). Introduction: Medicine and health from the patient's perspective. In M. Gerteis, S. Edgman-Levitan, J. Daley, & T. L. Delbanco (Eds.), *Through the patient's eyes: Understanding and promoting patient-centered care* (pp. 1–15). New York: John Wiley & Sons.

Graham-Pole, J. (2007). Applications of art to health. In J. Sonke-Henderson, R. Brandman, R., I. Serlin, & J. Graham-Pole (Eds.), *Whole person healthcare: Volume 3: The arts & health* (pp. 1–22). Westport, CT: Praeger.

National Coalition of Creative Arts Therapies Associations, Inc. Retrieved from www.nccata.org

Palmer, J. (2001). *An introduction to the arts-for-health movement, or how the arts sneaked in on the medical model.* Retrieved from the Art in the Public Interest Community Arts Network Reading Room: http://wayback.archive-it.org/2077/20100906195258/http://www.communityarts.net/readingroom/archivefiles/2001/11/introduction_to.php#

Perlstein, S. (1999). *Really caring: Why a comprehensive healthcare system includes the arts.* Retrieved from the Community Arts Network Reading Room: http://wayback.archive-it.org/2077/20100906203903/http://www.communityarts.net/readingroom/archive files/1999/12/really_caring_w.php#

Sadler, B. L., & Ridenour, A. (2009). *Transforming the healthcare experience through the arts.* San Diego: Aesthetics, Inc.

Society for the Arts in Healthcare, Retrieved May 1, 2012 from www.thesah.org

Sonke-Henderson, J. (2007). History of the arts and health across cultures. In J. Sonke-Henderson, R. Brandman, I. Serlin, & J. Graham-Pole (Eds.). *Whole person healthcare: Volume 3: The arts & health* (pp. 23–42). Westport, CT: Praeger.

Sonke, J., Rollins, J., Brandman, R., & Graham-Pole, J. (2009). The state of the arts in healthcare in the United States. *Arts & Health, 1*(2), 107–135.

State of the Field Committee. (2009). *State of the field report: Arts in healthcare 2009.* Washington, DC: Society for the Arts in Healthcare.

Thornton, L. (2013). *Whole person caring: An interprofessional model for healing and wellness.* Indianapolis, IN: Sigma Theta Tau International.

Warren, B., (Ed.). (2008). *Using the creative arts in therapy and healthcare: A practical introduction* (3rd ed.). New York: Routledge.

2

MAPPING THE ARTS IN HEALTHCARE FIELD

Katie White

The field of arts in healthcare is a varied and rapidly growing one. For both new and established organizations, connecting to peers in the field and accessing information about developments and resources can be a challenge. While numerous resources exist for arts in healthcare practitioners, no comprehensive geographic map of programs in the field was available until 2013, when I began developing the PlaceStories online field map and community, "The Arts in Healthcare Field in the United States." The project was initiated in response to the need for such a resource and was originally a component of my graduate work at the University of Oregon. As of 2015, the University of Oregon Arts in Healthcare Research Consortium is beginning the process of hosting and updating the map. This chapter provides a geographic and organizational map of the arts in healthcare field in the United States based on the PlaceStories project and the data gathered from the mapping process.

The pages that follow introduce the potential of PlaceStories to serve as an online base for further community expansion, present the data that was gathered during the creation of the community, discuss growth trends in arts in healthcare, and position the field as an essential, vital part of the American cultural sector. Objectives for initiating the PlaceStories web-based community included: researching the arts in healthcare programs and resources in existence throughout the country; providing information on program typology, geographic concentrations, and growth trends; and building an interactive geographical map in an accessible format that facilitates user contributions and information exchange. The result is an interactive map that shows locations, descriptions, and program websites for over ninety programs across the United States. While that number is undoubtedly quite small when compared with the large number of organized and informal efforts that must presently exist in the United States, there were several research parameters in place to make the project more feasible within a graduate thesis timeline. For example, the research took place by using several different "arts in healthcare"-based keyword groupings and conducting internet searches by state to find programs. Other resources, such as the State of the Field Report developed jointly by the State of the Field Committee (2009) for the National Endowment for the Arts and the Society for the Arts in Healthcare, provided lists of programs that were helpful. However, many organizations lack a substantial web presence, and it is hoped that in addition to updates through the University of Oregon Arts in Healthcare Research Consortium, practitioners will take the initiative to create profiles and put their own organizations on the map.

The map (see Figure 2.1) can be referenced interactively while reading this chapter by accessing its project link on PlaceStories (http://placestories.com/project/145991), or by creating a free account with http://placestories.com/ and using the search keywords "arts in healthcare" to locate the map. PlaceStories is an online community space maintained by FeralArts, an Australian cultural mapping organization, and was selected for the project due to its ease of use, attractive interface, and its potential for facilitating interaction with the map using its unique "story" format for map entries.

Using the PlaceStories platform, practitioners can contribute to the map, edit and expand their own organizational accounts, network with other professionals, and find other programs in their region or typology. In addition to providing a community resource, the simplicity of the platform and space for individual profiles allows organizations to promote their own work. It is hoped that this map and community will serve as the first geographic resource for the American arts in healthcare field, and will expand both nationally and internationally into a great tool for networking, research, and field-building.

With the PlaceStories community map and growing resources through organizations such as Americans for the Arts, the arts in healthcare field can unite and collaborate on a greater level than before. A sense of national community is necessary for information sharing, research exchange, and awareness of the field. Arts in healthcare is on the cusp of great development and progress, but if organizations do not promote themselves and connect with others in the field, this progress can be impeded. The PlaceStories community offers a way for organizations and practitioners to make field connections and further this process of development.

Regional program concentrations

When interacting with the PlaceStories map, regional concentrations of activity can be observed. The highest regional concentration of programs is found on the Northeast coast, which may be due to a large number of established arts programs in thriving metropolitan areas. Within this region, certain areas display prevalent types of programming. For example, Washington, DC contains a high amount of healthcare system-based programs, such as hospital and care facilities with on-site offerings, while the New York City area features a large number of nonprofit organizations working in partnership with healthcare systems as complementary resources, rather than facility-housed programs.

When surveying the PlaceStories heat map (see Figure 2.2), it is apparent that the Eastern half of the United States houses a greater number of programs than the

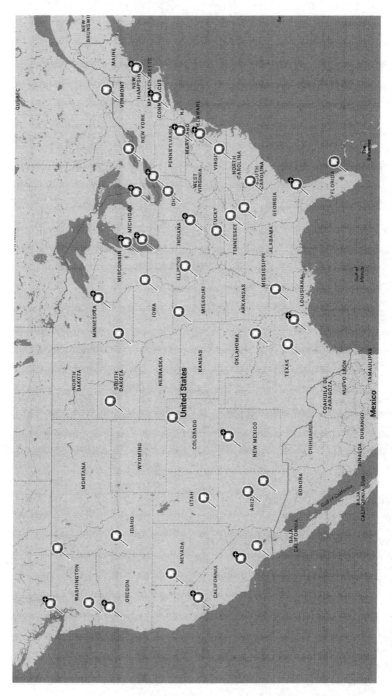

FIGURE 2.1 The Geographic Map for the PlaceStories Online Community

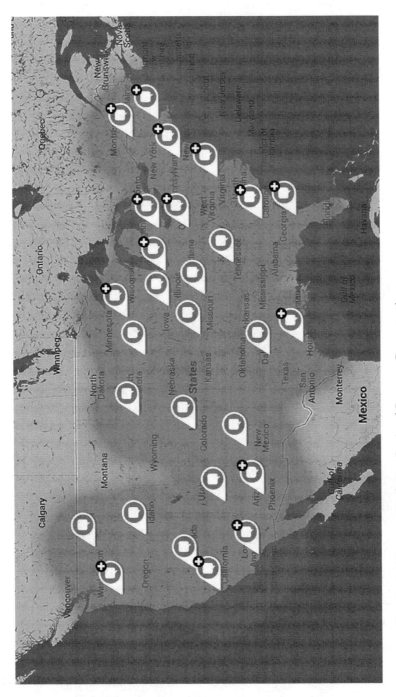

FIGURE 2.2 PlaceStories Heatmap Displaying Regional Program Concentrations

West. While some major cities in the Midwest (such as Chicago) contain highly developed programs, the area's relative lack of activity can likely be attributed to the prevalence of larger rural areas (this also applies to states such as Wyoming and Montana). On the Western side of the map, a growing amount of activity in the Pacific Northwest and California can be observed.

It is likely that large cities, in particular, have much more programming than can be found through web-based research efforts. Healthcare outreach is a growing trend in nonprofit activity, and informal collaborations between community organizations and healthcare systems are most likely taking place on a larger scale than is documented on the PlaceStories map.

Growth trends in arts in healthcare programs

The data gathered from the mapping process point to new developments in arts in healthcare organizations. These organizations illustrate several growing trends in the arts in healthcare movement: arts resources for veterans and their families, creative aging programs, community arts in healthcare education for schoolchildren, and evidence-based design for arts-friendly hospitals. The trend of beautification in hospitals is on the rise (Schweitzer, Gilpin, & Frampton, 2004), and incorporating visual art and landscaping that promote an atmosphere of healing is generally the first step for a facility creating an arts in healthcare program. An additional trend that has come out of the evidence-based design movement is a renewed emphasis on using local art in building remodels or design. Particularly for hospitals in rural areas that often function as shared meeting spaces as well as healthcare facilities, having such a centralized building reflect local arts offerings can create a greater sense of satisfaction and involvement for community members.

In response to the growing need for arts in healthcare programs, government resources are now being allocated for research and support. While the most notable players in this process are the National Initiative for Arts and Health in the Military and the National Institutes of Health's National Center for Complementary and Integrated Health, funding and research are also taking place through the National Endowment for the Arts and other groups. These nascent initiatives hold great potential for impact on both policy creation and future funding for arts in healthcare organizations.

Common types of arts in healthcare programs

From the research process, two types of art forms emerged as the most prevalent: visual arts (including exhibits and participatory art) and music (large space performances and bedside sessions). Other popular mediums include journaling, dance, and drama. Across these mediums, two common modes of expression can be found: *environmental expression*, in which the medium exists as part of the surroundings in a healing environment, and *participatory expression*, in which active engagement is required of both the producer and receiver of the medium. For example, environmental expression could include a healing garden located outside patient windows or soothing music piped in over loudspeakers in common areas. Participatory expression could include attending a drumming group, creating a painting, or engaging in a bedside music session.

Using common spaces, such as foyers or waiting rooms, for concerts or other performances could be considered *environmental participation*, as patients and community members choose to experience these programs even though active participation is not required. In public spaces, both visual arts activities and music activities are frequently found.

Some programs can be described as *comprehensive*, as they offer a spectrum of activities besides music and visual art, including creative movement and dance, poetry, journaling, and storytelling. Examples of comprehensive programs include Gifts of Art at the University of Michigan, UF Health Shands Arts in Medicine at the University of Florida, and Parker Adventist Hospital's programs in Parker, Colorado. While many programs achieve excellence and gain community reputation through focusing on one art form, such as music or visual art, the programs that offer multiple arts resources seem best suited for community enrichment.

Other programs are hosted by nonprofits, such as community arts organizations, which expand their offerings to include arts in healthcare programs. Some nonprofits exist solely for the purpose of working with healthcare and rehabilitation systems to incorporate healing arts into medical and emotional care. Others provide resources, such as arts in healthcare curriculum or training programs.

A growing sector of nonprofits exists to bridge the gap between artists and healthcare providers. Some contract with musicians or artists to provide programming in hospitals, others act as liaisons between arts organizations and health systems, and some even create curriculum or program tools for arts in healthcare programs. Others function as consultancies or design firms with expertise in hospital art and wayfinding. Examples of these organizations include Musicians on Call and RxArt in New York, New York; Aesthetics, Inc. in San Diego, California; and Healing Healthcare Systems in Reno, Nevada.

The sector of arts in veterans' care is rapidly developing, although not quickly enough to address the growing need for the benefits and services that these initiatives meet. The previously mentioned National Initiative for Arts & Health in the Military is a key force in directing fundraising and program creation in this sector. Two important partnerships currently participating in this initiative are the National Endowment for the Arts and Walter Reed National Military Medical Center's Healing Arts Partnership, and the National Center for Creative Aging and the Washington, DC Veterans Affairs Medical Center's Healing and Creativity collaboration. Programs offered for veterans include creative arts healing, resources, and career guidance for veterans reentering the arts field. While traditional art therapy has been used for years in veterans' programs, many organizations are seeing positive results in veterans' healing simply from involvement in the arts (Rollins, 2012).

Arts in healthcare organizations are becoming involved with local veterans' resources, and are being used to consult and create programs that address their specific needs. With the increase of federal involvement, some funding available for general arts in healthcare activities may be redirected toward programs that focus on veterans. While there may be less funding available to arts in healthcare organizations targeting other demographics as a result, the amount of publicity and research devoted to arts-integrated veterans' care can only be beneficial for raising awareness of the arts in healthcare field in general.

The aging "baby boomer" generation is a consumerist, experience-driven demographic (Herzlinger, 2004). As these older adults care for elderly parents and face their own aging process, their demands for a customizable healthcare environment are beginning to include arts and continuing education programs. In particular, programs for the arts in aging are on the rise, and several replicable models for repeated program construction have also emerged. Gene Cohen's and the National Endowment for the Arts' 2006 study on arts in aging care revealed that older adults in professionally administered arts programs reported fewer falls and doctor visits compared to a control group, among other quality-of-life benefits. As the type of care available for the aging continues to evolve past the dated nursing-home model, more facilities are offering community arts programs to their members. The vast majority of arts in aging programs are located in the New York City area, with Washington, DC and San Diego coming in second and third respectively. Due to the varied living situations that aging adults can experience, most organizations offer flexible locations, and visit assisted living centers or community centers where adults are already attending programs. While many of these programs are not housed in actual healthcare facilities, they offer essential health benefits to older adults.

The majority of these programs are focused on Alzheimer's or memory care, but integrating arts experiences into general community wellness for the aging is also a growing trend. Partnerships with museums, local primary schools, and family organizations are increasingly common as community stakeholders learn the importance of integrating aging care into daily social activities. Examples of these programs include Sweet Readers in New York, New York, Songwriting Works in Port Townshend, Washington, and Arts for the Aging in Rockville, Maryland. The National Center for Creative Aging (NCCA), founded in 2001, is the leader in research and innovation for arts in aging care. Its website features an extensive directory of programs, program evaluation reports, and resources for professionals, including a free online training module for artists working with aging populations.

Mapping the organization of the arts in healthcare field

When discussing the organization of the arts in healthcare field, the role of the Arts & Health Alliance immediately comes to mind. From its inception in 1989 as an organization for healthcare arts administrators, and its rapid growth in the early 1990s into the Society for the Arts in Healthcare, the organization functioned as a leader in the field for research and resources as well as a professional association for practitioners. The organization went through several changes through the years before becoming the Arts & Health Alliance. In 2015, the organization filed for dissolution due to financial challenges and declining membership. Members of the Alliance were offered new opportunities as members of Americans for the Arts through a joint agreement between the two organizations in 2015. This agreement worked to ensure continued access to information and resources for arts in health practitioners (M. Chambers, R. Cohen, & M. Walker, personal communication, January 2015). It is hoped that this new arrangement will allow for the continuance of resources for arts in healthcare practitioners in the years to come.

The field of arts in healthcare reflects trends in the fields of arts, humanities, and design, as well as developments in the medical field and healthcare industry. The very makeup and focus of arts in healthcare gives it a unique position to influence the formation of policy and cross-sector collaboration in the years ahead. For that reason, it is of great importance that arts in healthcare practitioners and leaders in the field understand the complex organizational infrastructure of their sector. While some relationships are obvious (collaborations between national entities such as the National Endowment for the Arts and Americans for the Arts, for example), others are more subtle and result from a symbiotic relationship between community organizations and larger health networks. The roles of government organizations as leaders in the field are obvious, but when the sector of arts in healthcare is closely examined, one finds a much more organic, evolutionary structure than many traditional fields with longstanding professional standards and organizations.

The Figure 2.3 illustrates organizational roots and some key governing players in the arts in healthcare field and their mutual relationships. These organizations advocate for the creation of favorable policy for arts in healthcare, undertake research in the field, publish works, and document the evolving sector. Over the years, the field of the arts in healthcare has developed relevant relationships with other cultural and medical sectors. The diagram also illustrates some of these relationships.

The diagram depicts some of the key organizational players in the arts in healthcare field: Americans for the Arts (which has incorporated the Arts & Health Alliance and hosts the National Initiative for Arts & Health in the Military), the National Endowment for the Arts (a major source for both research and funding), and the National Center for Creative Aging. As shown on the diagram, all aspects of the field influence one another in some way. Due to the constantly evolving nature of this field, this diagram should not be interpreted as comprehensive, as different national organizations are becoming involved at a rapid rate and charting the full extent of their current impact can be difficult.

As the organizational players in the field have evolved, so have the flagship programs that have shaped the practice of arts in healthcare: Gifts of Art (University of Michigan), UF Health Shands Arts in Medicine (University of Florida), Project Art (University of Iowa), and HAND (Duke University).

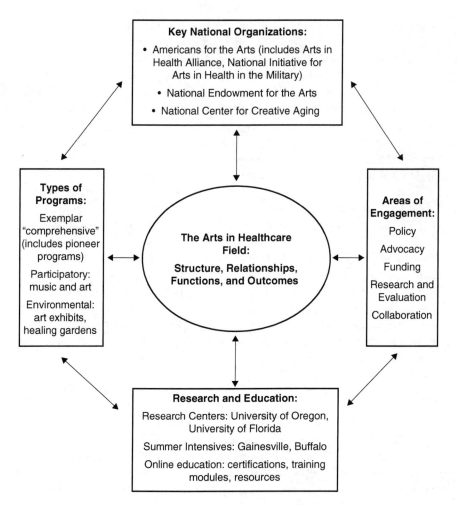

FIGURE 2.3 Organizational Map of the Arts in Healthcare Field

These "exemplar" programs have demonstrated the success of implementing arts in healthcare programming in hospital settings, and have served to inspire other programs and projects across the nation. As discussed previously, the typologies of programs have evolved in response to proven success in different settings, and are demonstrated on the diagram (participatory and environmental expression, the use of art and music, and "comprehensive" programs that include an array of expressive arts).

With the evolution of professional practice, some educational resources have been developed, although the need for more is still great. While small-scale research and education are doubtlessly taking place on a larger scale than is documented, two universities in particular have made great strides in developing educational programs and fostering research. The University of Florida in Gainesville hosts the UF Health Shands Arts in Medicine program, provides Summer Intensives for practitioners in both Gainesville and Buffalo, New York, and offers a degree and several certification options. The University of Oregon in Eugene offers a Master's in Arts Management with a concentration in Arts in Healthcare Management, and also hosts the Oregon Arts in Healthcare Research Consortium. In addition to university-based research and resources, the internet has become a great tool for practitioners looking to continue their education. The National Center for Creative Aging provides a training module for artists. Several "therapeutic musician" accreditations are also offered online, and the quality of instruction may vary, but with discretion the arts in healthcare practitioner could compare differing programs and decide if any may be beneficial for their goals.

Finally, the "areas of engagement" section of the diagram displays a few of the overarching functions and goals that participants in the arts in healthcare field may share. Creating arts in healthcare policy, conducting fundraising, advocacy for the field, research and evaluation, and collaborations shape the goals of organizations and practitioners and keep developments alive.

Meanwhile, developments in the art in healthcare field have also taken place outside of medical centers, as community arts organizations and university departments have begun offering arts in healthcare services and resources. Collaboration between these outside groups and healthcare centers is common, but not universal. As nonprofit organizations have increased their involvement with arts in health initiatives, community stakeholders have become involved. The result is a growing emphasis on community wellness and public health through shared artistic and life experiences, whether these take place in a healthcare facility or a general public setting. This increased emphasis is perhaps the key force that will continue to drive arts in healthcare innovation and development.

The venture into the public health sector presents many new opportunities for arts in healthcare organizations. Collaborations with public health officials, medical support groups, school systems, and senior living centers can take place with this shared goal of enriching lives – and health – through arts engagement.

The area of arts in aging is a prime example of developments in the field. With the 2006 study led by Gene Cohen and the National Endowment for the Arts, organizations can prove the health benefits (for example, decreased falls, fewer prescription medications, and fewer hospital visits) that regular participation in arts activities can provide senior citizens. In addition, museum and primary school programs are beginning to add collaborative series with older adults, with an emphasis on building cross-generational relationships through shared experiences with art. While the latter example may look very different from a "traditional" bedside arts intervention in a hospital, they both share the common aim of creating human connection and validation through art, with healing results.

The insertion of arts into community priorities, such as public health, lends traditional art forms new relevancy and value. As traditional arts organizations, such as symphonies and theaters, seek to reinvigorate their audiences and increase their level of community engagement, the prospect of collaborating with healthcare modalities makes increasing sense. In turn, for medical facilities and practitioners, the arts provide an increasing level of humanization and personal interaction that can be difficult to achieve using standardized healthcare procedures. In the growing culture of healthcare consumerism in the United States, providing healthcare with an individualized touch is in high demand. By incorporating individual arts experiences for patients and their families into standardized care, healthcare providers can imbue a sense of personal value and validation of experience to those seeking medical attention. Increased sense of worth as a patient results in favorable reporting for healthcare providers, which provides financial incentive to continue incorporating these services into daily procedure.

The increased emphasis on arts in medical care has resulted in a growing medical arts curriculum for preprofessionals in the field, which is addressed in Chapter 18 of this book. The desensitized, institutional practices of providing medical care that became standard in the 1970s are now proving unsuccessful for engaging physicians or patients. The demand for empathetic, expressive medical care is being addressed through training in medical narrative, in arts education for increased attention to detail, and to theater and storytelling work to develop skills of expressive compassion in new physicians and healthcare professionals. Once again, the arts in healthcare field is finding new allies in the areas of medical school curricular development and emerging hospital practice.

In addition to influencing medical school curriculum, the field of arts in healthcare is beginning to inform the study of traditional arts and their administration. Few degree programs exist, but the number is on the rise. Informal study is most likely taking place at a higher rate than is documented, as arts in healthcare programs located in university medical systems present excellent opportunities for collaboration with resident arts and music departments. Similar to the institutionalized approach of older medical school curricula, which are now being reexamined and shaped by the expressive arts and humanities, the field of traditional arts study has long been regimented and highly technical. Even in the twenty-first century, students earning traditional arts degrees, such as music performance, still face expectations of technical precision and a classical craft, in spite of the rapid decline of traditional employment in these fields. A growing need for students to be taught outreach and community engagement skills is being realized, and the arts in healthcare field has presented itself as an ideal candidate for blending traditional craft with a community outreach perspective.

Conclusion

As the field continues to grow, resources like the PlaceStories online community will only become more necessary. Through sharing knowledge, connecting with other field professionals, and reporting program developments, arts in healthcare practitioners can be truly connected to one another as they navigate this exciting and quickly growing field. The associational infrastructure of the arts in healthcare field will also continue to evolve and grow. In this ongoing state of field development, self-reporting and discussion among arts in healthcare practitioners and the communities that they engage is essential for further progress to be made.

The rapidly expanding initiatives taking place on multiple fronts in the arts in healthcare field bode well for the future of the work. It is hoped that the foundations laid by twentieth-century pioneers and innovators in the field will now be built upon to ensure a thriving, engaged, and relevant answer to the challenges that both traditional arts practitioners and healthcare providers face as they attempt to reinvent their craft in an increasingly self-aware society.

References and further readings

Bungay, H., & Vella-Burrows, T. (2013). The effects of participating in creative activities on the health and well-being of children and young people: a rapid review of the literature. *Perspectives in Public Health, 133*(1), 44–52.

Charmel, P. A. (2009). Building the business case for patient-centered care. In S. B. Frampton & P. Charmel (Eds.), *Putting patients first: Best practices in patient-centered care* (pp. 191–210). San Francisco: Jossey-Bass.

Clift, S. (2012). Creative arts as a public health resource: moving from practice-based research to evidence-based practice. *Perspectives in Public Health, 132*(3), 120–127.

Cohen, G., & the National Endowment for the Arts. (2006). *The creativity and aging study.* Retrieved from http://arts.gov/sites/default/files/CnA-Rep4-30-06.pdf

Heaphy, A., Bansal, A., & the National Endowment for the Arts. (2008). *Arts in healthcare: Best practices.* Retrieved from http://nac.nevadaculture.org/dmdocuments/Artsin Healthcare_handouts.pdf

Herzlinger, R. E. (2004). *Consumer-driven health care implications for providers, payers, and policymakers.* San Francisco: Jossey-Bass.

Raw, A., Lewis, S., Macnaughton, J., & Russell, A. (2012). A hole in the heart: Confronting the drive for evidence-based impact research in arts and health. *Arts and Health, 4*(2), 97–108.

Rollins, J. (2012, November). The arts: A promising solution to meeting the challenges of today's military. Summary report and blueprint for action presented in the Arts & Health in the Military National Roundtable, Washington, DC.

Sadler, B. L., & Ridenour, A. (2009). *Transforming the healthcare experience through the arts.* San Diego: Aesthetics, Inc.

Schweitzer, M., Gilpin, L, & Frampton, S. (2004). Healing spaces: Elements of environmental design that make an impact on health. *The Journal of Alternative and Complementary Medicine, 10*(1), S-71–S-83.

Sonke, J., Rollins, J., Brandman, R., & Graham-Pole, J. (2009). The state of the arts in healthcare in the United States. *Arts & Health, 1*(2), 107–135.

State of the Field Committee. (2009). *State of the field report: Arts in healthcare 2009.* Washington, DC: Society for the Arts in Healthcare.

Stuckey, H. L., & Nobel, J. (2010, January 1). The connection between art, healing, and public health: a review of current literature. *American Journal of Public Health, 100*(2), 254–263.

Wikoff, N. (2004, November). *Cultures of care: A study of arts programs in U.S. hospitals.* Washington, DC: Americans for the Arts.

3

PROFESSIONALIZING THE ARTS IN HEALTHCARE FIELD

Jill Sonke

Within the continuum of arts and health practices, arts in healthcare has emerged as a profession over the past three decades following, and in relationship with, established professionalism in the creative arts therapies. Pioneering innovation in the field of arts in healthcare has led to the development of training, continuing education, and most recently, certification to support professionalization. Arts in healthcare has evolved over this time from a grassroots movement dedicated to humanizing the experience of healthcare to a defined profession that engages the arts to enhance individual and population health as well as the healthcare system and delivery of care. While the field has grown rapidly over the past three decades, it also faces significant challenges today, as it approaches the major hurdles of professionalization, including certification and the adoption of a code of ethics and standards of practice. This chapter will address key challenges and opportunities for the field, including its definition and identity, credentialing and certification, training, scope and standards of practice, and employment opportunities.

Preamble: are we talking about a discipline, a field, or a profession?

The terms discipline, field, and profession can be difficult to assign to an emerging pursuit; however, they each apply to our discussion of arts and health. There is often debate over what terms apply along the way as a profession develops. The debate over how a profession, in particular, is defined and differentiated from other occupations has been ongoing for decades. While there are varying approaches to defining a profession that prevent us from arriving at one widely accepted set of characteristics, for the purpose of considering arts and health at the present time, it will suffice to note that a profession is generally defined by legal boundaries or regulations that delineate groups of those inside and outside the profession (Saks,

2012). Those boundaries and regulations, such as ethics and standards of practice, are typically established and maintained by a professional association or by governments. In that regard, arts and health moved into the realm of professionalism when the Society for the Arts in Healthcare was established in 1991. Additional important dimensions of a profession are well-defined areas of knowledge and expertise in a field, and these areas have been evolving organically through scholarship and praxis in the arts in healthcare field. As of this writing, however, no standards or ethics for practice have been adopted, but these are in development. Given these factors, arts in healthcare could be considered just on the cusp of arriving as a profession.

A field is defined as "a sphere of activity, interest, etc., especially within a particular business or profession" (Field, n.d.). The term "field" is widely used in key literature in reference to arts and health (Parkinson & White, 2013; Raw, Lewis, Russell, & Macnaughton, 2012; Sonke, Rollins, Brandman, & Graham-Pole, 2009), and is clearly a fitting term. Discipline is also an appropriate term, as it generally refers to academic study in a particular field or profession. As will be discussed subsequently, academic programs of study are available and define the scope of practice and professional competencies for the field. There is also a rapidly expanding body of literature that defines practice in the field within the realms of both healthcare and community-based practice. The literature articulates an array of practices, the prevalence and types of programs of study, impacts and outcomes, the emergence of policy, and some theoretical frameworks (Broderick, 2011; Clift, 2012; Dileo & Bradt, 2009; Sonke et al., 2009; Sonke, Rollins & Graham-Pole, in press; State of the Field Committee, 2009; Staricoff, 2004). Further definition is needed with regard to terminologies for the field, theoretical frameworks, and standards for practice (Dileo & Bradt, 2009; Raw et al., 2012; White, 2010).

Development of a professional field: a brief history

The use of the arts in healing practices is as old as mankind. In traditional cultures, dance, music, drama, art, and writing are core ingredients of healing rituals. History documents a long-standing "knowing" of how the arts – music, in particular – can enhance wellness and healing. Classical literatures, including the writings of Plato, Confucius, Pythagoras, Avicenna, and others, are rife with references to the healing power of music and recommendations for its use (Ruud, 2008; Sonke, 2011). Biomedical health systems in ancient Egypt and Greece document use of the arts for healing, and Western biomedical texts from as early as 1729 are dedicated to the prescriptive use of music for the treatment of physical injury and ailments (Sonke, 2007).

The spectacular accomplishments of biomedicine in the twentieth and twenty-first centuries have been accompanied by the growth of numerous supporting disciplines, or allied health professions, that use the arts as a part of patient care and contribute to a more holistic and patient-centered healthcare system. Between the 1930s and 1980s, the arts therapies (music, visual art, poetry, drama, and dance/movement), as well as child life, occupational therapy, physical therapy, and recreational therapy, emerged and became defined as allied health professions. In the 1970s and 1980s, arts in healthcare programs began to develop, and today likely are moving toward this same designation. A handful of programs developed independently of one another during this time and have spurred the development of what is now a defined discipline that includes arts programs in approximately half of the accredited healthcare institutions in the United States (State of the Field Committee, 2009).

The discipline has grown rapidly around the globe, with particular leadership in the United Kingdom, Australia, and the United States. There are programs on every populated continent, and professional networks in Australia, Europe, North America, South America, Asia, and Africa. In the UK, the field developed from a community and public health context and has expanded into healthcare settings, whereas in the United States, the field developed in healthcare settings with a focus on patient care and the environment of care, and is currently expanding rapidly into community and public health arenas.

Development of the field in the United States

Programs were established in the 1970s and 1980s at numerous major hospitals in the United States, including Duke University, the University of Michigan, the University of Iowa, and the University of Florida. These programs each began with a unique impetus to humanize the healthcare environment through the arts. In most cases, collaborations between caregivers and artists were developed to bring works of original art into the environment of care, to bring the arts to caregivers to help reduce compassion fatigue and burnout, and to provide patients with a means for enjoyment and stress reduction. These early programs included arts workshops for caregivers, exhibitions and permanent art installations, performances in public and patient care areas, and bedside arts activities provided for patients and their family members by professional artists.

The artists who began working in care environments in the 1980s and 1990s did so without formal education or training specific to the practice of using the arts in healthcare settings. These artists were often trained and supported by clinical personnel, such as nurses, social workers, or child life specialists. In this way, interdisciplinary teamwork was at the heart of the development of the discipline and remains crucial to the way artists work today in healthcare settings. These artists were the pioneers of the field, learning from experience, and developing the discipline from a grassroots level. Many have gone on to serve as educators and trainers, bringing a unique breadth of experience to match the theoretical foundations that now inform practice in the field.

Identity and terminologies

Today, there are significant inconsistencies in terminology within the field. These inconsistencies are challenging for professionals within the field, as they make it difficult for stakeholders to define and reference the field, and thus impede the field's progress. This issue has been noted in publications from several countries since 2009, yet the problem persists to date (Clift et al., 2009; Dileo & Bradt, 2009; Raw et al., 2012; Sonke, Rollins, & Graham-Pole, in press; Sonke et al., 2009).

In the UK, Australia, and other areas, the term *arts and health* is predominantly used, while in the United States, numerous terms are used, including *arts in healthcare*, *arts in medicine*, and *arts and health*. The Arts & Health Alliance, formerly the Society for Arts in Healthcare and the Global Alliance for Arts & Health, rebranded in 2012 and 2014 respectively, to align more closely with the global terminology. However, in the United States, there is at present no overall agreement or consistency in terminology for the field title. Even the field's primary educators use varying terms.

The University of Oregon uses the term *arts in healthcare* in its Master of Arts in Arts Administration with a concentration in Arts in Healthcare Management. Similarly, the National University of Ireland Maynooth offers a postgraduate program called the Postgraduate Certificate in Arts in Health Care Settings. In the UK, where the greatest prevalence of graduate programs focused on the arts and health can be found, program titles vary. The University of South Wales offers a Master of Arts degree in Arts, Health and Wellbeing, and the University of Central Lancashire offers a Master of Arts degree in Arts-Health. The University of Florida uses the term *arts in medicine* in its graduate programs, including the Master of Arts in Arts in Medicine and Graduate Certificate in Arts in Medicine. In its graduate curriculum, the University of Florida uses a defined set of terms to reference the field and its professionals in the United States:

- *Arts and health*: used to encompass arts in medicine, arts in public health, and the arts therapies.
- *Arts in medicine*: the discipline that engages the arts in healthcare fields and settings to enhance health, wellness, and the healthcare environment; *arts in healthcare* can be used interchangeably with *arts in medicine*.
- *Arts in public health*: the discipline that engages the arts in public health for health promotion and disease prevention.
- *Artist in Healthcare*: a professional artist trained and qualified to work in healthcare fields and settings. In 2015, the national certification, Artist in Healthcare–Certified (AIH–C), will be established.
- *Arts Therapist* or *Creative Arts Therapist*: a health professional who is trained to use the arts therapeutically to assess, establish and meet clinical goals, and evaluate outcomes.

The lack of terminology standardization contributes to unnecessary confusion, especially among those outside of the field. It can also prevent accurate comparisons across related disciplines and reduce opportunities for multicenter research and transdisciplinary collaboration. In the United States, there seems to be emerging agreement that the term *arts and health* may be the most relevant overall term to encompass the disciplines that engage the arts for health promotion. However, this term is technically problematic, as the purview of the discipline is not both arts *and* health, rather, arts *in* health. There are still many different titles being used to reference the field and overall agreement in terminologies, while urgently needed, remains a challenge.

Scope and standards of practice for artists in residence

Beginning in 2008, members of the Ethics Task Force and the Arts in Healthcare Professional Competencies Task Force, established by the Society for the Arts in Healthcare (which later became the Arts & Health Alliance), developed the *Code of Ethics for Arts in Healthcare* and *Standards of Professional Performance for Arts in Healthcare*. These standards were developed to guide certification and practice in the field, helping to define clear standards and scope of practice, but have not yet been adopted by a governing body or professional organization for the field. A clear understanding of both scope and standards of practice is essential for artists who work in healthcare settings and for the administrators who manage them, especially given the confusion that can arise between the similarities and differences between the arts therapies and arts in healthcare. It is critical, in particular, that artists do not cross boundaries into therapeutic or clinical engagement with patients.

In a healthcare setting, an artist in residence is a professional artist who uses the arts to enhance the environment of care and to bring creative opportunities that support health, recovery, and wellbeing to patients, their family members and visitors, and to staff. Artists in residence are not clinicians (nor are they therapists), but they can have a defined role on the care team. Artists in residence do not make clinical decisions or set clinical goals (as an art therapist might), but they may be involved in assisting clinicians in meeting their clinical goals. For example, a physician may call on a musician in residence to play music when a patient is undergoing a stressful or painful procedure that requires the patient to be calm and still. The intent of this kind of arts intervention is distraction, in contrast to the specific clinical goals that might be developed by professional creative arts therapists. The musician in residence is trained to identify a patient's musical preferences or select appropriate music for the moment, and to perform it at a high level of quality and in a way that is appropriate for the clinical environment. But, the artist would not be responsible for deciding when music is called for, and would not set a clinical goal for the patient. Clinical staff members who are familiar with the arts and the practices of artists in residence can, however, utilize the arts and the artist to reach their clinical goals. In this way, the medical and creative arts partner to optimize care, and each professional works within their own scope of practice. Appropriate education, training, and supervision are essential for artists to support a clear understanding of roles, and to facilitate effective collaboration within the interprofessional care team.

Education, training, and certification of artists

According to surveys conducted by the Joint Commission (the national accreditation organization for healthcare institutions), there are arts programs at approximately half of the hospitals and long-term care facilities in the United States (State of the Field Committee, 2009). Over the past decade, as program prevalence has expanded significantly, healthcare providers have begun setting higher standards for arts professionals regarding patient safety and professionalism. Arts programs are developing more substantial roles within healthcare institutions, including greater reach and visibility. Many programs operate as departments of hospitals, and as such, maintain practice protocols and hiring, supervision, and evaluation practices that are consistent with the standards of other departments.

Numerous articles published in field journals have articulated a need for advanced education and training for arts in healthcare professionals. In a review of literature related to arts in healthcare education, Moss and O'Neal (2009) note that education in the field, particularly at the graduate level, is needed and has arisen from a prevalence of arts programs in healthcare worldwide. Recently, in response to demand from both professionals and preprofessionals, there has been a significant increase in such programs.

A wide range of accredited and non-accredited training programs, degree programs, and certificate programs focused on various aspects of arts and health currently exist in the United States. Those programs include creative arts therapies degree programs, university-based training, degree and certificate programs, and non-accredited training and certificate programs offered by independent organizations. While the creative arts therapies possess a well-established system of professionalization, certification, and accreditation, the broader arts in healthcare field – the focus of this book – is in a nascent stage of professionalization. In this area of the arts and health continuum of practice, professionalization focuses both on artists who will be working in healthcare settings and on the administrative leaders of arts programs in healthcare.

In the United States, six universities currently offer full degree, minor, or certification programs designed to prepare artists to work in healthcare settings and administrators to start and manage programs. While an accreditation body for this professional field does not yet exist, the following universities are themselves accredited. These offerings include:

University of Oregon

- Master of Arts (MA) in Arts Administration with a Concentration in Arts in Healthcare Management: 64 quarter-hours, residential

Columbia College

- Arts in Healthcare Minor (undergraduate): 18 credits, residential

University of Florida (Center for Arts in Medicine)

- Master of Arts (MA) in Arts in Medicine: 35 credits, online
- Graduate Certificate in Arts in Medicine: 12 credits, online
- Graduate Certificate in Arts in Public Health: 12 credits, online
- Undergraduate Certificate in Arts in Healthcare: 12 credits, residential or low-residence
- Undergraduate Certificate in Dance in Healthcare: 14 credits, residential

The New School for Public Engagement

- Creative Arts and Health Certificate (undergraduate): nine courses plus 150 fieldwork hours, residential

Lesley University (Institute for Arts and Health)

- Advanced Professional Certificate in Arts and Health (post-Baccalaureate or post-Masters): 15 credits, residential

Five Branches University, California Graduate School of Traditional Chinese Medicine

- Certificate of Expressive Arts in Mind–Body Medicine (graduate): 9 units/135 hours of study

Individual courses not associated with certificate or degree programs are also offered at University of New Mexico, Georgetown University, San Francisco State University, University of Minnesota, the University of South Florida, and Baylor University, among others. Well-established training programs are offered by the Creative Center at University Settlement, the University of Florida, and the University at Buffalo.

Educational programs for creative arts therapists and for artists interested in working in healthcare environments are numerous. There are upward of 150 accredited degree programs in the creative arts therapies (C. Karlsson, personal communication, February 10, 2015). However, very few educational programs exist that are specifically designed to educate professional managers of the arts in healthcare settings. Dewey (2011) convincingly argues that "professionalization of the arts in healthcare field will not be possible without professionalization of the future leaders who will drive arts in healthcare policy and program administration" (p. 3). The nation's first specialized graduate program in this area was established within the University of Oregon's Arts and Administration Program in fall 2012 to address the field's need for "graduate-level study that concerns policy and administration of efforts that focus on how arts in healthcare contribute to quality of life, patient healing and wellness, and community health and well-being."

Please refer to Box 3.1 for a list of representative knowledge areas, skills, and abilities of a therapeutic artist in residence, and to Box 3.2 for a list of representative knowledge areas, skills, and abilities of an arts in healthcare manager.

BOX 3.1 REPRESENTATIVE KNOWLEDGE AREAS, SKILLS, AND ABILITIES OF A THERAPEUTIC ARTIST IN RESIDENCE

Knowledge of:

- Cultural diversity
- Evidence-based practice
- Environmental health principles
- Patient and employee safety regulations
- Professional practice environment
- Systems for patient safety

Skills in:

- Artistic competence
- Conversation facilitation, including difficult conversations
- Customer service
- Social competency
- Interpersonal, interprofessional communication
- Self-management

Abilities related to:

- Adapt with flexibility to situations, personalities, and tasks
- Appreciate balance between personal and professional life
- Be self-observant
- Commit to excellence
- Exhibit trustworthiness, honesty, and integrity
- Exhibit tolerance for cultural diversity and individual work style
- Inspire and motivate others
- Integrate ethical principles within practice

BOX 3.2 REPRESENTATIVE KNOWLEDGE AREAS, SKILLS, AND ABILITIES OF AN ARTS IN HEALTHCARE MANAGER

Knowledge of:

- Artistic practice and aesthetics
- Arts in healthcare research findings
- Arts management

- Artist relations
- Clinical arts therapy
- Healthcare administration
- Healthcare policy
- Holistic nursing
- Integrated care concepts
- Patient programs and services
- Specialized healthcare agencies and therapists

Skills in:

- Creativity
- Empathy
- Problem Solving

Abilities related to:

- Networking and forming coalitions and alliances
- Working with older adults and people with disabilities
- Advocacy, persuasion, and public speaking
- Community engagement and outreach
- Developing partnerships
- Event management
- Financial management
- Fundraising and development
- Marketing and communications
- Human resources
- Research skills

Certification of artists

Professional certification is an independent assessment of a person's knowledge, skills, and competencies to perform a specific professional role or work-related tasks and responsibilities. The proof comes in the form of a certificate that is earned when a professional passes an exam that is accredited by an organization or association responsible for monitoring and upholding prescribed standards for the particular industry involved (ICE, 2010). Professional certification shows employers that a professional is committed to their profession and is well trained. Certification makes employees more valuable to employers, and can provide professionals with better employment and advancement opportunities, a competitive advantage over candidates without certificates, and higher wages.

Despite the rapid expansion of the field, high prevalence of programs, and increase in education and training programs, as of this writing, there are no nationally established credentialing or certification requirements for artists to work in healthcare settings. However, a national task force was established in 2011 by the Arts & Health Alliance to explore the concept, and the Arts in Healthcare Certification Commission was established in 2011. The Arts in Healthcare Certification Commission is a nonprofit 501(c)6 organization incorporated in 2011 and governed by a Board of Commissioners who represent an array of artistic, academic, and professional disciplines. This Commission exists to establish credentialing mechanisms to promote patient safety and to improve the quality of care provided to participants of arts in healthcare services, and supports the philosophy that there should be a diversity of examinations that will effectively provide the opportunity for certification at various levels of professional roles in arts in healthcare.

As of this writing, an examination for certification of artists who work in healthcare settings is in development and has been piloted in four locations in the United States. Artists who meet eligibility requirements and successfully pass the examination will earn the Artist in Healthcare–Certified (AIH–C) credential (Arts in Healthcare Certification Commission, 2015). For the purpose of this certification, an artist is defined as *a person who produces work in any of the arts that is primarily subject to aesthetic criteria and who has been prepared through education and/ or professional experience.* Eligibility criteria for certification include: 1) an artist, as defined above; 2) a bachelor's degree in a related field (exceptions to the bachelor's degree requirement will be considered for applicants with a high level of professional achievement, and applicants appealing for this consideration must have clear documentation of a minimum of five years of related professional experience associated with significant professional achievement); and 3) a minimum of 800 hours of experience during the past five years facilitating an art form in a health context (Arts in Healthcare Certification Commission, 2015).

The intent of this certification is to help assure the public and employers that the artists working in healthcare settings have the essential knowledge, skills, and abilities needed to provide services safely. Training for all professionals who work in healthcare environments is essential, and employers must look for evidence of appropriate training and experience, particularly related to patient safety and professionalism. This expectation is in place for all professionals working in healthcare, and artists should be no exception. This certification process will establish the competencies required for professional artists to work in healthcare environments, help artists demonstrate competence to a potential contractor or employer, and help artists enter and follow a career path within healthcare.

In addition to the developing certification, several institution-specific and discipline-based certification programs exist in the United States, particularly for musicians. The National Standards Board for Therapeutic Musicians (NSBTM) has developed and maintains standards for therapeutic musician training programs and their graduates. NSBTM defines the courses of study, scope of practice, code of ethics, and other rules of conduct for certified therapeutic musicians. Musicians have opportunities to become certified therapeutic musicians through an array of existing distance learning programs, most of which require one or two years to complete. These programs result in certification titles unique to the educational program that was completed. For example, musicians working as therapeutic harpists can possess any of these credentials: a *certified therapeutic harp practitioner*, a *certified clinical musician*, a *certified music practitioner*, a *certified healthcare musician*, a *certified harp therapist*, or a *certified music-thanatologist* (Lambert, in press).

Within all of these certifications is the general expectation that a musician certified to work in healthcare settings possesses musical competency and skills as well as repertoire knowledge appropriate for bedside work and the needs of patients; is familiar with clinical deportment issues, monitoring equipment, and legal issues related to the work; understands that music serves medical care and that the focus is on the patient not on the musical performance; and possesses the professionalism, self-direction, and interpersonal skills required in a healthcare setting (Riley, n.d.).

Employment opportunities

Americans for the Arts (the nation's leading nonprofit organization for advancing the arts and arts education) reported in its 2013 National Arts Index that, despite the impact of the recent recession, arts employment has remained strong over the past decade. According to the report, "a variety of labor market indicators show relatively steady levels of employment, especially when compared to labor market difficulties facing all sectors of the economy" (Americans for the Arts, 2013). The report noted an increase of eight percent in the number of working artists from 1996 to 2011 (1.99 to 2.15 million), with artists remaining a steady 1.5 percent of the total civilian workforce. The report also noted that during ten out of the eleven years between 2000 and 2011, the self-employed artist workforce expanded.

As more healthcare institutions establish arts programs, employment opportunities for both artists and arts administrators increase. Published and unpublished field surveys suggest that many of the artists working in healthcare institutions do so as contracted employees (State of the Field Committee, 2009). In an unpublished University of Florida survey of twenty-five top employers in the field, one hundred percent of respondents reported having paid staff in their arts in healthcare program. The programs employed an average of 2.14 full-time and 2.4 part-time administrative staff members, an average of 1.0 full-time and 4.0 part-time staff artists (with benefits), an average of 15 contracted artists (without benefits), and an average of 11 paid visiting artists. Ninety-four percent of employers reported a need to expand their administrative staffs, while eighty-eight percent reported the need to expand their salaried or contracted artistic staffs. More are seeking salaried artistic staff members than contracted artists. Eighty-nine percent of employers · reported that they would be more inclined to hire administrative or artistic applicants who have an academic degree in arts in healthcare.

Arts programs in healthcare settings are positioned in a wide range of internal organizational locations within large healthcare institutions, resulting in great variety among the professional titles of arts in healthcare program directors. A survey conducted in 2011 identified that categories of arts in healthcare staffing "include various administrative positions (program director, coordinator, office management, communications, development), and artists (paid and volunteer). Administrative and artistic staff are hired as full-time, part-time, on-contract, on consultancies, as artists-in-residence, and as volunteers" (Dewey, 2011, p. 21).

Current pay scales in the field are consistent with, or higher than, other allied professions in healthcare, suggesting a viable level of compensation for artists and administrators who enter the field. A 2010 survey conducted by a Society for the Arts in Healthcare consultant of 220 arts in healthcare professionals showed a desire for higher pay scales and a need for graduate-level education and certification. The survey showed that while some artists are paid as much as $120/hour, the median hourly pay rate was $31–40/hour. Arts in healthcare administrators were similarly compensated, at an average hourly rate of $21–$30.

Conclusion

The field of arts in healthcare is growing rapidly and is at a pivotal stage of its professionalization. Developments in education, credentialing, and research are driving substantial and exciting growth in the field. Some of those same developments pose key challenges for the field, as it moves toward the establishment of certification, educational standards, and a code of ethics and standards for practice. These developments are critical to professionalization in the field, but are not yet in place. While the creative arts therapies end of the continuum of arts and health has achieved professionalization in this regard, arts in healthcare is in a much earlier stage in its development, but progressing in a very appropriate manner. Professional artists are playing important roles on interprofessional healthcare teams, and certification of these artists is necessary to ensure patient safety and appropriate scope of practice. Certification is likely to enhance the already expanding employment opportunities for artists in healthcare settings, and assist with further understanding of the field's scope of practice and utilization of its professional services.

References

Americans for the Arts. (2013). *2013 national arts index*. Retrieved from http://www.art sindexusa.org/national-arts-index

Arts in Healthcare Certification Commission. (2015). Retrieved from http://aihcertification. com/

Broderick, S. (2011). Arts practices in unreasonable doubt? Reflections on understandings of arts practices in healthcare contexts. *Arts & Health, 3*(2), 95–109.

Clift, S. (2012). Creative arts as a public health resource: Moving from practice-based research to evidence-based practice. *Perspectives in Public Health, 132*(3), 120–127.

Clift, S., Camic, P.M., Chapman, B., Clayton, G., Daykin, N., Eades, G., & White, M. (2009). The state of arts and health in England. *Arts & Health, 1*(1), 6–35.

Dewey, P. (2011). Arts in Healthcare Management: Feasibility study and program proposal. Unpublished internal report for the University of Oregon.

Dileo, C., & Bradt, J. (2009). On creating the discipline, profession, and evidence in the field of arts and healthcare. *Arts & Health, 1*(2), 168–182.

Field. (n.d.). In *Dictionary.com unabridged*. Retrieved from http://dictionary.reference.com/browse/field

Institute for Credentialing Excellence. (2010). *Defining features of quality certification and assessment-based certificate programs*. Retrieved from http://www.credentialingexcellence.org/p/cm/ld/fid=4

Lambert, P. D. (in press). The folk harp in healthcare: How to become a therapeutic musician. *Folk Harp Journal*.

Moss, H., & O'Neill, D. (2009). What training do artists need to work in healthcare settings? *Medical Humanities, 35*(2), 101–105.

Parkinson, C., & White, M. (2013). Inequalities, the arts and public health: Towards an international conversation. *Arts & Health, 5*(3), 177–189.

Pratt, R. (2003, June 26). *The arts in healthcare in the United States in the twenty-first century*. Keynote address presented to the VIII Music Medicine Symposium of The International Society for Music in Medicine. Hamburg, Germany.

Raw, A., Lewis, S., Russell, A., & Macnaughton, J. (2012). A hole in the heart: Confronting the drive for evidence-based impact research in arts and health. *Arts & Health, 4*(2), 97–108.

Riley, L. (n.d.). *How to start a healthcare music program in your local hospital or hospice*. Cypress, TX: Afghan Press.

Ruud, E. (2008). Reclaiming music. In M. Pavlicevic & G. Ansdell, (Eds.), *Community music therapy* (pp. 11-14). London: Jessica Kinsley Publishers.

Sadler, B. L., Ridenour, A., & Berwick, D. M. (2009). *Transforming the healthcare experience through the arts*. San Diego: Aesthetics.

Saks, M. (2012). Defining a profession: the role of knowledge and expertise. *Professions and Professionalism, 2*(1), 1–10.

Sonke, J. (2007). History of the arts and health across cultures. In J. Sonke-Henderson, R. Brandman, I. Serlin, & J. Graham-Pole (Eds.), *Whole person healthcare: Volume 3: The arts & health* (pp. 23–42). Westport, CT: Praeger.

Sonke, J. (2011). Music and the arts in health: A perspective from the United States. *Music and Arts in Action, 3*(2), 5–14.

Sonke, J., Pesata, V., Arce, L., Carytsas, F. P., Zemina, K., & Jokisch, C. (2015). The effects of arts-in-medicine programming on the medical-surgical work environment. *Arts & Health, 7*(1), 27–41.

Sonke, J., Rollins, J., Brandman, R., & Graham-Pole, J. (2009). The state of the arts in healthcare in the United States. *Arts & Health, 1*(2), 107–135.

Sonke, J., Rollins, J., & Graham-Pole, J. (in press). Arts in healthcare settings in the United States. In S. Clift & P. Camic (Eds.), *Oxford textbook of creative arts, health and wellbeing: International perspectives on practice, policy and research*. Oxford: Oxford Press.

Staricoff, R. L. (2004). *Arts in health: A review of medical literature*. London: Arts Council England.

State of the Field Committee. (2009). *State of the field report: Arts in healthcare 2009*. Retrieved from http://www.arts.ufl.edu/cam/documents/stateOfTheField.pdf

White, M. (2010). Developing guidelines for good practice in participatory arts-in-health-care contexts. *Journal of Applied Arts & Health, 1*(2), 139–155.

PART 2

Managing environmental arts in healthcare programs and initiatives

4

INTEGRATING ARTS PLANNING INTO HEALTHCARE DESIGN

Misty Chambers

What more perfect place to introduce the healing arts than in a healthcare environment? Much has been written about the built environment and its impact on the health and wellbeing of those who inhabit healthcare spaces. The concept of including the arts in healing rituals has been prevalent for centuries within indigenous cultures around the globe. More recently, the concept of including the arts in healthcare emerged in Italy in the fifteenth century with the inclusion of paintings and ceramic works in hospitals in Florence, Siena, and Milan (Baron, 1996). This practice gained momentum in the twentieth century and is exhibited in a variety of forms in today's healthcare facilities.

Pediatric healthcare environments have long embraced the concept of including the arts to enhance the patient experience, and positive distraction has been identified as a desirable evidence-based design strategy (Sadler, Joseph, Keller, & Rostenberg, 2009; Ulrich, Zimring, Joseph, Quan, & Choudhary, 2004). According to Ulrich et al. (2004), "Positive distractions refer to a small set of environmental features or conditions that have been found by research to effectively reduce stress" (p. 21). Positive interactive elements relieve anxiety and take a child's mind off negative associations and fear of medical procedures and tests. These elements, whether interactive or passive, evoke positive feelings from a patient's experience, spark the imagination, and create memorable moments of joy.

The practice of incorporating positive distractions has now become an accepted part of the modern design of adult healthcare environments. It is exemplified in the patient-centered Planetree philosophy (Planetree.org), defined by Charmel and Frampton (2008) as "a healthcare setting in which patients are encouraged to be actively involved in their care, with a physical environment that promotes patient comfort and staff who are dedicated to meeting the physical, emotional, and spiritual needs of patients" (p. 80). The term *patient-centered care* is often interchanged with the terms family-centered care and human-centered care to denote a healthcare practice that encompasses care for the whole person – body, mind, and spirit – inclusive of patients and their families, staff and physicians, and visitors within the healthcare environment. Incorporating the arts into healthcare facility design and arts programs into hospital operations are examples of bringing the body–mind–spirit connection to healthcare.

Similar to the movement toward evidence-based medicine and nursing to solve clinical problems, the healthcare design community has embraced the concept of evidence-based design put forth by Hamilton (2003), and further expanded upon by Stichler and Hamilton (2008) and the Center for Health Design (2010). Evidence-based design is defined as using the best available research to inform design decisions. It is also an important component of the arts selection process – basing decisions on research and evidence. This convergence of creativity and the arts with science and design is at the forefront of modern healthcare design.

Particularly important in healthcare environments, design should first be functional. Carter and Platt (2013) note that the healthcare environment can either support or hinder patient care and patient-centered practices. The physical environment should support the efficient flow of operations and safe patient care practices. It is possible to design architectural masterpieces that embrace creativity and the arts, while remaining true to the function of the spaces and supporting the activities for which a building is meant to operate. The real art of design is in the ability to create environments that support clinical and administrative tasks, while stimulating the senses and providing positive engagement, education, therapy, expression, and distraction through the arts (State of the Field Committee, 2009).

Research studies increasingly show the influence of the physical environment on stress, safety, and overall healthcare quality (Ulrich et al., 2004). Evidence-based design studies support the notion that access to the visual and performing arts contributes to reducing stress in healthcare environments (The State of the Field Committee, 2009; Sadler & Joseph, 2008; Ulrich, Zimring, Quan, & Joseph, 2006). Likewise, it has been shown that the arts have a positive impact on patient health outcomes, caregivers, and community wellbeing (State of the Field Committee, 2009; Ulrich, 1984). In addition, views of nature and positive distractions have been shown to reduce patient and caregiver stress (Ulrich et al., 2004). Art and architecture can independently provide access to nature, or they may work in harmony to enhance an individual's experiences and access to natural elements within the healthcare environment. All of these are important considerations when designing healthcare environments in conjunction with developing the arts programs offered within those environments.

In addition to the inclusion of evidence-based principles, the physical design of modern healthcare environments differs in other ways from the sterile landscape applied to the designed and built healthcare environments of the past. In today's holistic approach to healthcare design, the arts are integrated with architecture to create an environment that better addresses the needs of patients, their families, visitors, and caregivers. This seamless infusion of the arts within an architectural framework creates a healing environment, which includes: positive distraction;

opportunities for interaction; varieties of colors and textures; support for theming, branding, and storytelling; and varying scale and elements designed to stimulate the senses.

Patient experience

In recent years, patient experience has gained in importance to US healthcare leaders. The Advisory Board Company (2014) noted that many organizations have assigned patient experience leadership and accountability to senior directors, administrative leaders, or even senior executives. In addition, Medicare and other US insurers are tying reimbursement dollars to HCAHPS (Hospital Consumer Assessment of Health Care Providers and Systems) survey scores and patient satisfaction (The Advisory Board Company, 2014).

Although not specifically included on all patient satisfaction surveys, the physical environment does play a role in patient, family, and staff experience, and organizations are paying attention to the environment and to the convergence of architecture and the arts and their impact on users of healthcare environments.

According to Cahnman (2014), hospital design can impact elements that positively influence patient experiences. These experiences may be therapeutic, educational, or expressive in nature. Through experience with the arts and the healthcare environment, individuals may find a deeper understanding of self in the context of others, the hospital's culture, or broader healthcare issues.

It is important to be aware of the built environment's role in creating opportunities for positive patient experiences and the impact of the arts on positive patient outcomes, such as decreasing anxiety, reducing the perception of pain, and reducing stress. Designers, arts administrators, and artists should be aware of these outcomes and the implications for the business case or financial validation to justify arts programming and the inclusion of the arts in healthcare facilities (State of the Field Committee, 2009).

Planning and early commitment to the arts

Completing the design of a healthcare environment is not a simple process. It is a journey – from project conception through design, construction completion, move-in, and post-occupancy evaluation. The most successful environments that integrate the arts and architecture include interdisciplinary and inclusive planning and coordination of architecture and the arts with clinical and human-centered philosophies and work flows. Focused planning includes attention to clinical objectives, safety, patient and family needs, the creation of spaces with flexible uses, coordination with arts programming, the selection and installation of art, and coordination with construction details. Development of the project schedule and budget inclusive of the arts is critical during early project planning, and the arts should continue to be included at each pricing and design review milestone.

Planning begins with the development and statement of a clear vision, mission, and goals for the project, including those specific to the arts. The importance of committed leaders should not be underestimated. Project success is dependent upon visionary leaders who are willing to make a commitment to the established goals – leaders who understand the impact of the arts on healing, and the importance of creating a unique environment that incorporates not only the clinical and technological tools, but also healing arts elements into the design of a new facility. Community representatives and donors are also important partners on this journey and help support the vision through their gifts of time and resources.

The integration of arts planning into healthcare design should begin at project inception and involve a collaboration of design and construction team members, patients and their families, community representatives, artists, and arts administrators. From the beginning, this requires a different level of communication and collaboration with a dedicated project team who understands the project vision, the role of the arts, and their importance to the success of the project.

It is important to include the voice of the customer in discussions that help shape the facility's approach to the healing arts and the design of patient and public areas throughout the facility. Soliciting community and family feedback may include their participation in focus groups or as members of design committees. This approach illustrates a family-centered care philosophy, helps ensure community support for the project, and provides the opportunity to hear directly from customers and respond to their needs.

Site visits can be helpful tools during the planning and design process. When members of the design team participate in site visits to tour recently completed hospital projects around the country, they learn from the experiences of other healthcare facilities. Conversations about the importance of the healing arts in healthcare environments emerge as a result of these newly formed relationships, and a vision for arts in the new facility begins to form as dialogue continues between the participants from the healing arts department (or its equivalent within the organization), clinicians, administrators, donors, patients and their family members, and designers.

Guiding principles for art

Through this ongoing dialogue early in the life of a design project, goals and guiding principles for art begin to take shape. These help guide the overall direction of the arts program, the integration of arts within the architecture, and the final selection of art that will be included in the facility. Examples of guiding principles for art include the following:

- Infuse discussions of the arts throughout design, including interior and exterior planning discussions
- Create an environment that integrates the arts into architecture, creating a seamless and interactive environment between architecture, interior design, signage/graphics, and the arts

- Utilize varied art forms exemplifying artistic excellence (e.g., visual and performance arts, literary art forms printed and framed for display)
- Plan spaces to showcase the arts and to support arts programs
- Utilize varying mediums, such as textiles, sculptures, prints, paintings, glass, interactive, patients' works, and electronic/digital media
- Select art and art experiences that appeal to varying ages and developmental levels, particularly in spaces designed for pediatric populations
- Plan displays at varying heights with sensitivity to individuals of differing ages, those in wheelchairs or on stretchers, and those with limited vision
- Include original works from local, regional, national, and international artists
- Include culturally responsive pieces
- Involve the community in the process
- Include flexible and changing art options (e.g., rotating visual art displays)
- Include pieces that express the history and culture of the facility and the area
- Create opportunities to educate through the arts

Throughout planning and design, it is important to maintain an overall vision for the facility and its operations and an understanding of how the arts fit into that vision.

Space planning

When creating an environment in which art and architecture are synergetic, it is important early in design to determine specific space needs required to support the arts program. Opportunities for including the arts should be considered at entry and access points into the medical campus, around the exterior of the facility, within interior spaces, and throughout interior elements of the facility. These may include public spaces, patient care areas, performance areas, or conference and meeting spaces, which may be planned as multifunctional spaces to support performances or art events within the facility.

Many questions need to be answered early during planning. Will community donors support unique arts features or spaces within the facility? What spaces will be required to accomplish this vision? What is the arts budget for this facility project?

Visual art locations may include options for linear art gallery displays along public corridor walls or key destination points, rotating art displays, donor recognition features, sculptures in prominent locations or key navigation points within the facility, opportunities for branding and prominent logo displays, navigation or wayfinding points, and public waiting spaces.

Identifying the spaces for performance art venues should include accessibility considerations. Will the space(s) accommodate wheelchair, walker, and stretcher access? What types of programs should be accommodated within the venue(s) – for example, live or taped musical performances, zoo animal visits, gift shop sales, dance performances? What type of audio-visual accommodations will be required for the activities planned for these spaces? Will a sound system be required? Is there a need to plan space to accommodate large items such as a grand piano? Will the space(s) be required to accommodate arts events as well as other activities, such as meeting, dining, or training space accommodations?

Multifunctional spaces that encourage creativity, socializing, and use of imagination are important programmatic considerations when planning a healthcare facility. Planning spaces to meet the needs of multiple activities is one method for avoiding the duplication of spaces within a facility and the avoidance of additional square footage that leads to higher construction costs. This approach often provides a planning scenario in which expanded arts programming is possible through the economical use of space and resources.

Several examples of this creative use of multifunctional space to support arts programming can be found at the Monroe Carell Jr. Children's Hospital at Vanderbilt in Nashville, Tennessee:

1   A large, lineal segment of corridor wall in the entryway to the conference center was developed to support a rotating visual art gallery for the display of framed original art work as well as other art forms, such as framed poetry.
2   Within the conference center is a large, multifunctional space designed to resemble a movie theater and planned to accommodate movie nights for patients and families, large meetings and conferences, training and educational sessions, public receptions, and other large gatherings.
3   A performance area was also designed within the main public floor of the hospital. This space is embraced by an interactive art feature that doubles as a donor recognition element; this feature creates positive distraction and an environment in which children and families can experience healing arts performances from the community, while playing with an interactive art exhibit. This space is also used for additional functions, including visits from zoo animals, retail events, the hospital's fundraising radiothon, telethon activities, and press conferences. Wireless access and medical gas outlets are included in this area; space for beds, wagons, and wheelchairs is provided to maximize patient use of the space.

Leadership wanted to involve the community in the life of the children's hospital and understood the importance of the healing arts as a means of providing distractions for children undergoing treatments in the hospital and outpatient settings. Donor support was strong and available to provide funds for theses spaces as naming opportunities.

Conceptual plans

Once key questions are answered and spaces within a healthcare facility have been identified, the design team will develop conceptual architectural plans showing the relationship of departments and key spaces within the facility to confirm basic operational flow and identify functional and spatial relationships. This conceptual

FIGURE 4.1 Monroe Carell Jr. Children's Hospital at Vanderbilt in Nashville, Tennessee

design stage is the best time to begin identifying specific locations for key art features, particularly those requiring space, structural support, power, data, or other infrastructure requiring coordination with multiple design and construction disciplines. In addition to these considerations, many participatory arts programs also require locked storage for supplies, instruments, and sound system connections, and some require water connections.

For example, a large sculpture will require enough space to contain its physical dimensions, including clearances around the sculpture and access for maintenance and cleaning. Larger sculptures often require engineering expertise to design structural attachment details, in addition to structural supports, which may include a concrete stand, or additional structural support on the floor, ceiling, or walls to hold the weight of the piece. Accent lighting is often needed to highlight art features, and some pieces require power or data connections and coordination with the hospital's Engineering and Information Technology experts to coordinate connectivity to existing systems and software, as well as ongoing systems and software support.

These requirements should be determined as early as possible during the planning stages in order to address each of the components required and coordinate details with all disciplines within the correct construction sequence. Lack of this type of advance planning can lead to out-of-sequence construction work, schedule delays, and added cost to the project – all at a time when project schedules and budgets are typically strained and challenged to exceed expectations.

Careful planning and coordination with architects, engineers, interior designers, and construction managers are required to realize the vision, to create complementary indoor and outdoor relationships, and to successfully create a symbiotic relationship between architecture and the arts within the physical environment.

Key elements to address during design

Celebrate place and culture

Maintaining sensitivity to the local culture is an important design consideration. Both art and architecture create opportunities to cultivate human response and interaction. This begins with creating a sense of arrival at the entrance to the medical campus and continues along exterior travel paths, parking areas, and entryways. Outdoor applications and healing gardens create meaningful opportunities to connect with local culture, and they are discussed in more detail in Chapter 5 of this book.

Both exterior areas and interior spaces provide the landscape for utilizing native materials, images, familiar textures, culturally sensitive imagery, visual art pieces, and graphics. Providing familiarity through these elements may help decrease fear and stress and provide a sense of normalcy to the healthcare environment. This approach also affords the opportunity to celebrate individuals and the community, to express the hospital's culture through aspects of the physical environment, and to collaborate with community resources and local artists.

As an example, this cultural connection may be made through ambient music playing in parking or other exterior areas as well as within interior spaces of a facility.

The collaboration of the design team and the team at Resolute Health in New Braunfels, Texas, led to a design that created a flexible lobby space for large gatherings, receptions, and community functions, including the facility open house and staff kickoff party. Interior floor patterns create a transition from the lobby to the dining area and outside to a patio, simulating the flow of nature into the interior space. Custom mobile seating was designed to allow flexibility and provide a large gathering space for hospital or community functions. Similarities in interior and exterior finishes provide a familiar link to the community and the local area.

The Monroe Carell Jr. Children's Hospital at Vanderbilt in Nashville, Tennessee, chose to create a public persona during the construction process. This helped identify to the community that the facility would be something different – a special place for children that would embrace the arts both inside and outdoors. As the contractor made plans to fabricate the construction fence as a safety barrier for the building site, the design team and the arts committee collaborated to transform the fence into a community piece of art. Community members young and old, patients, families, staff, and physicians all came together to paint the fence. The fence itself became a popular interactive piece of art. Clear acrylic windows were added at multiple levels along the sidewalk in order to provide adults and children of all ages an opportunity to view the activity on the construction site and to engage with the facility even as the first shovels of dirt were being moved. Collaboration on many levels helped set the stage for this arts integration.

Regulatory requirements

Collaboration also extends to regulatory agencies, engineers, and acoustic consultants, among others. Requirements of local, state, and federal regulatory authorities must be followed in the selection of materials. This includes, but is not limited to, details related to infection control considerations, noise levels, safety, and maintenance.

The 2014 edition of The Facility Guidelines Institute's Guidelines for Design and Construction of Hospitals and Outpatient Facilities (2014 FGI Guidelines) addresses minimum architectural and engineering criteria in the design and construction of healthcare facilities. This document is recognized by federal, state, and local authorities across the United States as a code or a reference standard when licensing, certifying, or accrediting newly constructed healthcare facilities. The 2014 FGI Guidelines notes the importance of the effect of colors, textures, and patterns on safety, maintenance, and life cycle performance (The Facility Guidelines Institute, 2014). These same concepts are also important considerations when selecting works of art for the healthcare environment.

Safety

As noted above, the 2014 FGI Guidelines identify safety as a focus of concern within healthcare environments. This concept is shared by regulatory authorities, such as The Joint Commission, and it is included in the basic medical principle to do no harm. Architecture, interior design, and arts elements must adhere to safety principles, including fire and safety codes. Sprinkler heads must be planned according to standards, and they must be accounted for during the design process and coordination of architectural and interior design features as well as arts elements.

Visual art must be secured using safe mounting methods, such as placing special hardware on the backs of all hanging art work to securely mount each piece and keep individuals safe from the potential of falling art objects. Protrusions into corridors or spaces must be designed with safety issues in mind. In order to avoid the potential for injury to users of the spaces, sharp, dangerous edges should be avoided, and small features that may be easily removed and become choking hazards should also be avoided.

Lighting is another feature that can address safety needs and also create opportunities to aesthetically enhance the healthcare environment. Appropriate task lighting impacts safety (Joseph, 2006b), and it has been shown to decrease medication preparation errors (Joseph, 2006a). Lighting can also be used as an artistic feature or to accent artistic or architectural features within a facility. With varied lighting solutions from which to choose and an increased use of LED lighting within healthcare environments, it is important to specify performance requirements appropriate to each application.

The arts, architecture, and interior design may also coexist in creating functional elements to address the prevention of falls. For example, many facilities include a grand stair in the main public lobby to create a vertical connection between levels of a two-story atrium. Likewise, all facilities include handrails on corridor walls to assist patients with safe ambulation. Collaboration between the design team and artists can lead to creative solutions for functional handrail designs that also enhance the visual environment of the healthcare facility.

Infection control, cleanability, durability and maintenance

Infection control principles must also be followed in the design of healthcare facilities, and these principles apply in the installation of art and the implementation of arts programs. The Joint Commission and authorities that govern healthcare environments require specific guidelines to be followed to minimize the spread of infections, particularly through contact and water-borne agents. In fact, the 2014 FGI Guidelines no longer permit indoor, open-water features (The Facility Guidelines Institute, 2014). However, closed-water features are permissible. Another example for addressing infection control concerns is the encapsulation of pieces that utilize fabrics. Placing quilts and textiles in frames or plexi-glass boxes can assist with managing infection control concerns.

The ability to clean, repair, and maintain features over time is also an important consideration when selecting materials for use in the healthcare environment. Can the material or art work hold up to routine, daily interaction? How easily can the feature be accessed for dusting or cleaning? Can the finished product be routinely cleaned with the chemical agents used in healthcare environments? How will the artwork endure exposure to sunlight? Are the materials durable, and how will they be maintained?

In addition to the design team, the hospital's environmental services and plant services departments are important partners to include in finishes and art selection discussions, as they will be key players in the ongoing upkeep of the facility and its features.

Interior details and acoustics

Numerous opportunities exist for collaboration between architects, interior designers, and artists in the design of healthcare environments. With the progression of detailed facility planning and space layouts, interior design details and finishes become an important part of design discussions. The goal should include a careful layering of architecture, interior finishes, graphics, and signage with the arts to create a welcoming, healing environment – an environment that evokes the feeling, "I am going to get better here."

An example of this can be found at Mission Trail Baptist Hospital in San Antonio, Texas. Connecting with the local area, elements reminiscent of a river theme tie together both exterior and interior design features. Concepts are connected through a varied color palette, imagery, materials, textures, and curved and wavy shapes, and they are given vitality in art glass, landscaping, visual art, textiles, upholstery, and signage. Flooring patterns include subtle accent strips to mimic the flow of rivers. These features, along with changes in accent colors and signage details, are layered to create a seamless environment.

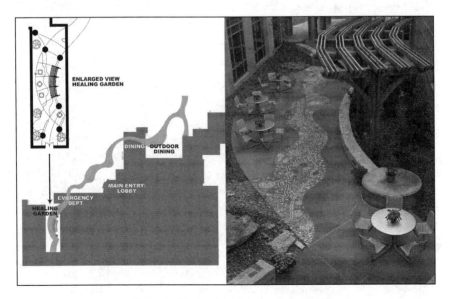

FIGURE 4.2 Mission Trail Baptist Hospital in San Antonio, Texas

The harmonious blending of art with architecture and interiors may be partially realized through coordination of the color palette (Tofle, Schwarz, Yoon, & Max-Royale, 2004) or the use of varying textures in the materials utilized. Through biomimicry, which the *Oxford Dictionary* defines as "the design and production of materials, structures, and systems that are modeled on biological entities and processes" (Biomimicry, n.d.), art, architecture, and interior design may come together to provide an experiential connection with nature.

It is important to find a balance that engages the senses and avoids over-stimulating them. Within the healthcare environment, there are numerous opportunities to design artistic interior elements that also serve functional needs. Examples include casework or cabinet details, interior and exterior doors, windows, flooring patterns, ceiling details, features in elevator cabs, accent lighting, signage, and large, linear wall sections.

In addition to the emphasis placed on selecting the appropriate materials to address safety, infection control, cleanability, durability, maintenance, and safety concerns, management of sound levels within the healthcare environment has also gained importance. High sound levels in healthcare settings have been identified as negative environmental stressors and have been key areas of concern in recent years, evidenced by the attention given to this topic in the popular media as well as by regulatory agencies. Quietness of the hospital environment is one of nine areas included in the HCAHPS (Hospital Consumer Assessment of Healthcare Providers and Systems) Survey to measure patients' perceptions of their hospital experience. This is significant to healthcare facilities, as it is recognized by the U.S. Patient Protection and Affordable Care Act of 2010 and directly impacts the calculation of value-based incentive payments received by healthcare facilities (HCAHPS, 2013).

Design features, materials, finishes, and furnishings have an impact on perceived noise levels within healthcare spaces. Noise-reducing finishes benefit patients and staff, improve satisfaction, and have an impact on reducing medical errors (Joseph & Ulrich, 2007; Sadler, Joseph, Keller, & Rostenberg, 2009; Solet, Buxton, Ellenbogen, Wang, & Carballiera, 2010; Ulrich, et al., 2008). Designers should carefully consider noise-absorbing options (Chambers & Bowman, 2011). This is another opportunity for collaboration with artists – to develop sound-absorbing solutions that combine interior finish materials with artistic options.

Flooring materials, high-noise-reducing-coefficient (NRC) ceiling tiles, and sound-absorbing wall panels can be used to improve sound buffering. For example, patient care environments within critical care units and imaging departments include numerous solid surfaces that reflect (rather than absorb) sound. Sculptural, artistic elements, such as panels with acoustical properties, may be used to absorb sound within these noise-intensive areas. Acoustical panels may be infused with colorful nature photographs, images of the local area, graphic patterns that fit within the overall interior design theme of the facility, or even literary phrases that tie in with local culture and fit with the theme of the facility. Acoustic panels have been used successfully within healthcare environments. Though it has not been scientifically quantified, the NICU team in one nationally-ranked children's hospital has anecdotally observed a perceived decrease in the amount of sedation medication required by patients in new patient rooms that featured noise-reducing acoustical panels, rubber flooring, and high NRC-rated ceiling tiles.

Visual art decisions

Similar considerations regarding color, imagery, patterns, materials, and textures are required in the selection of visual art. Coordination between visual art and interior design finishes is required. This process requires careful planning, as the selection of visual art pieces may consist of multiple components. For renovation projects or replacement facilities, art in an existing facility must be carefully evaluated, refurbished as necessary, and prepared to be moved to the new facility. New pieces of art may include commissioned pieces. "Calls for artists" may be sent out for other pieces, targeting groups such as local and state arts commissions, hometown newsletters, newspapers, and arts organizations.

Responding to the needs of various ages and cultural backgrounds of facility users, artwork should be planned to be mounted at varying heights, and include contrasting colors, textures, and materials scattered throughout the facility.

Forming an arts committee with a defined role early in the design process is recommended. The committee's role may be to give counsel and advice to the Healing Arts Director and the project team and to endorse the hospital's arts projects. The committee should have a diverse membership, which may include affiliations to arts organizations, community nonprofits, artists, frequent patients, and their family members.

It is desirable to develop a written art policy that includes goals, key determinants for choosing art, and standards to address such issues as donations, art on loan, and rotating exhibitions. For example, will the goal be to select from a broad range of art representing a diverse cross-section of artists and media? The creation of a policy and maintenance of standards in art selection is critical in evaluation and selection of pieces submitted for review and approval. This is particularly true when staff, patients, and community members submit work for consideration. (Additional details about art collections and sensitive curation in choosing art images are addressed within other chapters of this book.)

The final art selection process, parameters, budget, and the compensation for artists should be established with administration early in the project and prior to securing the first piece of art. Before the facility opens, it is also important to establish a plan for ongoing maintenance of the collection.

Major large-scale commissions and acquisitions make for excellent donor naming opportunities. The design team and healing arts department representatives often work with Hospital Foundations or Development Office liaisons to identify potential donors who might like to underwrite the cost of unique works planned for interior and exterior spaces of a new facility. Artist renderings or giclée prints may be used to help donors understand the piece of art under consideration. In addition, renderings are often used to assist potential donors in understanding the design intent of donor naming opportunities related to spaces and to generate community support for the overall design project as well as for individual elements within the design.

Many pieces of art collections in healthcare facilities across the United States have been given by donors who embraced a vision of the importance of integrating the healing arts into healthcare environments. They began the journey with a healthcare leadership team and designers and, through those strong relationships, many continue to support the work and mission of those facilities.

Wayfinding

Featured art pieces, when carefully planned with architectural and interior design elements, can also be used to define environmental cues and assist with navigation or wayfinding within a healthcare campus or facility. As defined by the U.S. Department of Veterans Affairs' 2012 VA Signage Design Guide, wayfinding is "the ability of a person to find their way to a given destination in a built, or planned environment, using information provided throughout that environment." The guide goes on to say that it "can involve signs, colors, objects, materials, and architecture" and that wayfinding is "a broader, more inclusive way of assessing all the environmental issues which affect our ability to find our way" (Veterans Health Administration, 2012, p. 13–2–19).

Simplified wayfinding contributes to a decrease in excess motion, which occurs when one is able to find their way within a facility. According to Ulrich et al. (2004), clarity in wayfinding and integrated wayfinding systems offer an increased sense of control and can decrease stress of users in healthcare environments. This has become particularly important with the growing trend toward fewer construction projects that include full replacement hospitals. The increase in hospital renovations and additions can lead to challenges in finding one's way through a facility that has grown in square footage over time. This requires careful planning and attention to details in developing creative wayfinding solutions to enhance navigation, avoid confusion, and facilitate movement through a facility.

Directional wayfinding is more than a clever signage system or well-developed room numbering system. It serves to improve both movement and communication with those traveling through a healthcare campus or facility. Ease of navigation can be facilitated through architecture in the layout of a building or through the standardization of layouts between floors (Veterans Health Administration, 2012). Exterior views can create wayfinding landmarks within a facility, and artistic features may serve as destination points at the intersection of corridors or decision points along key paths of travel within the built environment (Huelat, 2007). These artistic features are not limited to creative signage and graphics features; they may take various forms, including sculptures, significant wall art, ceiling or floor features, changes in color schemes or theming, digital or animated imagery, or artistic lighting.

Coordination details and communication

Coordination of all of these elements requires detailed communication during design, construction, and installation. The importance of coordination and communication to the success of a project should not be underestimated. Many architectural, engineering, construction, and artistic details must be carefully coordinated in order to successfully complete a healthcare design project.

Visual arts and performing arts spaces often require detailed planning and installation of lighting, power, and data connections in addition to structural supports in walls, ceilings, or floors. These structural and infrastructure requirements must be carefully planned and sequenced within the construction schedule. Other key issues that should be communicated within the design and construction team, and planned and coordinated carefully with the rest of the construction details, include the size, medium and materials of the art feature, installation location, degree of integration with the architecture, and means and methods required for installation. Variances around the feature for future cleaning and maintenance access must be planned, and installation details such as safety mounts are important considerations.

An example of this can be found in the new chapel completed in 2014 at CHI Memorial Hospital Chattanooga in Chattanooga, Tennessee. This chapel is located in an area of the hospital connecting new construction to existing spaces and involved the relocation of four historic stained glass panels, which were removed from a chapel in an older facility and stored for years prior to being revitalized for this project. The glass panels were then transported across two states, carefully stored during construction, and reinstalled in the newly designed chapel space.

The process required extensive planning and coordination on the part of the project team. The new space had to be prepared to accept the exact measurement of the panels. An architectural building envelope specialist provided detailed structural support recommendations, and the contractor reviewed these with the metal framework subcontractor responsible for securing the panels within the exterior wall. Budgetary allowances were measured against real costs, and necessary adjustments and provisions were found.

Panel conditions were assessed, and a local stained glass artisan was hired to restore the panels to their original beauty. These panels were finally installed and aligned with another set of uniquely designed exterior windows, which allowed the stained glass panels to shine with daylight, while being protected from potential damage from exterior elements. The other set of windows also provided acoustical properties that buffered the chapel from outside traffic noise.

As with many artistic and special architectural features, key donors generously provided monetary gifts as the process developed. They were recognized with special signage. Through detailed planning and coordination efforts, these panels found a new home where patients and their families, physicians, staff, and visitors are comforted on a daily basis by their inspirational beauty.

FIGURE 4.3 CHI Memorial Hospital Chattanooga in Chattanooga, Tennessee

Conclusion

Architecture and the arts working in synergy create opportunities within the built physical environment to celebrate an area, its culture, and its people. The process of completing a healthcare design and construction project is not simplistic in nature. It is a journey, and its successful completion requires forward-thinking leaders with a clear vision, a dedicated and committed project team, careful planning, clear communication, and thorough coordination of design, construction, and installation details to meet established programmatic, schedule, and budget targets.

The built healthcare environment offers many opportunities for integrating the arts with architecture and interior design features to evoke emotional response through a variety of creative and artistic expressions. Integrating arts planning early into the architectural design process presents a multitude of opportunities for creative collaboration and varied artistic expression to be infused within the architectural framework, creating a seamless healing environment. This integration of the arts into planning, design, and construction of a healthcare setting provides the environmental canvas to support healing of the *whole* person. It is through this integrated canvas that the built physical environment has the most positive impact on patient outcomes and patient, family, staff, and physician satisfaction.

References

The Advisory Board Company. (2014, March 25). Hospitals put patient experience officers in the C-suite. *Daily Briefing.* Washington, DC: The Advisory Board Company. Retrieved from http://www.advisory.com/daily-briefing/2014/03/25/hospitals-put-patient-experience-officers-in-the-c-suite

Baron, J.H. (1996). Art in Hospitals. *Journal of the Royal Society of Medicine, 89*(9), 482–483. Retrieved from http://www.ncbi.nlm.nih.gov/pmc/articles/PMC1295908/pdf/jrsoc med00051–0008.pdf

Biomimicry (n.d.) *Oxford dictionaries online.* Retrieved from http://www.oxforddictionar ies.com/us/definition/american_english/biomimicry

Cahnman, S. F. (2014, May 28). Designing for the patient experience. *Healthcare Design Magazine.* Retrieved from http://www.healthcaredesignmagazine.com/article/designing-patient-experience

Carter, R., & Platt, L. (2013). Healing environment: Architecture and design conducive to health. In S. Frampton, P. Charmel, & S. Guastello (Eds.), *The putting patients first field guide: Global lessons in designing and implementing patient-centered care* (pp. 149–172). San Francisco, CA: Jossey-Bass.

Center for Health Design (2010). *An introduction to evidence-based design: Exploring healthcare and design* (2nd ed.). Concord, CA: The Center for Health Design, Inc.

Chambers, M., & Bowman, K. (2011). Finishes and furnishings: Considerations for critical care environments. *Critical Care Nursing Quarterly, 34*(4), 317–331.

Charmel, P. A., & Frampton S. B. (2008). Building the business case for patient centered care. *Healthcare Financial Management, 62,* 80–85.

Facility Guidelines Institute. (2014). *Guidelines for design and construction of hospitals and outpatient facilities.* Chicago, IL: American Society for Healthcare Engineering.

Hamilton, D. K. (2003). The four levels of evidence-based practice. *Healthcare Design, 3*(4), 18–26.

HCAHPS: Hospital Consumer Assessment of Healthcare Providers and Systems. (2013, August). *HCAHPS fact sheet.* Retrieved from http://www.hcahpsonline.org/files/August_2013_HCAHPS_Fact_Sheet3.pdf

Huelat, B.J. (2007). *Wayfinding: Design for understanding* (Position paper for the environmental standards council of The Center for Health Design). Concord, CA: The Center for Health Design.

Joseph, A. (2006a). *The impact of light on outcomes in healthcare settings* (Issue paper # 2). Concord, CA: The Center for Health Design.

Joseph, A. (2006b). *The role of the physical and social environment in promoting health, safety, and effectiveness in the healthcare workplace* (Issue paper # 3). Concord, CA: The Center for Health Design.

Joseph, A., & Ulrich, R. (2007). *Sound control for improved outcomes in healthcare settings* (Issue paper # 4). Concord, CA: The Center for Health Design.

Planetree. (n.d.). About us – Planetree.org. *Planetree.org.* Retrieved from http://planetree.org/about-planetree/

Planetree. (n.d.). Planetree Selected to Partner with VA Office of Patient Centered Care. *Planetree.org.* Retrieved from http://planetree.org/wp-content/uploads/2012/01/VA%20 announcement%20press%20release%20final%20May%2010.pdf

Sadler, B.L., & Joseph, A. (Eds.) (2008). *Evidence for innovation: Transforming children's health through the physical environment.* Alexandria, VA: National Association of Children's Hospitals and Related Institutions.

Sadler, B.L., Joseph, A., Keller, A., & Rostenberg, B. (2009). *Using evidence-based environmental design to enhance safety and quality.* (IHI innovation series white paper # 18).

Cambridge, MA: Institute for Healthcare Improvement. Retrieved from http://www. IHI.org

Solet, J. M., Buxton, O. M., Ellenbogen, J. M., Wang,W. & Carballiera, A. (2010). *Evidence-based design meets evidence-based medicine: The sound sleep study.* Concord, CA: The Center for Health Design.

State of the Field Committee. (2009). *State of the field report: Arts in healthcare 2009.* Washington, DC: Society for the Arts in Healthcare.

Stichler, J. F., & Hamilton, D. K. (2008). Evidence-based design: What is it? *Health Environments Research and Design Journal, 1*(2), 3–4.

Tofle, R. B., Schwarz, B., Yoon, S. Y., & Max-Royale, A. (2004). *Color in healthcare environments.* San Francisco, CA: The Coalition for Health Environments Research (CHER).

Ulrich, R. (1984). A view through a window may influence recovery from surgery. *Science, 224*(4647), 420–421.

Ulrich, R., Zimring, C., Joseph, A., Quan, X., & Choudhary, R. (2004). *The role of the physical environment in the hospital of the 21st century: A once-in-a-lifetime opportunity.* Concord, CA: The Center for Health Design.

Ulrich, R., Zimring, C., Quan, X., & Joseph, A. (2006) The environment's impact on stress. In S. Marberry (Ed.), *Improving healthcare with better building design* (pp. 37–61). Chicago, IL: Health Administration Press.

Ulrich, R., Zimring, C., Zhu, X., DuBose, J., Seo, H., Choi, Y., Quan, X., & Joseph, A. (2008). A review of the research literature on evidence-based healthcare design. *Healthcare Environments Research & Design Journal, 1*(3), 61–125.

U.S. Department of Veterans Affairs. (2013, May 22). *Veterans Health Administration: Patient centered care.* Retrieved from http://www.va.gov/health/newsfeatures/20120827a.asp

Veterans Health Administration (2012). *VA signage design guide.* Washington, DC: U.S. Department of Veterans Affairs.

5

HEALING GARDENS

Annette Ridenour

The importance of nature as a source of physical, psychological, and spiritual wellbeing is so widely recognized today, and so thoroughly supported by careful research, that it is common for decision-makers to seek ways to incorporate nature into the design of healthcare facilities, particularly in the form of healing gardens.

A healing garden (sometimes referred to as a therapeutic garden or a supportive garden) can be understood as "any green outdoor space within a healthcare setting that is designed for use" (Cooper Marcus & Barnes, 1995, p. 4). Although the design of healing gardens typically focuses on serving a healthcare facility's patients, the benefits of healing gardens generally also extend to staff, physicians, visitors, family members, and even, at times, members of the broader community.

After presenting evidence regarding nature's positive effects on individuals, this chapter will principally discuss how art can amplify the appeal and impacts of healing gardens (providing three case examples) and describe a process for managing the selection and inclusion of art in healing gardens.

The healing effects of nature

The idea that nature has healing properties has a long history. It can be seen in Japanese gardens dating back to the first century CE and in medieval monastic gardens. The distinguished scientist E. O. Wilson (1984) has proposed a "biophilia hypothesis," which states that humans are genetically drawn to other living things. Regarding nature, Wilson has said, "I think that an attraction for natural environments is so basic that most people will understand it right away" (Tyson, 2008).

Careful research has shown that a connection with nature helps people cope with difficulties (Kuo, 2001), increases feelings of safety and connectedness with others (Maas, van Dillen, Verheij, & Groenewegen, 2008), improves overall wellbeing (Kaplan, Kaplan, & Ryan, 1998), and increases longevity (Takano, Nakamura, &

Watanabe, 2002). The connection with nature can be direct or indirect: as a foundation report asserted based on an extensive literature review, "More than 100 studies now confirm that stress reduction and mental restoration are significant benefits associated with living near green areas, having a view of vegetation, and spending time in natural settings" (Wolf & Housley, 2013, p. 1). With regard to children, another research summary concluded: "Current evidence suggests that . . . contact with nature is supportive of healthy child development in several domains – cognitive, social, and emotional. Until proven otherwise, we may continue to assume that, just as they need good nutrition and adequate sleep, children may very well need contact with nature" (Faber Taylor & Kuo, 2006, p. 136).

Specific conditions, such as asthma (Kimes et al., 2004), ADHD (Faber Taylor & Kuo, 2009), and dementia (Ottosson & Grahn, 2005) can be improved by contact with nature. Recovering breast cancer patients who undertook nature activities three times a week for ninety days had far less tendency to complain of mental fatigue, depression, marital problems, or a general inability to cope than patients who did not engage in those activities. They scored significantly higher on tests of cognitive acuity than their counterparts. They were far more likely to go back to work full-time and tackle new projects, such as losing weight or learning a foreign language (Cimprich & Ronis, 2003).

Nature in healthcare settings

In 1984, Roger Ulrich – a leader in the evidence-based design movement that is discussed elsewhere in this book – published the influential paper, "View through a window may influence recovery from surgery," in *Science* magazine (Ulrich, 1984). He compared the post-surgical experiences of two groups of hospital patients: one group whose hospital room windows had a view of trees, and the other group whose view was of a brick wall. Summarizing the results, Ulrich stated: "The patients with the tree view had shorter postoperative hospital stays, had fewer negative evaluative comments from nurses, took fewer moderate and strong analgesic doses, and had slightly lower scores for minor postsurgical complications" (1984, p. 421).

In subsequent studies, Ulrich and others showed that even nature-related artworks within healthcare facilities can affect healing outcomes – art showing natural scenes had a more positive effect on patients than any other kind of art (such as portraits, urban scenes, or abstract art) (Poggi, 2006; Ulrich, Lunden, & Eltinge, 1993).

Actual natural spaces within healthcare settings are, of course, a fully logical application of all the research findings, just as they are an outgrowth of humans' intuitive awareness of the power of nature to restore and heal.

In contrast to the very extensive general research about nature's restorative and health-giving influence, there is not a large body of research concerning the therapeutic effects of healing gardens in healthcare settings. In a post-occupancy evaluation of four hospital gardens in California, Clare Cooper Marcus and Marni Barnes (1995) concluded that patients, nurses, and other healthcare workers achieved pleasant escape and recuperation from stress from visiting the gardens. Another post-occupancy study, by Sandra Whitehouse and others (2001), determined that a children's hospital garden "was perceived as a place of restoration and healing, and use was accompanied by increased consumer satisfaction" (p. 301).

Design of healing gardens

Ulrich (1995) has proposed that healing gardens will effectively achieve their purposes insofar as they foster four elements: "a sense of control and access to privacy; social support; physical movement and exercise; and access to nature and other positive distractions" (p. 36). He added that for a garden to provide those elements, it must convey a sense of security: "If the design or locational characteristics of a garden engender feelings of insecurity or even risk, the setting will likely have stressful rather than restorative influences, and many patients, visitors, and staff will avoid the space. Patients who undergo medical treatment often feel psychologically vulnerable, which has been demonstrated to heighten their sensitivity to insecurity in an environment" (p. 36). The need to take into account patients' heightened sensitivity is illustrated by these experiences of healing-garden artwork, as described by one author: "Patients thought that a large gazing ball in one garden was the 'evil eye.' A somewhat abstracted sculpture of birds was seen as 'vultures that scrape flesh' " (Kreitzer, 2013).

The 2013 book edited by Clare Cooper Marcus and Naomi Sachs, *Therapeutic Landscapes: An Evidence-Based Approach to Designing Healing Gardens and Restorative Outdoor Spaces*, contains extensive recommendations for designing gardens for many specific types of facilities, including acute care hospitals, children's hospitals, cancer centers, and hospices. The Horticulture Therapy Association, Horticultural Therapy Institute, and other organizations possess substantial experience and expertise in the design of healing gardens.

Art within healing gardens: three examples

Art within a healing garden can augment the positive effects of the garden's natural greenery in many ways. It can catch the eye and invite individuals in. It can frame the entrance and borders of the space in a way that increases its specialness or even its sacredness. Art creates positive distractions in many forms, including captivation by beauty, by becoming engrossed in constructive wonderment, or by enabling carefree physical activity. Designed properly, art offers private spaces for contemplative restoration, and art can promote or facilitate socially supportive interactions, whether between companions or between strangers. Art can make statements, either directly or indirectly, about important aspects of life's journey. It can exalt the spirit, stimulate or calm the mind, and engage the body.

Properly envisioned, art does not just supplement or complement the effects of a garden; it amplifies those effects. Virtually every aspect of the garden is an art component or a potential art component – walkways, furniture, walls, gates, and other elements are as much part of the art aesthetic of the garden as are such items as sculptures, fountains, and murals. It is this holistic approach, in which the whole garden environment is in fact an integrated art experience, that will make the garden experience exceptional.

Here are three examples from Aesthetics, Inc. – an organization based in San Diego, California that collaborates with healthcare institutions and the communities they serve to create patient- and family-focused evidence-based design in healing environments.[1]

1. Children's Hospitals and Clinics of Minnesota – St. Paul

For the 6,000-square-foot Children's Hospital Rooftop Auxiliary Storybook Garden, at the St. Paul campus of Children's Hospitals and Clinics of Minnesota, six primary user groups were identified:

1 Children who were in the hospital and had the ability to leave their rooms to attend an outdoor performance.
2 Children who were in physical therapy, either outpatient or inpatient.
3 Siblings of children who were in the hospital who could engage in more active play.
4 Families of children in the intensive care unit that was adjacent to the garden.
5 Other family members who needed to get away for restoration, solace, or contemplation.
6 Staff that would choose the space for respite.

From this identification of users, it was determined that spaces within the garden would need to accommodate small groups as well as individuals, and include areas for active play, passive play, gardening, socialization, and reflection. This is truly a multipurpose garden.

A large mural was commissioned for the hospital corridor leading to the garden entry. This mural, a very detailed depiction of an imaginary community having many aspects of St. Paul's landscape and demographics, designates the start of a journey of discovery and positive distraction. A portal treatment further announces the beginning of the experience. An artistic privacy fence, topped with words that cumulatively tell a story, separates the garden from the patient units and provides safety.

The different areas of the garden are articulated by different flooring materials, including screened tile, hand-painted tile, inlaid rubber, and artificial grass. For active play, areas in the flooring create a pathway for tricycles and wagons the children can ride, and there is also a hopscotch pattern. A labyrinth in the corner provides an area for more quiet reflection.

Three large play areas contain sculptures, which provide opportunities that include sitting on ladybugs, hopping from mushroom to mushroom, talking into

FIGURE 5.1 Storybook Garden, Children's Hospitals and Clinics of Minnesota – St. Paul

Photographer: Wendy Zins Photography

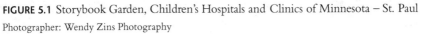

a flower that is also a sound tube, and exploring how a chrysalis turns into a butterfly.

The central design feature of the garden is a very large fountain with a water play area for boats where water is turned on for play and recycled, as well as highly sculpted areas for plantings that include playful depictions of leaves, flowers, bugs, and a giant sculpted rose.

Art – the fence, the fountains, and even the shade structures that house seating areas, bronze sculptures, and planting space – becomes the play environment.

Performing and participative programs also take place within the garden. An area was created that allows for movie nights and also accommodates mobile television equipment to produce short pieces that can be broadcast into the patients' rooms. Tables are included so an artist in residence can lead art therapy activities with a small number of patients under umbrellas in the garden. Outdoor audio speakers shaped as rocks are distributed around the garden to assist with ambient music and performance. Children's Hospitals and Clinics already has a robust lineup of artists in residence and performers on a regular basis, so accommodating spaces for them to move into the garden was important.

The garden also features quiet sitting areas for parents and staff, including a rose bench and fountain in the center of the garden and a five-circuit labyrinth. Arbors create quiet places for intimate conversation and shade for plants and sculptures. Expansive plantings throughout the garden provide ample green spaces.

FIGURE 5.2 Storybook Garden, Children's Hospitals and Clinics of Minnesota – St. Paul
Photographer: Wendy Zins Photography

2. Scripps McDonald Center

Scripps McDonald Center, a treatment center in La Jolla, California focused on adults and adolescents dealing with substance abuse, provides an example of how artwork enhances the healing gardens in an adult facility, supporting the therapeutic purposes of a facility of this type. (The center and the garden were recently torn down as part of a new building plan.)

The garden transformed an underutilized outdoor concrete basketball court into a tranquil and contemplative environment. Working closely with staff and past program graduates, a vision for the garden emerged in which the space became a teaching tool and a place of respite for the center's residents. The garden experience was based on the twelve steps and twelve traditions of the Alcoholics Anonymous program.

Entered over a symbolic ridge, the garden contained twelve outdoor meditation alcoves, each representing one of the program's twelve steps. At each alcove, one of the twelve steps was engraved in paving, surrounding a labyrinth, and each alcove had either inspirational architectural features or works of art specifically commissioned to reinforce each step's core values and principles. Elements included fountains, seating, and stone and glass artwork. The artists worked with the staff and program graduates to create artwork that would resonate with the patients. A local landscape architect was hired to develop and refine the plan, the art, and the plantings into a lush and vibrant garden.

FIGURE 5.3 12–Step Garden – McDonald Center, Steps 4–5, Scripps Memorial Hospital, La Jolla

Photographer: Schmidt Design Group (Landscape Architect)

FIGURE 5.4 12–Step Garden – McDonald Center, Step 6, Scripps Memorial Hospital, La Jolla

Photographer: Schmidt Design Group (Landscape Architect)

3. Cottage Hospital

Cottage Hospital of Santa Barbara, California is an adult hospital with a children's wing. Cottage Hospital included five separate gardens, at street level and as rooftop gardens, in a large expansion of its downtown campus. The landscape design team, Arcadia Studio, designed the gardens to reflect their different uses by patient populations and by the general community.

The overall theme of the gardens was respite and restoration. Art benches were created for a small pocket park where the public was invited to enjoy the newly landscaped space with large shade trees and bountiful plant life. A large "River of Life" was designed for the outdoor seating area of the cafeteria. Contemplative artworks by many different artists were chosen to reinforce the peaceful feeling of the space. A child-attracting mosaic totem was commissioned for the pediatric terrace, and a large bronze mother-and-child sculpture was commissioned for the women's center. A beautiful Spanish garden, with stone walls and symmetrical patterns, was designed as a place for patients to get away. A large bronze globe was commissioned from Sandra Kay Johnson, representing a bouquet of symbols – a bas-relief sculptured sphere of multicultural symbols of hope, joy, love, and comfort.

Managing the design and implementation process

This section of the chapter will describe four elements of planning and implementing art within healing gardens: (1) leadership; (2) the overall design process; (3) selecting, contracting with, and overseeing artists; and (4) evaluation. Key aspects of each element are listed in Box 5.1.

1. Leadership

Aesthetics, Inc. has been fortunate to contribute to the visioning, planning, and implementation of art in healing gardens in many healthcare environments. It found that most healthcare facilities will start the planning process for a healing garden with only a landscape architect, but it is important to include an art consultant at the table from the beginning, so that the art is fully integrated with the design.

Ideally, a committee of stakeholders is assembled to envision and plan the new garden, along with the landscape architect and the art consultant. This group will be referred to as "the design committee" or "the committee," to differentiate it from the consultant's design team. The committee should include representatives of most stakeholder groups; members might include a physician, a nurse, a patient advocate or a patient or former patient, and key representatives from marketing, the foundation, administration, chaplaincy, and facilities, as well as a community master gardener, and any philanthropic stakeholders that have been identified. Aesthetics, Inc. has generally found that the committee becomes less effective when there are more than fifteen members.

While various authority structures can be established, it is most workable for the committee to be advisory to the art consultant, and for the consultant to report

BOX 5.1   KEY CONSIDERATIONS FOR ART WITHIN HEALING GARDENS

Leadership

- Involve the art consultant from the beginning of the process.
- Create a strong design committee that reflects all stakeholders, including patients (maximum committee size of fifteen).
- Budgets must be regularly updated to reflect all relevant cost considerations.
- Fully document all aspects of the project.

Overall Design Process

- Visioning and goal setting should take place at the earliest possible point in the process.
- Designs must be thoroughly reviewed by the committee and by representatives of the garden's likely users.
- The design must reflect the requirements of the various garden users – patients and others.
- Plans for the art must be integrated with the overall design and construction process for the garden.
- All required approvals and permissions must be obtained.
- The art must have no potential to cause physical or psychological harm.

Working with Artists

- It should be the art consultant's responsibility to manage relationships with the artists who are selected to provide the works, from contracting to installation.
- Contracting is generally divided into two phases – concept design and design development, fabrication, and installation.
- Using local artists adds an important element of commitment and community interest and support.
- Do not underestimate the capacity to attract donors to a project.

Evaluation

- Conduct outcome studies that assess the attainment of the original goals (focusing generally on quality of life improvements), and use those studies to consistently improve users' experience of the garden.

directly to the executive or executives responsible for the garden. Whatever the structure is, it should be clearly defined and understood by all participants from the first days of the project.

The duration of committee meetings is important. The committee members are generally very busy people with crowded schedules. Two-hour meetings are often ideal, but usually not feasible. A ninety-minute meeting is far preferable to a one-hour meeting – typically, more will be accomplished in one ninety-minute meeting than in two one-hour meetings. The meetings described in the sections below are assumed to be ninety-minute meetings.

It is also important to identify a budget target early in the process, and to state how the funds for art will be obtained – through the capital budget or through philanthropy. Properly managed, fundraising can greatly increase the opportunities for garden artwork. At Children's Hospitals and Clinics of Minnesota – St. Paul, for example, each art piece and area of the garden was funded through the generous philanthropy of the community. This method also creates a strong sense of community ownership in the creation and maintenance of the garden itself.

Even though patients or former patients may participate on the design committee, a larger input process involving patients is appropriate in many cases. In children's hospitals, for example, there are often peer review councils, in which about a dozen children of different ages meet to review design concepts for additions and remodels of that hospital. In many cases, the children chosen to participate are ones who have been coming back to the hospital for extended stays and multiple operations for most of their life. At Children's Hospitals and Clinics of Minnesota – St. Paul, it was the children who wanted to make sure that movies could be shown outdoors in the summertime. Several of the children also wanted to be sure that there was flexibility for the garden to change over time so that they could experience new elements each time they came back. At another facility, many of the artists' concept drawings were shared with the children and families in the inpatient play room. The children were shown the options and given stickers to vote their preferences; along with input from the families and nurses, that information influenced the art committee's final decisions. And at another facility, a team of child life therapists who worked with the children on a daily basis had a strong influence on the final decision-making about artwork for the gardens.

We recommend that at each phase of design the art consultant and the client create a written agreement of completion before proceeding with the next phase. With some projects taking years to complete, consistent and well-maintained documentation is essential.

2. The overall design process

Visioning. It is important to begin with an engaging visioning process. Before the first meeting, each committee member is asked to think about the garden that they most love, and to bring photographs of that garden and be prepared to share with the group what aspects of the garden are special to them. The first committee meeting begins with an introduction by each member of the group, including a description of his or her favorite garden. After those introductions, a guided meditation occurs in which the committee members are invited to enter the newly completed garden for the first time, looking around it, walking through it, and noticing what they see and feel. This individual information is then shared with the whole committee and recorded as part of the meeting minutes.

After that sharing of thoughts, an overview of evidence-based best practices in healing garden art is provided. Then the committee members are asked to start listing the physical components they want in the garden, the feelings they would like the garden to evoke, and the experiences they would like to occur for users of the garden. This information is compiled and the first meeting concludes with the committee members sharing information about the different patient populations and any special considerations based on those patients' physical, emotional, and cognitive states.

Preliminary Design. From the information gathered in the first meeting, the design team starts mapping a preliminary design for the art elements. That design usually starts with a block diagram of spaces for a variety of functions, which might include walking, eating, sitting in intimate groups, sitting in large groups, quiet reflection, gardening, and engaging in some type of physical activity or therapy. The design team creates image boards that include furniture, artwork, plantings, planters, fountains, and paving materials, and it prepares a statement explaining how the design supports the physical, emotional, and cognitive requirements of the different garden users. At this point, the design team would begin compiling lists of artists who might be approached for various elements, and acquiring portfolios of the potential artists' work.

Considering and Refining the Preliminary Design. The second committee meeting begins with an opportunity for the members to share any thoughts they have had about the garden since the first visioning session. After this discussion, the preliminary designs and image boards are shown and discussed by the committee members, who then vote on their favorite design elements so that the design team can leave the meeting with clear direction regarding all of the aspects presented.

Concept Design. With the favorite elements identified and discussed, the design team creates an initial concept design articulating the plans and siting the different elements. The types, media, and sizes of the artwork are concretely defined in this stage. Where appropriate, the design team identifies artists that might be approached for commissioned works – three to five artists for each possible commission.

Review of the Concept Design. At a third meeting of the design committee, the concept design, including a proposed art budget, is presented by the design team, along with the portfolios of the final candidates to create works of art for the garden. A plan should be developed that further articulates the number, type, and placement of artwork, and the artist selection process should be narrowed down to one or two artists for each potential commission. For purposes of assessing and pursuing philanthropic support, each art element should be priced and budgeted separately.

Even if some or all of the art will be paid for through philanthropy and therefore might be somewhat uncertain, it is necessary to ensure that all required structural, civil, lighting, electrical, and plumbing coordination is carried out for each possible art element. If a pad is needed for the artwork, for example, or water and a drain are needed, this has to be included in the design of the garden (and included in the budget).

Selection of Artists and Initial Design Development. In this phase, the artists are selected (see section three below for more detailed information) and they begin concept designs of the art pieces. The artists are usually asked to sketch two designs that are based on previous works or ideas that have been approved by the client. A contract is created with each artist for this phase only.

Design Review. The artists' designs are reviewed by the design team to determine which will work best in the overall design concept, and then they are presented to the overall design committee for its consideration. It is not uncommon for committee members to like some parts of one design by an artist, and some parts of another design by the same artist. In this case, the artist might be asked to provide a new concept design for the artwork. Once the concept design is accepted, a new contract (or series of contracts) is created related to further design development, fabrication, and installation (see section three, below).

The work of the design committee is generally considered complete when the artists have been selected. In subsequent stages, the art consultant works directly with the architect of record and with the client's designated executive or executives.

Required internal and external reviews and approvals must also be identified and pursued. For example, most hospitals will have a department of life safety and infection control that will scrutinize the proposed artwork for sharp edges, tripping or falling hazards, infection control, ease of cleaning, ability to be maintained, fire safety, and overall compliance with the Americans with Disabilities Act. A prominent sculpture might require approval by the architectural review board of the community. In California and other states, such a sculpture might also require approval by a statewide office of health planning and development.

3. Selecting, contracting with, and overseeing artists

The Role of the Art Consultant. Art consultants are the liaisons who shepherd the relationships with artists through to a successful installation. The art consultant is responsible for ensuring that the artwork is properly integrated into all construction and installation documentation – this is a large and complex responsibility.

In most cases, the art consultant is paid a fee, which might be a percentage of the art budget or a flat fee for services rendered. In some cases, the art consultant will sell the artwork and be paid a commission within the sale price of the art.

Commissions and Calls. While it is possible on rare occasions to identify existing works that will fully fit with a garden's design, usually the art will be custom-made for the garden setting. There are two principal ways of selecting artists. One is through commissioning, in which a particular artist is directly approached and asked to create a specific work. The other is the issuance of a call for artists, in which a need is identified and proposals are sought from multiple artists. A call is the preferred way of seeking artists, but it can add as much as four to six months to the duration of the project. Even the time for commissioning should not be underestimated – a responsible art consultant will review many artists' work before recommending a small number of artists to the committee for consideration.

Aesthetics, Inc. has found that working with local artists – where "local" might mean the immediate surrounding area or perhaps an area as broad as the state in which the facility is located – adds an important distinctive energy to the design process and can increase the in-house and community "buzz" related to the garden.

Contracting. Contracts may be direct contracts between the artist and the client; three-way contracts among the art consultant, the client, and the artist; or contracts between the artist and the art consultant as agent for the client. The client's preferred arrangement needs to be established at the beginning of the project.

Contracting is generally divided into two phases – concept design and design development, fabrication, and installation.

After the art consultant negotiates a price for the artwork that is approved by the client, a contract is created that delineates the concept design phase for the artist. The artist is usually paid ten percent of the full price of the artwork as a fee for concept design. The artist is usually asked to sketch two designs based on previous works or ideas that have been approved by the client. Models are rarely created in concept design, although some artists prefer to create models to express their concept ideas. In those cases, a model will be the deliverable for the concept design phase.

In the concept design contract, it is made clear that if the client does not like the designs, the client is not obligated to continue working with the artist – the design will be returned to the artist if the client decides not to accept it. This contract specifies that the artist is an independent contractor and that this design is not work for hire by the client. It is also important for the client to understand whether the commissioned work of art will be a unique piece or will be part of a limited edition. If it is part of a limited edition, then the number of copies must be agreed upon in the contract. Some clients prefer to pay more to have unique pieces created just for them. If the client is requesting a unique piece, the price might be higher, especially if it is a cast piece.

Design Development, Fabrication, and Installation. Once the concept design for the artwork is accepted, a new contract (or series of contracts) is created related to design development, fabrication, and installation. Many artists are not familiar with this phase, so the process needs to be spelled out in detail based on the kind of artwork, where it is going, how it is being integrated into the environment, and any governmental or other relevant regulations.

In some cases, the construction process of the artwork itself may need to be calculated and submitted by a structural engineer. In most cases, materials, colors, foundations, attachments, and lighting are standard requirements that are approved in the design development phase before the artist is allowed to go into the fabrication phase.

Once the artwork has been approved for fabrication, a contract is created that details the timelines and approval processes required during the fabrication and installation phase. Among other things, the art consultant will generally review photographs of the progress of the artwork, approve the artwork, make installation arrangements, and provide on-site supervision of the installation.

4. Evaluation

It should be standard practice to conduct outcome studies on healing gardens, and to use the results of those studies to improve the effectiveness of the garden. Healthcare programs are usually evaluated principally with regard to either health outcomes or quality of life improvements. For art in gardens, the principal evaluation questions ought to address quality of life matters. The evaluation should be anchored in the goals that were established for the garden and that guided the selection and placement of the art. Some sample topics for an evaluation might include the following, depending on the guiding goals:

- To what extent does the garden provide a place of peace and restoration? How do the art elements and themes contribute to or distract from that experience?
- To what extent does the garden inspire therapeutic activity? How do the art elements and themes contribute to or distract from that experience?
- To what extent does the garden inspire persistence in the health journey? How do the art elements and themes contribute to or distract from that experience?

Conclusion

Art is not just a means to include additional healing elements within a garden that is already healing – properly envisioned and executed, art amplifies the healing effects of the garden. It creates an encompassing environment that – more fully than a garden by itself – removes garden visitors from the troubles and stresses they are experiencing and provides nourishment and restoration. Holistically affecting body, mind, and spirit, the art creates visual and tactile experiences, promotes wonder and contemplation, and lifts the soul.

A healing garden that fully makes use of art will, more than virtually any other aspect of healthcare facility design, create the "positive distraction" from cares and worries that is demonstrated by evidence-based research to be an essential element of the health journey. Using the processes in this chapter, healthcare art leaders can join with consultants and stakeholders in an immensely creative endeavor that will have vast impact on the wellbeing of patients, family members, physicians, staff, visitors, and community members.

Note

1 Annette Ridenour is the founder and owner of Aesthetics, Inc.

References

Cimprich, B., & Ronis, D. (2003). An environmental intervention to restore attention in women with newly diagnosed breast cancer. *Cancer Nursing, 26*(4), 284–292.

Cooper Marcus, C., & Barnes, M. (1995). *Gardens in healthcare facilities: Uses, therapeutic benefits, and design recommendations.* Martinez, CA: Center for Health Design.

Cooper Marcus, C., & Sachs, N. (Eds.). (2013). *Therapeutic landscapes: An evidence-based approach to designing healing gardens and restorative outdoor spaces.* New York: Wiley.

Faber Taylor, A., & Kuo, F. (2006). Is contact with nature important for healthy child development? State of the evidence. In C. Spencer & M. Blades (Eds.), *Children and Their Environments: Learning, Using and Designing Spaces* (pp. 124–140). Cambridge, U.K: Cambridge University Press.

Faber Taylor, A., & Kuo, F. (2009). Children with attention deficits concentrate better after walk in the park. *Journal of Attention Disorders, 12*, 402–409.

Kaplan, R., Kaplan, S., & Ryan, R. (1998). *With people in mind: Design and management of everyday nature.* Washington, DC: Island Press.

Kimes, D., Ullah, A., Levine, E., Nelson, R., Timmins, S., Weiss, S., & Blaisdell, C. (2004). Relationships between pediatric asthma and socioeconomic/urban variables in Baltimore, Maryland. *Health & Place, 10*(2), 141–152.

Kreitzer, M. J. (2013). *What are healing gardens?* Retrieved from http://www.takingcharge. csh.umn.edu/explore-healing-practices/healing-environment/what-are-healing-gardens

Kuo, F. (2001). Coping with poverty: Impacts of environment and attention in the inner city. *Environment and Behavior, 33*(1), 5–34.

Maas, J., van Dillen, S., Verheij, R., & Groenewegen, P. (2008). Social contacts as a possible mechanism behind the relation between green space and health. *Health & Place, 15*(2), 586–595.

Ottosson, J., & Grahn, P. (2005). Comparison of leisure time spent in a garden with leisure time spent indoors on measures of restoration in residents in geriatric care. *Landscape Research, 30*, 23–55.

Poggi, E. (2006, November 1). Beyond traditional treatment: Establishing art as therapy. *Healthcare Design Magazine.* Retrieved from http://www.healthcaredesignmagazine. com/article/beyond-traditional-treatment-establishing-art-therapy

Takano, T., Nakamura K., & Watanabe M. (2002). Urban residential environments and senior citizens' longevity in megacity areas: The importance of walkable green spaces. *Journal of Epidemiology and Community Health, 56*, 913–918.

Tyson, P. (2008, April 1). A Conversation with E. O. Wilson [Edited interview transcript]. *NOVA.* Retrieved from http://www.pbs.org/wgbh/nova/nature/conversation-eo-wilson.html

Ulrich, R. (1984). View through a window may influence recovery from surgery. *Science, 224*, 420–421.

Ulrich, R. (1995). Effects of gardens on health outcomes: Theory and research. In C. Cooper Marcus & M. Barnes (Eds.), *Gardens in healthcare facilities: Uses, therapeutic benefits, and design recommendations* (pp. 27–86). Martinez, CA: Center for Health Design.

Ulrich, R. S., Lunden, O., & Eltinge, J. L. (1993). Effects of exposure to nature and abstract pictures on patients recovering from heart surgery. Paper presented at the thirty-third meeting of the Society for Psychophysiological Research. Rottach-Egern, Germany.

Whitehouse, S., Varni, J. W., Seid, M., Cooper Marcus, C., Ensberg, M. J., Jacobs, J. R., & Mehlenbeck, R. S. (2001). Evaluating a children's hospital garden environment: Utilization and consumer satisfaction. *Journal of Environmental Psychology, 21*(3), 301–314.

Wilson, E. O. (1984). *Biophilia.* Harvard University Press: Boston, MA.

Wolf, K., & Housley, E. (2013). *Feeling stressed: Take a time out in nature.* Annapolis, MD: TKF Foundation.

6

MANAGING ART COLLECTIONS IN HEALTHCARE ENVIRONMENTS

Donna Glassford

Art is for the Spirit, a print by artist Jonathan Borofsky, is a whimsical and inspi-rational depiction of a barefoot man standing on the planet Earth surrounded by an aura of white light and swirling cosmos. His arms and hands are raised toward the cosmos in a gesture of empowerment and connectedness. Although he is a small player in a vast universe, he is central to the event as a powerful conductor of energy and action. Through art, his heart and spirit are radiant, transformed and connected to all things seen and unseen.

Borofsky's print can be found on display in several hospitals that recognize the intrinsic relationship between art and healing. Research attests to the fact that engagement through the arts can enhance health outcomes and provide therapeutic opportunities for patients. Because of this, over the past twenty-five years, a new breed of art collection has emerged: art specifically curated for the wellbeing of patients in healthcare environments. These collections are designed to honor the humanity of the patient and to recognize that the patient is a whole person, as opposed to a part of a person that is diseased or disordered. "The visual arts offer a means of non-verbal communication, often bringing order and clarity to mixed-up, poorly understood feelings. While providing a vehicle for catharsis, the artwork itself offers a tool to monitor the individual's emotional and/or developmental state and progress" (State of the Field Com-mittee, 2009, p. 16).

In healthcare art collections, we find unique themes of hope, inspiration, empowerment, recovery, peace, resolve, resilience, and celebration. The presented art is accessible to all and intended to resonate with viewers who are often anxious, afraid, and in pain.

Healing arts collections are curated with respect to sociological factors such as age, cultural preference, and the special needs of the patient population. All hospital art collections have one guiding principle: the needs and viewpoint of

FIGURE 6.1 *Art is for the Spirit*

the patient come first. Once considered and present, this factor will influence the appropriate types of art to present and collect.

This chapter addresses how healing art collections in the United States are defined, built, managed, and funded. We will look at the best practice leaders within the field of hospital arts programs for inspiration, direction, and descriptions of collections. These model art collection programs include the mission statement crafted by the institution to guide curators and art selection committees to select art that will enhance the patient experience and benefit the medical staff.

Examples of healing art collections

The Cleveland Clinic, Cleveland Ohio

> The mission of the Cleveland Clinic Art Program is to enrich, inspire and enliven our patients, visitors, employees and community and to embody the core values of the institution: collaboration, quality, integrity, compassion, and commitment. The collection evidences a commitment to supporting the national and local arts communities. An emphasis on contemporary art fosters an environment of creative excellence, encourages dialogue and challenges viewers to experience diverse points of view. The art reflects an interest in underlying concepts such as innovation, teamwork and service, which are fundamental cornerstones of the Cleveland Clinic.
>
> (Cleveland Clinic Art Program)

One of the most prestigious contemporary art collections residing within a healthcare environment can be found at the Cleveland Clinic. The collection is composed of modern and contemporary art and, according to curator Jennifer Finkel, (personal communication, June 5, 2014) "focus is placed on the impact not the intent of the artwork" when interpreting an object for acquisition. Because the Cleveland Clinic is a world-class hospital with an outstanding reputation for care, patients of diverse ethnicities and cultures travel to it from all over the world to receive medical evaluation and treatment. The diversity of the patient population is represented in the works of art displayed, and many of the artists collected have artworks in major art collections throughout the world. The overall feel of the collection projects a level of sophistication, yet the art is still accessible, thought-provoking, and intriguing to the viewer.

According to the Arts & Medicine Institute's Art Program's executive director, Joanne Cohen, (personal communication, June 5, 2014) artwork is selected that is unique, metaphorical, progressive, and encouraging. Of the over 6,000 objects of art, the bulk of the collection is comprised of prints, works on paper, photographs, as well as paintings and other media. Works created by internationally and nationally known artists such as Alyson Shotz, Jaume Plensa, Vik Muniz, and Catherine Opie hang throughout the hospital in public spaces, corridors, and patient rooms.

There is a saying in the art world – "plop it and drop it" – which means taking an existing work of art from one location and transporting it to another location for quick installation. The Cleveland Clinic is keen to not fall into the "plop and drop" trap, having commissioned over twenty site-specific art pieces that are rich in metaphor, suggestive of the interaction between art and science, and emphasize the connectivity between cultures and health. The overall patient and staff favorite work of art is a permanent video installation by Jennifer Steinkamp, entitled *Mike Kelly 1*. This is an eight-minute video loop of an animated, lissome tree that smoothly sways and twists in the wind. The video sparks interaction from its viewers, who are often seen moving in unison with the tree or reaching out to the wall trying to touch the magical tree.

One work that is an unexpected surprise at the Cleveland Clinic is the mammoth thirty-foot sculptural depiction of an iceberg by artist Inigo Manglano-Ovalle, entitled *Blueberg* (r11i01), which hangs in the Great Hall between the Miller Pavilion and the Glickman Tower. *Blueberg* (r11i01) is intriguing in a healthcare environment. Manglano-Ovalle's work speaks to the intersection between local and global communities emphasizing the intricate nature of ecosystems (About, n.d.).

University of Kentucky Medical Center, Lexington Kentucky

Our mission is to create an environment of care and to focus on the spiritual and emotional well-being of our patients, families, caregivers and staff. The program recognizes the arts and the artists as powerful and positive forces in the healing process.

(The University of Kentucky Arts in HealthCare Mission)

The newly constructed Albert B. Chandler Hospital Pavilion at the University of Kentucky houses a notable art collection that features internationally renowned contemporary artists and celebrates the rich tradition of Southern folk art. Most of the collected or commissioned artwork emphasizes the relationship of Kentucky's people to the local landscape and to long-held agrarian traditions, and it honors the medical center's mission of healing and research. All work was purchased through philanthropy and a committee of art and healthcare professionals determines the artwork selected.

The majority of art was thoughtfully commissioned or purchased during the design phase of the construction project. Through a call-to-artists competition, five key areas of the hospital were identified to feature significant works that provide moments of awe, inspiration, and calm. Warren Selig's sculpture, *Gingko*, greets all upon entering the main lobby of the medical center. This impressive three-story construction, composed of stainless steel and mesh, references the indigenous gingko trees of Kentucky. British artist John Reyntiens designed and created chapel windows that energetically depict Kentucky's colorful spring. Guy Kemper's beautifully tiled mosaics in central elevator lobbies are excellent examples of how public art can gracefully assist in wayfinding.

The Monroe Carell Jr. Children's Hospital at Vanderbilt, Nashville, Tennessee

The mission of Vanderbilt University Medical Center Arts is to present the healing arts in a context that makes the medical center a more compassionate and comfortable environment for patients, their families, and staff.

(Vanderbilt University Medical Center Arts)

The Monroe Carell Jr. Children's Hospital at Vanderbilt University has an impressive collection of paintings, sculptures, and installations. Artworks are themed around the flora and fauna of Tennessee, as well as the universal values of family, love, nurturing, play, caregiving, and nature. Original, commissioned, and limited edition artwork was selected at the inception of designing the new hospital. The art was fused into the architecture. Regional to international artists of all ages, including children, contributed to make the facility a place of healing, awe, celebration, and hope.

Dominating the children's hospital art collection are the vibrant and youthful paintings and three-dimensional installations of internationally known painter-poet DeLoss McGraw.

The centerpiece of the collection is Maurice Blik's iconic fountain sculpture, *Splishsplash*; the fountain depicts an adolescent boy and girl in joyful play, beckoning patients and their families to enjoy a bit of fresh garden air in the Friends Healing Garden. Phil and Mary Farris Martin commissioned *Splishsplash*. The family sought to memorialize their son, Alexander, who died at the age of 10. After Blik showed the maquette of *Splishsplash* to the family, Alexander's mother, Mary Ferris Martin, died unexpectedly. "I wanted to produce something spirited and strong to give encouragement and optimism to children – many of whom would be facing daunting prospects," Blik said (M. Blik, personal communication, December 2003). While the sculptor was working on the piece, he was diagnosed with cancer. He maintains that on some days the only thing that propelled him through this challenge was finding solace in his studio while completing the sculpture he knew would bring the Martin family comfort.

Upon the dedication of *Splishsplash*, Phil Martin, father and husband said, "From tragic circumstances, hope eventually blossoms. *Splishsplash* is a victory and a symbol of hope for every parent" (P. Martin, personal communication, 2005).

Playful whimsy brightens the children's hospital's radiology department walls. Lanie Gannon's brilliant, interactive sculptures of garden elements tempt children to open doors, press levers, and turn knobs to find bugs, distracting them from the anxiety of an upcoming procedure or test. Celebrating the innocence and unique viewpoint of youth, tempera paintings created by elementary school children are featured in the main lobby. This changing exhibition wall is replenished yearly through collaboration between an artist and local school art specialists.

Art collections flourish in children's hospitals and are unique to the pediatric environment, both in the hospital and in outpatient clinics. Any development officer will attest to the fact that it is easier to raise money for bricks and mortar (and art) to construct a children's hospital than to build an adult facility. In many children's hospitals, the art correlates to themed hospital floors or medical specialties. Emphasis tends to be placed on whimsical themes, bright colors, education, and interaction or play. These collections focus on artwork that is appealing to all age levels, creates a sense of wonder, and invites interpretation. Better collections steer away from the predicable commercial trademark super heroes, princesses, and fantasy icons, which are banal and will not stand the test of time.

FIGURE 6.2 *Splishsplash*

How to build a healing arts collection

These creative and prestigious model collections are only a few examples of many others found throughout the United States, such as The Mayo Clinic (Minneapolis, MN), The Bloomberg Children's Hospital (Johns Hopkins, Baltimore, Maryland), Stanford Hospital (Palo Alto, California), and the University of Iowa Hospitals and Clinics Project (Iowa City, Iowa).

There are many steps to building an art collection for a healthcare audience, and what makes each process unique is that two entirely different worlds, art and healthcare, come together to honor and celebrate creativity and healing. The man in the Borofsky print, *Art is for the Spirit*, offers a nice metaphor, as we see him bridging the earth and cosmos to unite both worlds. The remainder of this chapter offers structuring information in a somewhat chronological order of tasks relevant to the special physical requirements needed in presenting art in healthcare environments, including art policy suggestions, managing tips, and funding strategies.

Often art collections are assembled at the onset of a new construction project or major renovation. Usually an enthusiastic group of people involved in the project form a committee whose vision shapes the overall aesthetic, theme, and feel of the collection. The first question often posed by healthcare administrators and committee members who are out of their area of expertise is, "Where do we begin?"

The best place to begin is to hire an experienced arts consultant or arts program manager who understands the mechanics and politics of working in healthcare. The consultant's expertise can help guide the project through the many steps involved in creating a healing art collection:

1 Identify and know your patients and staff.
2 Form an art committee.
3 Write the collection's mission and vision statement.
4 Craft a collections policy germane to healthcare requirements for art acquisitions, loans, de-accessions, and disposal.
5 Create a physical arts master plan.
6 Identify funding for art and yearly program costs.
7 Acquire art through purchase.
8 Hire a curator or program manager.
9 Solicit loans of art.
10 Insure and inventory art.
11 Install the art.
12 Care for the collection.
13 Design collection support materials.

1. Identify and know your patients and staff

Most hospitals have a patient advisory board that will be happy to express their preferences about the aesthetics of the hospital environment. Patients at medical facilities in rural areas will likely have very different opinions from those in urban areas as to the kind of art they prefer and feel comfortable viewing. Socioeconomic, geographic, cultural, and demographic factors can influence the interpretation and accessibility of the art. Art of a religious nature is perfectly appropriate in a faith-based healthcare provider, such as the Hebrew Home for the Aged in Riverdale, New York, which has over 5,000 art objects. Of these, 1,400 are Jewish ceremonial objects. For a complete composite of patient users, ask the marketing department, whose job it is to know who their patients are, what they are being treated for, and the average length of stay.

2. Form an art committee

Most healing arts programs have art committees whose duties might include selecting acquisitions, identifying artists for commissioned work, reinforcing the boundaries set by the arts policy, promoting the program's mission, and advocating for the significant relationship between art and healing within the committee. Ideally, the committee is comprised of diverse members representing both areas of art and medicine. Committee numbers can range from five to twenty members, depending on the size of the institution and the duties of the members. To ensure institutional buy-in, invite colleagues from across the medical center or hospital to sit on the committee. Creating term limits is optional. All members like to be engaged and informed.

Having a development or foundation officer on board is advisable. He or she can identify donors who have a keen eye and a passion for collecting art. It may be helpful to consult with the regional philanthropic community and invite a few big name "movers and shakers" devoted to the cultural landscape of the community. Invite physicians and nurses who are advocates of integrating art into the fabric of the healthcare environment. Ask a patient or survivor to join for his or her intimate viewpoint. Recruit a member of your local arts commission who can assist in identifying artists.

It is very important to identify key members of medical departments who can internally support the art collection program and ensure sustainability. Tap into the talents of your local architects, grateful patients, artists, curators, and educators from the local art museum and members of the craft council. These community members all make resourceful and good candidates who would be eager to contribute their time, ideas, support, and energy and serve as your local ambassadors.

3. Write the mission and vision statements

Next, the committee's task is to create a mission statement for the art program that complements and supports the medical institution's overall mission. The best mission statements tend to be clear, short, and memorable, describing the essence and purpose of the collection program. List the purpose and intention of the collecting program. State its tenants and values and recognize the patient population you serve. The vision statement differs from the mission statement and describes the change resulting from the program work. The Cleveland Clinic Art Program's mission statement, for example, clearly defines the purpose of their collection and for whom it is intended: "to enrich, inspire and enliven our patients, visitors, employees and community" (Art Program, n.d.).

Here is another example of an excellent mission statement, from the Dana-Farber Art and Environment Committee: "The mission of the Art Program is to provide an art collection that engages patients, families and staff, and at the same time brings comfort, provides an opportunity for contemplation, and humanizes the hospital experience."

4. Craft an art collections policy

Ideally, a thorough and carefully constructed collections policy should be in place before the artwork arrives. The institution's arts committee or arts consultant can write the arts collection policy. A well thought-out arts policy supports the art program's mission specific to the needs of the healthcare environment and describes the goals of the collection. The arts collection policy is a living, flexible document that can be adapted over time to best serve the patients and the institution. Many policy documents state that the collection was established for a humanitarian purpose in keeping with the institution's mission, not for the advancement of art or for investment value.

The art collections policy ensures that:

- there are criteria for the art selected and processes for the accession of artwork;
- the artwork is documented, inventoried, and insured;
- the artwork accepted is maintained and properly secured;
- the artwork can be de-accessioned for an appropriate reason.

The criteria for selecting art describe the overall aesthetic quality, content, media, and subject matter for desired art, and these can be explicitly stated in the collections policy. One should select art for patient areas that achieves a healthy and harmonic outlook and is accessible to an audience of diverse race, income, and education. Avoid art that is hostile, obviously depressing, has any negative medical connotation, or is surrealistic. Obviously, such themes may disturb viewers or make patients uncomfortable. Some policies state that artwork depicting body parts will not be accepted. The University of Michigan Gifts of Art program is very clear in their policy on what types of art will not be considered. They state: "We take into consideration the medical and emotional sensitivities of our viewers. Overt sexual content, violence and nudity will not be considered. We will also avoid pieces that are confrontational, chaotic, obviously depressing or contain negative medical connotations" (Gifts of Art, 2015–2016).

Whereas the display of religious art at the Hebrew Home for the Aged is greatly appreciated by its residents, placing iconic religious art in a nondenominational healthcare facility may be offensive to patients from other cultures and religious affiliations. The collections policy can also provide the criteria for acquisition of religious or non-religious artwork and objects. Clearly defined policies protect the integrity of the collection and provide a gracious way for the curator or committee to decline well intentioned, but unsuitable, gifts of art. Once the policy is approved by the institution's legal department and leadership, it can then be added to the institution's policy and procedures manual.

Many of the collections policies for healthcare visual arts collections subscribe to evidence-based research conducted over the past twenty years. *A Guide to Evidence–Based Art,* by Kathy Hathorn and Upali Nanda (2008) and published by the Center for Health Design, reviews significant research and describes how the viewing of art can facilitate or enhance healing. The former Arts & Health Alliance hosts the largest online database of research on the topic of arts in healthcare. Many collection programs have reached beyond the prescriptive parameters of evidence-based research and have successfully created art collections that are a bit more abstract in thought and genre, to the approval of their patient base.

5. Create an art master plan and acquisitions budget

Knowing how much art is needed and where requires coordination with the project architect, project manager, and interior designer. The design team reviews the blueprints to identify potential art opportunities in both public and private spaces and notes are made on specific architectural or physical requirements for designated areas. Discuss with the design team what types of art media would work best in certain areas. For instance, placing a large fountain sculpture in an atrium area may cause problems with humidity or sound. Or an uncovered textile work may create infection control issues; fibers, exposed to touch, can harbor germs. Discuss anticipated needs for significant artwork with the design team; support or lighting requirements may affect the construction documents and budget. Will a rebar pad be needed to accommodate a sculpture or will lighting enhancements be required at any art locations? Learning where the fire alarm units are placed on the walls will influence the placement of art. It is always better to know ahead of time rather than on installation day.

At this point, the first draft of the physical art master plan – the blueprint indicating places for art – can be created. The first draft of the plan will determine approximately how many pieces of art are needed for the project. The plan should include sizes of each individual piece, framing needs, installation costs, sculpture bases, display cases, transportation costs, additional site work, and hardware for three-dimensional work. Once all these factors are compiled, the project's art budget can be forecasted.

Public spaces – atriums, lobbies, food service areas, and patient waiting areas – usually feature large-scale, high-dollar artwork. The semi-private and private areas – sub-waiting rooms, corridors, exam and procedure rooms, and patient rooms – are subject to more wear and tear. Moving gurneys, wheelchairs, and medical equipment can damage artwork, which will need to be refreshed periodically. Because semi-private and private spaces are smaller, they can accommodate smaller-scale, less expensive art, such as posters, limited-edition prints, and photographs.

In a spreadsheet, the art procurement budget can be broken down into specific categories: units per floor, units for public spaces, units for private spaces, units for corridors and large-scale public art. When funding is tight for acquiring art, create a plan that provides a strategy to incrementally place works in key areas of the hospital. Strategic planning will strengthen the integrity of the overall collection.

Ask the project manager or interior designer if any allotments have been made for art in the interior's furniture budget. Sometimes a piece of art or decorative element has already been included as a line item in the patient room furnishings budget. Knowing might yield a pleasant surprise and lower the cost of the art budget.

When considering acquisitions, remember that art storage space is minimal or non-existent within a hospital. Rotating and resting work seasonally is usually not an option. Knowing this may prohibit acquiring delicate watercolors, photos, and prints. The majority of the art collection will remain in-situ except for designated changing exhibitions spaces.

6. Identify funding for art and the arts program

It takes money to build and sustain an art collection. Many collection programs are strictly supported through philanthropy. Others are funded through state percent-for-art mandates, or money has been earmarked as a capital expense in the construction budget. Oftentimes the art budget is a combination of all of these funding options. Arriving at the total budget number can be calculated in several ways:

- It can be created from the blueprints of the art master plan.
- A budget number may be assigned as part of the overall construction cost.
- The institution can commit to a percentage of the construction cost for art.

Many states have a percent-for-art program for public new construction and renovation projects. Percent-for-art programs require that a certain percentage of the cost on large-scale development projects be allocated to fund and install art that is accessible to the general public. This percentage generally ranges from 0.5 to 2 percent, with most programs adopting the classic 1 percent. A list of states with percent-for-art programs can be found on the Americans for the Arts (AFTA) website under the Public Art Network. Also available on AFTA are tools and resources such as sample RFQs (Request for Qualifications), art administrator tips, public artist registries, and sample contracts.

Philanthropic gifts of art or funds that can underwrite art purchases may provide highly visible naming opportunities for donors. The institution's development officer is the liaison between the donor and the institution and will guide the art program curator throughout the gift process. The development officer's responsibility is to oversee the logistics of accepting the gift.

In addition, maintenance expenses are considerable and crucial to include in the program's budget. Art collection programs need a yearly budget to pay the curator, to build inventory, and to physically maintain the collection and support therapeutic and educational programming and collateral materials.

BOX 6.1 DEVELOPMENT OF THE ART COLLECTION AT CEDARS-SINAI IN LOS ANGELES

Cedars-Sinai in Los Angles has a collection of over 4,000 objects that was built on philanthropy, beginning with a key donor, Marcia Simon Weisman. In 1966, Frederick R. Weisman slipped into a coma after suffering a head injury and was taken to Cedars-Sinai for treatment. Mr. Weisman's recovery was slow and he had yet to recover his speech. Mrs. Weisman decided to bring his favorite Jackson Pollock painting from their art collection to his bedside to give him something to enjoy and contemplate. Still not able to speak his wife's name, Fred exclaimed, "Pollock!" Always a champion of the arts, Marcia knew then that her new mission would be to bring the highest quality art to Cedars-Sinai for the benefit of patients, their families, and staff. Marcia and Frederick Weisman enticed collectors and artists such as Andy Warhol, Ellsworth Kelly, Frank Stella, and Roy Lichtenstein to donate works of art to Cedars-Sinai, which marked the beginning of a world class collection in the heart of a medical center worthy to be in any top-rated art museum.

(Mullin, 2012)

---

7. Acquire art

Who selects the art for acquisition to the collection varies at every institution. The predominant method is for the curator to make recommendations to the art collection committee on what artwork to purchase, borrow, or accept as donation. It's the curator's responsibility to guide the committee on what types of art are suited to the mission of the healthcare institution, what will enhance the overall aesthetic of the built environment, and what will assist in creating a supportive environment to all users of the facility.

The manner of accessioning art for a healthcare facility is similar to that of collecting for a museum or corporate or private collection. Standards, best practices, and resources relating to building and maintaining art collections are available from the museum industry. Through the nonprofit organization, The American Alliance of Museums (AAM), information from ethics to collections management can be found and adapted for healthcare audiences, programs, and environments.

> Acquisition is the act of acquiring an item or object for any of the museum's collections. Accessioning is the formal act of legally accepting an object or objects to the category of material that a museum holds in the public trust, or, in other words, those in the museum's permanent collection. Because of this, it is important that acquisition/accession policies are written with the museum's mission in mind. The museum must ensure that each accession not only enhances or strengthens the museum's collections but also can be

properly cared for, stored and used. This section outlines the specific criteria and decision-making process for adding objects to the collection. Having a thoughtful accession/acquisitions policy will yield a strong and cohesive collection, in addition to helping avoid any misunderstanding between potential donors and the museum.

(American Alliance of Museums, *Alliance Reference Guide*)

Methods for the acquisition of art include:

- Negotiating directly with the artist.
- Working with a gallery that might offer a 10–25 percent discount depending on the price point of the art or the quantity of work purchased.
- Bidding on art through auction houses.
- Employing an arts consultant to find the art and handle the sale.
- Accepting gifts of art or loans from donors. A third party appraiser must appraise donated art if the donor would like a tax deduction. The institution's development office can help with gift credits for tax purposes.
- Placing a call-for-art out to the arts community.
- Commissioning art for site-specific spaces. Calls-for-art should clearly communicate the appropriate genre, media of work wanted, and include the mission of the art program.

What makes collecting for a healthcare environment different from collecting for a museum or corporation is that the hospital's mission is to provide quality health services and facilities for the community, to promote wellness, to relieve suffering, and to restore health. The art collection should uphold these tenets. The criteria for art should be guided by the demographics of the patient population and overall mission of the institution and arts program, not art for art's sake. The work should provide a place of respite for the patient. It should convey calm, hope, and inspiration. Consider that patients may be stressed by their illness or their treatment. Be mindful that certain medications can affect patients psychically and psychologically and affect their perception or interpretation of a work of art. The physical and psychosocial needs of patients must be considered first. Also remember that families, staff, physicians, and caregivers may all be under a lot of stress.

The physical properties of artwork in hospitals must be able to meet Joint Commission Standards. The Joint Commission is an "independent, not-for-profit organization that accredits and certifies more than 20,500 healthcare organizations and programs in the United States. Joint Commission accreditation and certification is recognized nationwide as a symbol of quality that reflects an organization's commitment to meeting certain performance standards" (About the Joint Commission, 2015). Requirements applicable to art are infection control, cleaning, and safety requirements for installing artwork. Also, all physical installations of art must meet Americans with Disabilities Act (ADA) requirements applying to access and visual impairment.

Factors to weigh before acquiring the art are the durability of the medium, installation requirements, and the cost of installation or site work. Are there any special methods for cleaning or yearly maintenance requirements? Will cleaning the art create problems with the housekeeping department? Will installing the work create egress issues by having to block a public space or corridor, inconveniencing patients and staff?

Declining a donation of art is quite simple: just say, "No thank you, the artwork does not meet our collections criteria."

8. Hire a curator

The characteristics of a curator or arts manager working in a healthcare environment can be likened to the octopus that has two hearts and eight arms. The curator should possess one heart for healing and empathy, and one heart for the love of art. Eight arms juggle and balance the duties that unite the two distinctly different disciplines. The healthcare art curator is a hybrid who must know the medical setting's arduous systems of rules, procedures, and protocol, as well as be attuned to the value and care of art. In smaller healthcare environments, the curator often has to perform the duties of not only a curator but also those of the registrar, preparator, educator, fundraiser, and exhibit designer. Every object in the collection needs to be documented and inventoried, which involves recording provenance, date of acquisition, condition of work, size, and value. Other duties include overseeing the preparation, installation, and care of work, managing volunteers, writing grants, and preparing RFP's (requests for proposals). At a large medical center like the Cleveland Clinic, a curator may be responsible for one specific area of the collection, with help from a support staff.

9. Solicit loans of art

Loans of art can supplement the existing collection and can give the owner great pleasure in knowing their loan is bringing comfort to patients and enhancing the aesthetic of the healthcare environment. The office of contracts or the lender can write up the loan agreement. Because the logistics of accepting a loan of art can include many steps and require planning time, it is wise to make the duration of the loan for three years or longer. In accepting a loan, there are associated costs, which can include signage, shipping, installation, site preparation, insurance, and sometimes crate storage. These expenses can be planned for in the art program's yearly operating budget, or the artwork owner can be asked to make a monetary gift to cover such costs.

10. Insure and inventory art

All purchased and loaned artwork becomes property of the healthcare facility and must be insured immediately. In many medical facilities, the curator or arts program coordinator submits the appraised amount of the artwork to the office of risk management or to the legal department. Throughout the year, the insurance schedule is updated by listing new art works, loans of art, de-accessioned art, and disposed works of art. When an object is damaged, lost, or stolen, the office of risk management or the insurance company must be informed immediately and a report must be filed. Insurance should cover the cost of repairs of the object and the cost of the stolen merchandise.

Each object of art needs to be immediately recorded once it has been purchased or accepted as a gift within the permanent collection. There are many ways to keep and manage an inventory list. For larger art collections, a museum inventory software program might be a good option. Some software packages include training. For smaller collections or when budget restrictions prohibit the purchase of a museum registrar program, an inventory schedule can be created in a spreadsheet program.

11. Install the art

Careful logistical planning in anticipation of the arrival of an object is always wise.

Pay attention to the installation requirements of the work and have any prep work completed in advance. Always check in with the project architect or the space and facilities department regarding any special requirements for major installations before an object is delivered. Determine where the work will be unloaded and if special parking passes are needed. Will installing the work demand a bucket truck? Will it fit through the door? If an object is heavy, will additional structural support be needed to safely hang the work? Will the existing floor supports be able to support the weight of a sculpture? Does a concrete pad need to be poured in preparation for the delivery of the work? These questions should be considered and answered early in the planning process.

Security hardware on two-dimensional work is mandatory for the safety of hospital users and to protect the artwork. The hardware deters theft and tampering with art hanging in public spaces. There are several vendors that sell this specialized hardware that can be used on wood and metal frames. An artist or professional installer can easily apply the hardware to the back of the painting, print, or photograph. A quick internet search on security picture hardware can quickly identify vendors who carry this specialized product.

12. Care for the collection

Caring for the art collection comes under the auspices of the curator or program director's work, whose responsibility is to oversee the interpretation, documentation, and preservation of the collection. Some duties can be assigned to professionals on a fee-for-service basis. For instance, art conservators can perform yearly maintenance on sculptures, paintings, and prints. Museum professionals and professional art handlers can oversee installations or pack artwork for storage or transit.

13. Design collection support materials

Collection support materials or collateral materials are created to support the collections program. Through the use of collateral materials, patients, staff, and the community can learn about artists in the collection, recent acquisitions, tour times, and where to find more information. Collateral materials can include a web presence, maps, walking tours, acoustic guides, and brochures. Some programs provide a virtual tour of the collection on the web, which is ideal for bed-bound patients. Many institutions provide guided maps that direct viewers to discover where the artwork is located and provide information about the work of art. The program manager, the marketing department, or a consultant can create collateral materials. Materials can be written, auditory, web-based, or designed for smartphone use.

Conclusion

We have always known that the arts can enrich our lives. Now we are learning that the arts can support us in healing. Specifically, the visual arts can heal passively as well as through creative action. In a hospital waiting area, patients can have their attention diverted from their own issues and anxiety by the art around them. In therapeutic art sessions, patients can release emotions that might otherwise go unexpressed. Staff members participating in an employee art show can promote a feeling of community and work satisfaction. The arts can also heal through the act of giving; it can be deeply rewarding for a donor to know that art given in appreciation for care for a loved one will continue to provide comfort to other patients and their families.

The interdisciplinary nature of building and managing a healing arts collection and program – where healthcare providers, art lovers, and patients come together – is an enriching experience for all involved. A well-structured collection and program can comfort patients, enhance healing, and improve medical outcomes. For patients, medical staff, and arts program personnel, the shared knowledge that a healing arts program can be transformative is sustaining and rewarding in itself.

References

About Iñigo Manglano-Ovalle. (n.d.). *Art21.* Retrieved from http://www.pbs.org/art21/artists/iñigo-manglano-ovalle

About the joint commission. (2015). *The Joint Commission.* Retrieved from http://www.jointcommission.org/about_us/about_the_joint_commission_main.aspx

American Alliance of Museums. Developing a collections management policy. Reference guide retrieved from http://www.aam-us.org/docs/continuum/developing-a-cmp-final.pdf?sfvrsn=2

Art program. (n.d.). *Cleveland Clinic*. Retrieved from http://my.clevelandclinic.org/services/arts_medicine/art-program

Cleveland Clinic Arts & Medicine Institute. http://my.clevelandclinic.org/services/arts_medicine

Dana-Faber Art and Environment Committee. Retrieved from http://www.dana-farber.org/How-to-Help/Leadership-and-Advocacy/Friends-of-Dana-Farber/Friends-Programs/Friends-of-Dana-Farber-Art-Program.aspx

Gifts of art call for entries. (2015–2016). *Gifts of art home, University of Michigan health system*. Retrieved from http://www.med.umich.edu/goa/liveonline.htm

Hathorn, K., & Nanda, U. (2008). *A guide to evidence-based art* (Position paper for the Center for Health Design Environmental Standards Council). Retrieved from http://www.healthdesign.org/chd/research/guide/-evidence-based-art

Mullin, Sheppard. (2012, October 10). Public art programs: 1% for the 99% – Part one [Blog post]. *Art Law Blog*. Retrieved from http://www.artlawgallery.com/2012/10/articles/artists/public-art-programs-1-for-the-99-part-one/

State of the Field Committee. (2009). *State of the field report: Arts in healthcare 2009*. Retrieved from http://www.arts.ufl.edu/cam/documents/stateOfTheField.pdf

University of Kentucky Arts in HealthCare Mission. (n.d.) *Arts in Healthcare*. Retrieved from http://ukhealthcare.uky.edu/arts/

Vanderbilt University Medical Center Arts. Retrieved from http://www.culturalenrichment.com/

7

EXHIBIT GALLERIES IN HEALTHCARE FACILITIES

Elaine Sims

The author and illustrator of the *Madeline* books, Ludwig Bemelmans, nearly suffered a breakdown while serving in the US Army during World War I. What saved him was what he called imagining "islands of security." As he wrote in his memoir, "I have started to think in pictures and make myself several scenes to which I can escape instantly when the danger appears, instant happy pictures that are completely mine, familiar, warm and protective" (Rothstein, 2014). Bemelmans was instinctively using art to console himself and create a safe haven. He could have been describing the mission for introducing art into the healthcare environment: to create a place of respite using visual cues to help make patients, visitors, and staff feel they are in a space that is familiar, warm, protective, and above all, safe.

Placing art in healthcare and other public buildings in the last century began with the Works Progress Administration during the Great Depression, and was re-energized in the 1960s with the creation of the National Endowment for the Arts. Early attempts at the inclusion of art in hospitals focused on the environment of care. It was thought that art exuded an aesthetic that could reduce stress by calming and comforting patients, visitors, and staff in what were seen as increasingly sterile and impersonal hospitals. If stress was harmful, the reduction of stress was hypothesized to be beneficial and thus supportive of healing.

Over time, we have come to understand more about the impact of and preferences for color, subject, and design in art among hospitalized populations. Research has strengthened this body of knowledge, as have theories such as those by anthropologist Ellen Dissanayake, who takes an ethological and bio-evolutionary approach in her book *What is Art For?* Dissanayake (1988) sees art as having a selective or survival value: "An ethological view presumes that art contributes something essential to the human being who makes or responds to it – not in the usual sense of being good for his soul or pleasurable for his mind or spirit (though these benefits are not denied), but beneficial to his biological fitness" (p. 8).

This chapter will examine the use of art galleries in healthcare in which the exhibits are changed out regularly, using the terms changing art galleries, rotating art galleries, exhibits, or galleries interchangeably. We will focus our exploration on the comprehensive exhibit program at the University of Michigan Health System's Gifts of Art program.

Early programs

Early hospital arts programs did not tend to have generous funds available for the purchase of art. Nor were those hospitals designed as they now are with comfort, functionality, safety, and aesthetics as guiding principles. Today, by contrast, most hospitals are designed by healthcare design specialists and expect to seek philanthropic support for amenities including art. Nonetheless, hospitals operate on tight margins, and support for the arts still varies greatly across the country. As a consequence, many hospitals seek affordable solutions for bringing the arts into their facilities.

The pioneering healthcare arts programs dating to the 1970s and 1980s often had their roots in community arts organizations. As in the case of Duke Medical Center, enlightened CEOs invited community arts directors into their hospitals to create similar programming, usually focusing on the visual arts (Palmer, 2001). Several of these pioneering programs have continued to thrive and have become recognized as best practice models. Examples include Duke Medical Center's Cultural Services, the University of Iowa Hospitals and Clinics' Project Art, the National Institute of Health, and the University of Michigan Health System's Gifts of Art program.

While the aforementioned hospitals all have permanent collections of various sizes, Iowa's being the most extensive thanks to the statewide Percent for Art program (Art in Public Buildings), each has also maintained a program of rotating art galleries. In the case of the University of Michigan, the galleries have always been the primary focus for their art on display in public spaces. Over the years, numerous other programs have emerged as the field of arts in healthcare matured and spread across the industry. This growth was aided by support from local and state arts councils, and from the National Endowment for the Arts (NEA), which has a very strong commitment to community arts with a special focus on underserved populations and accessibility. The Society for the Arts in Healthcare, founded in 1991, aided the growth of the field with annual conferences, grants, consulting services, and the dissemination of research and resources.

The mission for arts in healthcare

The University of Michigan Hospitals and Healthcare Centers's comprehensive arts program, Gifts of Art, was conceived as an enhancement to the new 1986 hospital facility then being designed. This program was developed specifically to focus on the hospital's environment of care as referenced in the following policy:

> The University of Michigan Hospitals and Healthcare Centers maintain an environment of care which is mindful of key elements and issues that the Joint Commission [for the Accreditation of Hospitals and Healthcare Centers] has identified which contribute in creating the way a space feels and works for patients, families, visitors and staff experiencing the health care delivery system. They go beyond traditional physical comfort and safety issues to include maintaining an environment:
>
> - which is sensitive to patient needs for comfort, social interaction, positive distraction, and self-control,
> - which minimizes unnecessary environmental stresses,
> - which respects human dignity,
> - which supports the development and maintenance of patient's interests, skills and opportunities for personal growth, and
> - provides orientation and access to nature and the outdoors.
>
> Examples of enhancements to the environment of care maintained by UMHHC include:
>
> - Permanent artwork and galleries of changing artwork,
> - Public performances of music, theater and artist demonstrations,
> - Live music at the bedside,
> - Lending libraries of poster art for patient rooms,
> - Accessible courtyard, and
> - Meditation garden
>
> (The University of Michigan Hospitals and Health Centers, n.d.)

The benefits of galleries

Why does art in hospitals have such a profound effect on us? We might say it is because art in healthcare has a job to do. It is not intended to merely hang on the wall and look pretty. It is a workhorse whose job is to distract, engage, comfort, calm, maintain a presence, provide clues to social support, and help retain personal identity. Some permanent pieces of art stand the test of time and perennially retain their appeal – but additional energy, pleasure, and surprise come from art that is ever changing.

While initially there may have been financial and practical reasons for introducing art into hospitals through the practice of changing exhibit galleries, the gallery model has been retained and replicated. Galleries provide continuous renewal and variety, helping to maintain an air of freshness and interest for staff and patients alike. In addition, exhibit content can serve to make patients feel more at home by visually connecting them with their communities. Exhibits can be a powerful tool for "place making," helping a hospital environment reflect the community or region's values and character, making it feel familiar and safe.

Exhibit programs are excellent vehicles for showcasing emerging talent and providing a high level of visibility for artists. As the field of arts in healthcare has grown, an increasing number of artists find meaning in sharing their art with those who have a true need for healing and the comforts and benefits of a positive distraction.

> A young woman came to my booth this past Saturday. She told me she was at her doctor's appointment at University of Michigan and the doctor gave her some bad news. She was beside herself and thought "How am I going to get through this?" . . . While sitting in the lobby she looked around and saw she was surrounded by this beautiful artwork. . . . She told me: "I am here today because it was your artwork that helped get me through my diagnosis and I had to buy a piece of your art." She thanked me over and over again. What an important and powerful role your Gifts of Art program plays in people's lives! This story made my day and will remain with me for a long, long time.
> (K. Fenwick, personal communication, July 16, 2013)

Exhibition programs also help give a voice and forum to artists who may be outside the mainstream due to physical or medical challenges. Hospitals or other healthcare organizations have coordinated traveling art exhibits with an educational or awareness component. An example is *Mind Body Spirit* by Erin Worsham Brady, an artist before and after her diagnosis with Lou Gehrig's Disease, who changed her expressive medium to computer generated paintings as the illness progressed. Adapting her creative practice helped her rediscover her freedom and gave new meaning to her life. That show was organized by Vanderbilt University Medical Center and traveled under the umbrella of the Arts and Health Alliance.

FIGURE 7.1 *Mind Body Spirit*

FIGURE 7.2 Employee Art Winner

Hospitals mount employee art exhibitions to showcase and celebrate the creativity of their staff. Some are organized by outside services such as the National Arts Program, which provides an opportunity for employees and their family members to participate in a professional visual arts exhibition. They currently sponsor eighty-two exhibits annually in thirty-eight states (Our mission, 2015). The University of Michigan has been hosting an annual employee art exhibition since its inception. Employee art exhibitions typically bestow awards and prizes during a public reception. In many cases, they also include a people's choice award determined by the viewing public. Upon winning the Best in Show award, one artist was quoted as saying, "Really, next to the birth of my children this has been the best experience in my life" (S. Collins, personal communication, July 13, 2010).

Additional benefits of exhibit galleries

Exhibition programs also serve staff as purchase galleries in complex medical centers where it can be difficult to leave during the workday for errands and shopping. Patients, too, are drawn to art that speaks to them. They may celebrate a successful surgical or medical outcome by purchasing an art piece that comes to have special meaning for them. Patients who know they are not going home sometimes want to leave a legacy gift to a loved one and see an art piece that embodies a lasting or intangible connection to that person.

Artwork can be used to emphasize the mission and vision of a medical center. For example, exhibits may celebrate organizational values such as diversity, showcase stories of nursing, explore scientific discovery, display patient art, or provide a venue for student initiatives. Medical school curricula increasingly provide students the opportunity to create and display artwork as part of their training on the arts of observation and empathy.

Some hospitals devote gallery spaces exclusively to patient art, especially cancer centers and children's hospitals. These specialty hospitals are more likely to have artists, child life specialists, or art therapists on staff to facilitate art-making opportunities for patients. Some patient galleries are located within patient care areas, but some are in public spaces such as the Voices Gallery at the University of Michigan Comprehensive Cancer Center. There, the art therapist selects and mounts shows made by cancer patients.

Today's healthcare facilities can feel like small towns. They house a sizable population made up of staff, visitors, and patients on any given day. A large academic medical center, for example, may have a staff of 25,000 and 1,000 beds in addition to numerous clinics and outpatient surgery sites. Many are tertiary centers to which patients travel long distances and spend a fair amount of time navigating the facility and waiting between appointments. With the quality of "time out of time," medical centers can feel like self-contained space stations for time travelers. In this environment, art is a powerful presence and is experienced quite differently from when viewed in a museum. The relationship between the viewer and the art object is more visceral, immediate, and intimate. It can best be summarized in this patient comment: "Being able to look up and see the picture on the wall helped reassure me that things would eventually return to normal" (C. Durocher, personal communication, January 22, 2002).

Managing galleries in healthcare facilities

Exhibit galleries in healthcare facilities run the gamut from those operated entirely by an outside entity such as a community art center, private gallery, or independent art consultant, to those run entirely in-house, or some combination of the two. When a program is run by an outside gallery, the artists are selected by the gallery and all contractual and financial arrangements are handled by the gallery. The shows are installed by gallery staff, and if work is sold, a ten percent to forty percent commission is retained by the healthcare organization to help support the program. Commissions vary by institution. The National Institutes of Health, for example, retains twenty percent of the sale price for a Patient Emergency Fund which is used to support patients and families in need (National Institutes of Health, 2014). The commission may be split between the gallery and the hospital. Sometimes, the artist's name and contact information is on the title block and purchasers are directed to contact the artist directly. The artist then handles the sale and donates a percentage to the healthcare organization. In some cases, the exhibiting artist may donate a piece to the permanent art collection of the institution.

At the other end of the spectrum are programs operated entirely by the healthcare organization. The University of Michigan Gifts of Art program is an example of an extensive hospital arts program that has been mounting shows since 1987. It has an exhibit coordinator on staff. The program sends out an annual Call for Entries (CFE), generating responses from which to select exhibits for the coming year. It maintains an extensive list of artists and arts organizations in the multi-state region. With the advent of the internet, the CFE has achieved an international circulation. Gifts of Art pays for annual memberships in state and regional arts organizations, which then list the CFE in their online calendars and newsletters. It also maintains its own extensive electronic artist database. Hard copy brochures go to individual artists without email, and promotional packets go to key arts organizations for distribution to members.

Some, but not all, organizations convene a formal art committee to assist with the selection process. The Gifts of Art schedules all fifty-four shows for its nine galleries once a year. Contracts are sent as part of a very extensive packet of materials, which also includes blank inventory templates, gallery diagrams, and framing and packing instructions, as well as a checklist of key calendar deadlines leading up to the exhibit installation. The Gifts of Art communications coordinator handles all the advance publicity and also corresponds with the artists. The business manager arranges insurance through the university's risk management office and processes all art sales. This includes credit card transactions, checks, payroll deduction, and sales tax reporting. Gifts of Art then pays the artists for any sales minus a thirty-five percent commission, and pays and files the sales tax reporting with the state.

Locating galleries within the facility

Hospital and healthcare center galleries are located in well-traveled public spaces within the institution. An exception is galleries intended for special populations, such as medical students or staff-only exhibits of a sensitive nature. Exhibits may change monthly, bi-monthly, or at longer intervals. Work may be for sale, or not. Mounting methods vary from institution to institution. Art may be mounted directly on the walls, as in museums, and the walls patched and painted between shows. It may also be installed with a track system, which can accommodate varying sizes of art. Some systems have a locking feature and an alarm system. Other galleries are made up of permanently mounted frames that can be easily opened to change out the artwork, all of a standard size. The installation of specialty track lighting varies. Such lighting has greatly improved in recent years, but remains costly.

Some galleries' works of art are housed inside built-in wall units secured with locking glass doors. They can accommodate wall-mounted art as well as three-dimensional art. Duke University Medical Center uses such display cases. These galleries are spared dealing with security hardware and regular dusting. However, they do put another layer between the viewer and the art – at least in the case of two-dimensional art. They can offer more flexibility, though, in the size of three-dimensional objects verses standard pedestal display cases.

A few hospitals house their changing exhibits within self-contained gallery spaces or small museums, such as the Medical Historical Museum at the University of Iowa Hospitals and Clinics. The McMullen Gallery within the University of Alberta Hospital in Edmonton, Alberta, Canada is located next to the main entrance of the hospital and maintains gallery hours and functions much as a free-standing art gallery might. These types of galleries are more commonly found in community-based arts and health centers, such as the Joan Hisaoka Gallery within the Smith Center for cancer patients in Washington, DC. Free-standing community centers for cancer patients or dementia patients that provide arts classes often have galleries for the art made there, or artists representing that population. For example, a geriatric center may display the art of artists fifty-five and older.

Some hospitals and healthcare centers maintain virtual galleries online so that patients in their rooms and staff in off-site locations can view the art. Virtual galleries may contain images of pieces currently on display in the physical galleries. They may also contain images of the permanent collection of the hospital. Or, in the case of the Creative Center in New York City, the virtual sales gallery promotes the work by artists with cancer who take art classes or participate with the Creative Center.

Gallery systematics

Receiving and returning artwork to artists presents its own set of challenges. It can be as easy as an artist delivering their work to the gallery on the day of installation and perhaps assisting or installing the artwork themselves, to as complex as delivery to a busy hospital loading dock. On occasion, exhibits are shipped. All sold artwork is wrapped and distributed to the purchaser by appointment. Artwork stays on display until the show ends. But when the purchaser or recipient of the art is a patient, everything is done to quickly get the artwork into the hands of – or support the needs and wishes of – the patient.

Gifts of Art maintains a large work/storage room containing all tools, transport carts, and ladders for managing the gallery program. Such space is not always easy to secure within healthcare organizations. Empty boxes and packing materials are often barcoded and stored off-site between shows due to the lack of adequate storage space. Although it was not always the case, construction services staff help install the artwork under the supervision of and alongside Gifts of Art staff. All nine galleries are changed out over a four-day period every two months.

The industry standard for installation hardware is a security system that locks a piece of art directly to the wall or onto specially installed art panels. The panels are typically plywood sheets covered with a fire-retardant sisal product. The panels can be finished with decorative trim or framed to cover an entire wall surface.

They are extremely durable and forgiving. When used with plywood panels, the security hardware is the most difficult to dislodge by casual theft. Likewise, display cases for three-dimensional works of art use countersunk, special security screws to lock the hoods to the pedestals.

While it may sound tongue-in-cheek in the context of a hospital, there are art emergencies. The emergency can come from a patient or visitor who sees a piece of art and is drawn to it in a powerful way and wants to purchase and receive it RIGHT THEN. It should be no surprise that the complexity of a large hospital system adds layers of complexity to a gallery program. Artists and gallery visitors alike expect the arts program office to be "on the premises" for questions, assistance, and service. More often than not, that is not the case.

Inquiries about the art or how to purchase it are typically handled by phone. At the Gifts of Art program, art sales are handled in accordance with the cash and credit handling policies of the larger University of Michigan. Art can also be purchased by check or payroll deduction. In some programs, purchases are handled directly by the artist or an independent gallery, which then pays the commission fee directly to the hospital exhibit program.

Delivering sold artwork to purchasers can also be complicated. In the case of the University of Michigan, the work/storage room for the exhibit program is not in a public area and can be challenging even for staff to locate. As a result, many purchased pieces are delivered to offices and clinics, or coordinated with patients' return medical visits. When the purchaser is a patient who does not live locally or has special needs, Gifts of Art will ship the artwork to them. Receipts are numbered, and like all business operations at the University, subject to audit.

Like a private art gallery, hospital galleries may hold receptions for the opening of new exhibits. Some hospitals host and fund the opening receptions. Others may allow the artists to hold openings at their own expense within well-defined parameters. When galleries are located in main corridor thoroughfares, the reception must take place at low traffic times such as early evenings or weekends. Hospital corridors must remain clear as built by regulation, so installing artwork or holding a reception must be scheduled so as not to impede traffic flow or egress within a building. Galleries in lobby spaces or atria accommodate receptions more easily.

Marketing and communications

With the advent of digital media, publicizing exhibits has become both easier and more complicated. While one no longer sends out hardcopy mailings, there are now a plethora of communication avenues that are largely uncoordinated. Some arts in medicine programs produce their own publicity, while others are supported by hospital marketing and communications departments. If a hospital gallery is managed by a community organization, they typically handle all publicity. Thoughtful branding and graphic identity clarifies the relationship of the gallery to the arts program, and the arts program to the institution. This coordination allows patients and others to more easily locate galleries, make inquiries, or contact the right department to purchase art.

Managing gallery materials for art exhibits in healthcare facilities is challenging. They must compete for online, wall, and counter space as well as for the attention of passersby. In addition to signage, there are fliers, brochures, QR codes, or gallery maps to consider at multiple placements within the facilities. Someone must distribute and restock these locations on a regular basis. Online and digital displays must be programmed and updated. Galleries are typically unstaffed and must be regularly monitored and checked for cleaning and maintenance as well as restocking printed materials. This is complicated by the fact that, in many cases, the arts program office is located at a significant distance from the gallery sites.

Protecting the art

The University of Michigan uses special hardware systems to secure the art on the wall and within display cases. If artists decline attaching security hardware to their frames, they must sign a waiver, but the art is nonetheless insured. All attempts are made to keep the art safe because hospitals can be harsh environments for art. They are typically open 24/7 to vast numbers of people who are often stressed or distracted. Wheelchairs are notorious for scraping walls and display cases. Large equipment is used to clean and polish floors, and housekeeping staff clean and disinfect surfaces with harsh products. For this reason, Gifts of Art monitors its nine galleries regularly, and dusts, cleans, and maintains the artwork itself. On the rare occasion there is loss or damage, reports are filed with hospital security and claims are submitted to the University risk management department. Any repairs are made by professionals.

Just as there are critical incidents for patients in healthcare, so too are there are critical incidents for art. Not only are hospitals harsh environments for art, but they are places of constant change. The coordination of care for the artwork can be as challenging as the coordination of care for patients. Outside contractors often wash windows and pay little attention to dripping on artwork. Periodic floor waxing necessitates that display cases get moved. Large lifts and other construction equipment and supplies get parked in galleries. Sometimes areas in which galleries are located are closed for remodeling. The gallery program needs to be able to accommodate change instantly. That may mean emptying display cases or taking down or moving an exhibit with little or no notice. There can be trickle-down effects, which may include modifying publicity, altering contracts, or seeking temporary, safe storage for art.

Although some programs do not provide any or only partial insurance coverage for the art they exhibit, it is desirable do so. Damage and loss are rare, but they do happen. Typically, a security officer creates an incident report as the first step for filing a claim. If the individual art pieces are itemized (scheduled) on the insurance, there will be no deductible. The gallery or arts program may have to pay for the repair or replacement cost up front, and then be reimbursed from the insurance or the risk management department if the organization is self-insured. Artists typically set the sale price or replacement value (if not for sale). If a damaged work is considered a total loss, the insurance company will not return the piece to the artist. They may also dispute the value, although that is rare.

Art beyond the gallery

Gifts of Art regularly invites artists whose work is on display to lead informal artist demonstrations and workshops. Supplies are provided for patients, visitors, and staff to drop in and try their hand at art-making. The artist demonstrations are usually scheduled for the hours spanning lunchtime. Popular demonstrations include snowflake paper-cutting, clay tiles, Chinese calligraphy, kite making, origami, and just about anything else that is simple to make on a drop-in basis. Artist demonstrations can also be a time to watch and ask informal questions. Hospital audiences are not shy and reward artists by showing real interest and authentic engagement.

Art exhibits can help shape bedside art experiences. In today's world, hospitalized patients are extremely sick and usually discharged to complete their recovery at home. For this reason, only a small number of inpatients are able to visit the public galleries in hospitals. A bedside art program can make the exhibits accessible to patients in several ways. Laptops or iPads make it possible to view a show online

FIGURE 7.3 Exhibits Coordinator, Kathleen Talley, installing artwork in one of the Gifts of Art galleries at the University of Michigan Health System.

Photo by Carrie McClintock

and engage in conversation about art. The art on exhibit can be the jumping-off place for art-making projects or art kits available at the bedside. Exhibiting artists, accompanied by a staff artist, may also visit inpatient units where they can give bedside gallery talks or lead simple art-making activities related to their shows.

The role of philanthropy

Naming galleries within healthcare institutions is a way of securing funding or creating an endowment for an exhibition program. Standard gift amounts vary and they continue to rise, but this is usually set by the institution's development department and is seldom less than seven figures. Be sure to establish boundaries and gallery guidelines before the donor is invited to the table. Donors might see their gift as an invitation to participate in the running of the galleries or the selection of artwork. Such agreements need to be carefully articulated and structured to prevent misunderstandings and future problems.

The future

Dr. Iva Fattorini, chair of the Global Arts and Medicine Institute at the Cleveland Clinic says, "I can't imagine the hospitals of the future without some form of the arts: visual, performing and literary – with their latent therapeutic powers fully activated. . . . In a hospital setting art is not a commodity, it's a necessity." She goes on to say, "The same artwork that you might see in a gallery or at the exhibition radiates completely different energy when you interact with it in a hospital. In places where people come to heal, different communication channels are open" (Fattorini, 2014).

The digital revolution will undoubtedly continue to transform the hospital/ healthcare art experience. It should help make gallery art more accessible to bed-bound patients and off-site workers. Might gallery visitors soon be able to enter a virtual space and experience art in a more immersive manner? Might patients order up virtual art spaces in the same manner they order their meals – spaces perhaps not unlike those islands of security Bemelmans conjured up to comfort himself during World War I?

Whatever form these art galleries evolve to, there will always be a place for the arts in healthcare to nurture and engage those who otherwise travel a lonely path fraught with fear, distress, and pain. For them, the art will provide shelter and refuge within the context of the great unknown in the journey through illness and healing. The biological basis of how and why the arts support health and healing we leave to the future to illuminate.

References

Arts and Health Alliance. Retrieved from http://www.artsandhealthalliance.org/about/
Art in State Buildings. Retrieved from http://www.uihealthcare.org/content.aspx?id=1636
Dissanayake, E. (1988). *What is art for?* Seattle, WA: The University of Washington Press.

Fattorini, I. (2014, June 24). Arts and Medicine. Do it. [Blog post]. Retrieved from http://www.huffingtonpost.com/iva-fattorini/arts-and-medicine-do-it_b_5526700.html

Our mission. (2015). *The National Arts Program*. Retrieved from http://www.national artsprogram.org/our-mission

National Institutes of Health. (2014). *Fitzgerald Fine Arts*. Retrieved from http://ffinearts.com/?ffa_portfolio=national-institutes-of-health

Palmer, J. (2001). An introduction to the arts-for-health movement, or how the arts sneaked in on the medical model (Paper published online on the Art in the Public Interest Community Arts Network Reading Room). Retrieved from http://wayback.archive-it.org/2077/20100906195258/http://www.communityarts.net/readingroom/archivefiles/2001/11/introduction_to.php

Rothstein, E. (2014, July 3). At 75, still stepping out of line: Ludwig Bemelmans's Madeline celebrates a milestone. *New York Times*. Retrieved from http://www.nyt.com

The University of Michigan Health System Gifts of Art program Mission Statement. Retrieved from http://www.med.umich.edu/goa

The University of Michigan Hospitals and Health Centers. (n.d.) UMHHC Policy 05–01–001 (Internal Policy).

PART 3

Managing participatory arts in healthcare programs

8

PERFORMANCES IN PUBLIC SPACES

Jill Sonke

Throughout the world, healthcare facilities of all kinds are engaging the performing arts as a means of making healthcare environments more welcoming and uplifting (State of the Field Committee, 2009). The field of arts and health is providing more professional opportunities for fine and performing artists alike, and many healthcare settings are more like community cultural centers as they host daily arts activities and performances.

Artists have been performing in healthcare settings, such as hospitals, nursing homes, and long-term care centers, for many decades, both independently and through arts and health programs and partnerships. More than twenty years ago, as I established a hospital-based performing arts series, a physician fondly recounted to me his memory of Carol King coming into the hospital where he was undertaking his residency in the 1960s to perform for patients. As he described it, she just walked in, sat down, and played. Today, as experience, research, and professionalism have significantly advanced programs that bring the arts to healthcare settings, best practices are emerging that can guide program leaders and artists in using the performing arts to yield clear benefits to patients, caregivers, and the environment of care.

Presentation of performing arts in healthcare settings requires a significant level of consideration, planning, and oversight. There are two types of venues in hospital settings – public spaces and clinical spaces. This chapter will focus on performances that take place in public areas, and will not address the parallel issues of presenting performances in clinical spaces. However, many of the concepts presented will be useful in planning performances in clinical areas. The chapter will discuss some of the general concepts that program planners can benefit from understanding and will address specific topics, including developing performance protocols, selecting, preparing, and supporting artists, selecting appropriate venues within healthcare facilities, partnerships between performing arts presenters and healthcare organizations, and the importance of artistic excellence in healthcare settings. While the chapter will refer primarily to performances in hospital settings, the concepts presented are applicable to an array of healthcare settings.

Foundational concepts

Cultural engagement and wellbeing

Engagement in cultural activities, such as performances, has a long history in Western and other societies. The performing arts are so much a part of many cultures and people are so drawn to them that clinical and social sciences researchers have investigated their impact on health. Investigators have found that participation in cultural activities not only can contribute positively to health and wellbeing, but can also contribute to our longevity (Bygren et al., 1996; Castora-Binkley, Noelker, Prohaska, & Satariano, 2010; Cuypers et al., 2011; O'Niel, 2010; Putland, 2008).

Bygren, Konlaan, and Johanssen (1996) conducted a nine-year study of 15,198 individuals to examine the possible life-extending implications of regular attendance of cultural events, such as performances and art exhibits, as well as reading and listening to or making music. When controlling for confounding variables, including age, sex, education level, and income, the investigators found that people who regularly attend cultural events had a better chance of survival (a longer lifespan) than those who do not. Following this study, Johanssen, Konlaan, and Bygren (2001) conducted a study to assess how changes in the habit of attending cultural events might predict self-reported health. They studied a sample of 3,793 adults over an eight-year period, controlling for type of residence, socioeconomic status, and level of education, and found a sixty-five percent increase in the risk of impaired perceived health among people who were not culturally active as compared with those who were culturally active.

In Norway, a survey of 50,797 adults found a significant association between participation in receptive and creative cultural activities and good health, good satisfaction with life, and low anxiety and depression (Cuypers et al., 2011). Wilkenson, Waters, Bygren, and Tarlov (2007) followed up on these findings with a cohort of 1,244 individuals in the United States and found a significant association between cultural activities and self-reported health. They found, specifically, that the more cultural activities people reported attending, the higher was their self-reported health. So, if we can conclude that the performing arts can be beneficial to health, why not make them a part of the healthcare environment, where we aim to improve health and extend life?

Performing arts in the workplace

More recently, investigators have begun to examine how cultural activities in the workplace, including healthcare settings, can benefit workers and others. Tuisku,

Pulkki-Råback, Ahola, Hakanen, and Virtanen (2012) reported that a higher frequency of cultural activities was positively associated with wellbeing at work. The study examined the associations between frequency and type of cultural activities (active/receptive), and found that participation in art-making and creative expression was associated with creativity in work, while receptive participation (such as attending performances) was associated with work engagement. Both types yielded benefits to wellbeing.

Performances in hospital lobbies and other public areas can be very exciting and can also significantly enhance a healthcare environment. For healthcare workers, performances can be a major perk. Many healthcare professionals work long, exhausting hours and don't often get to take in the cultural offerings of their community. By investing in the performing arts, a hospital can provide its employees with cultural enrichment, enjoyment, and stress-reduction, and also enhance organizational satisfaction and retention. Studies have found that when given a choice, nurses are inclined to choose or retain employment in a hospital that offers the arts (Staricoff, Duncan, Wright, Loppert, & Scott, 2001; Staricoff & Loppert, 2003). For patients and family members, being welcomed into a hospital by a live performance can completely change a healthcare experience and the perception of a healthcare institution.

A 2008 survey of 800 arts programs in healthcare settings revealed that 162 programs offer performances in public spaces (State of the Field Committee, 2009). These findings are consistent with results of a 2007 survey by the Joint Commission, which documented that the performing arts represented the second highest prevalence in arts in healthcare program offerings, following the permanent display of art (State of the Field Committee, 2009). While there is little literature focused specifically on staff or patient outcomes related to arts performances in public areas in hospitals, in one study of visual and performing arts in hospitals in the UK, seventy-five percent of respondents reported that the performing arts greatly diminished their stress levels, changed their moods for the better, and helped take their minds off immediate worries or medical problems (Staricoff, Duncan, Wright, Loppert, & Scott, 2001).

Adding to the complexity of the healthcare environment

While the performing arts have the potential to provide healthcare populations with very positive benefits, it must also be noted that the arts, like any other input, add to the complexity of a healthcare environment (Kannampallil, Schauer, Cohen, & Patel, 2011) and can potentially be a positive or negative distraction. Hospitals are very complex systems with many layers of activity that are carefully balanced to create the highest possible levels of order, effectiveness, and safety. The addition of anything to this complex system must be approached with awareness and consideration of how the proposed input will affect all the existing factors.

A recent study of how arts activities impact short-term inpatient care revealed that, while most nurses on a medical-surgical patient care unit experienced live music as a positive distraction for themselves and their patients, six percent of nurses (two out of thirty-one) experienced it as a negative distraction, describing a reduced ability to perform their work effectively and expressing a clear concern that the distraction caused by music could cause them to make an error in patient care (Sonke et al., in press). Similarly, Preti and Welsh (2012) found both positive and negative impacts of music exposure, with five out of twenty (twenty-five percent) of the medical staff interviewed describing music to be a negative element in the environment of care. These findings are consistent with literature that identifies distractions as a factor in medication errors (ASHP, 1993; Sears, et al., 2012; Tang, et al., 2007), and underline the importance of knowing that the performing arts can impact an environment of care in significant ways, both positively and negatively. Program managers and performers alike must plan performances with this in mind.

Developing performing arts programs

There are two primary ways that most institutions approach the development of a performing arts program, either by structuring it within an internal program or department or by establishing a partnership with a performing arts presenter or arts organization, such as a symphony orchestra. Programs that are run internally are typically managed by an institution's art program or by another service department, such as volunteer services, patient and family services, or pastoral services. These programs may feature daily performances of ambient music in public areas, a defined series or season of events, weekly formal performances of music, dance, theatre, poetry, or other performance art, or performing artist residencies. Some institutions provide all of these types of programs. Internally managed programs typically have a dedicated coordinator or director, who develops protocols and policies, schedules performances, acts as a liaison with other departments, and prepares and supports artists. These coordinators may also undertake fiscal management, including grant writing, fundraising, and program evaluation.

Formal performing arts programs have been established internally at University of Iowa Hospitals and Clinics, Duke University, Dartmouth-Hitchcock Medical Center, UF Health Shands Hospital, Penn State Hershey Children's Hospital, Mayo Clinics, and many other healthcare organizations. Some hospitals also feature dedicated performing arts centers or stages in their facilities. For example, at Penn State Hershey Children's Hospital, children can attend performances in the Jeanne and Edward Arnold Atrium and Performing Arts Center or view them through a closed circuit television station (About us, 2015).

Partnerships between healthcare institutions and performing arts presenters can be an excellent means for developing a performing arts program in a healthcare setting. Such partnerships allow each organization to contribute their specialized expertise and systems to a collaboration that can yield effective resource sharing and often a higher level of performance programming than a healthcare institution could achieve independently. Such partnerships have been established between University of Florida Performing Arts and UF Health Shands Hospital, the University at Buffalo Center for the Arts and Roswell Park Cancer Center and Women's and Children's Hospital, and The Alys Stephens Performing Arts Center and UAB Medicine at the University of Alabama at Birmingham, to name just a few. The Kentucky Center for the Performing Arts partners with more than a dozen healthcare facilities, including major hospitals, in Louisville, Kentucky. These partnerships bring world-class performers to these healthcare facilities.

A unique model in this arena is Hospital Audiences, Inc. (HAI), in New York City, New York. HAI has been providing access to the performing arts to hospital and underserved audiences in New York since 1969. HAI partners with many area hospitals and schedules more than 100 performances by professional artists every month at health and social service facilities in the New York City area (Live performances, 2013).

Partnership-based performing arts in healthcare programs bring high-level arts events to healthcare facilities, where audiences tend to be made up of highly diverse populations, many of whom have limited access to the arts due to illness, disability, and geographic or socioeconomic circumstances. For performing arts presenters, these partnerships can serve to expand programmatic reach to underserved and new audiences, and can greatly expand access to the arts for these populations.

Also of note are programs that engage caregivers themselves in the performing arts. Recognizing that many medical professionals are also musicians and that engagement in the arts can reduce stress and enhance wellbeing, numerous medical centers also develop their own orchestras and choirs. The University of Michigan's Life Sciences Orchestra employs a conductor and performs three times annually at the University's historic Hill Auditorium. Similarly, the Texas Medical Center Orchestra presents full seasons of performances that are affordable and accessible to diverse audiences and that financially benefit medical institutions and charities. The orchestra also provides special performances during the holidays at area hospitals. Both of these orchestras are made up of health professionals and are dedicated to providing these professionals with a high-quality outlet for creative expression.

Creating performance program protocols

Every department in a healthcare organization, including an arts program, is responsible for creating and maintaining protocols that guide practices. Clear protocols for performance programs can help garner support from administrators and decision-makers, guide program staff in effectively managing performances, and guide performers in having meaningful and impactful experiences. The development of performance program protocols should include consideration of:

- program structure, including where, when, and why performances might take place;
- program leadership, oversight, and reporting, including organizational charts and responsibilities;

- program planning procedures, including interdepartmental communications, notifications, forms, approvals, management of equipment, media plans, record keeping, etc.;
- artist qualifications and requirements, including the steps taken in selecting and preparing artists, such as interviews, background checks, health or other screenings, training, orientation, and reporting;
- event procedures, including staffing, set-up of seating and technical equipment, signage, infection control procedures, consent, and incident reporting; and
- other procedures, as might apply to PR/media, patient privacy, particular locations, populations served, or types of performances.

Program protocols should be made available to institutional leaders, partners, staff, and artists, and should be maintained as living, evolving guidelines that reflect understanding of patient safety, privacy, and other key healthcare policies and concerns.

Selecting artists

It takes a particular set of skills and attributes for performing artists to be effective in a healthcare environment. Performing in a healthcare setting is very different from performing in an arts venue. The cultures are highly disparate, and the "rules of engagement" are entirely different. In a professional performing arts venue, the ultimate goal is to produce the highest quality performance possible for a paying audience with high expectations. The artists set the parameters under which they can achieve the highest level of artistic excellence. In a healthcare venue, the goal is to provide people in the environment with positive distraction and enjoyment that is supportive of caring and healing. Artistic excellence is extremely important in the healthcare environment, and must be achieved in accord with the more essential needs of the setting and the individuals in it. The healthcare system sets the parameters under which the artist must function. Some artists would see the healthcare environment as an impossible venue, while others are happy to creatively adapt their performance in order to provide a benefit to healthcare populations. The latter are the artists who will work well in healthcare. Program planners must be able to recognize artists with this potential and also orient performers effectively to the healthcare environment.

Several mechanisms can be employed for screening and selecting performing artists. Auditions are an essential step in the screening process, and should be used as the initial gateway. Artists should be asked to perform several pieces that they feel would be appropriate to the setting. In this way, their skill, artistry, and initial judgment can be assessed. If an artist has suitable artistic skill and their performance style fits the needs of the environment, other skills and attributes – as will be discussed below and are listed in Table 8.1 – can be assessed through interview and training or mentorship processes.

TABLE 8.1 Skills and Attributes of Successful Hospital Performers

Skills	Attributes
Artistic excellence	Desire to help others
A broad or flexible repertoire	Empathy
Ability to choose appropriate material	Compassion
Observation	Sensitivity
Responsiveness	Humility
Flexibility	Self-awareness
Adaptability	Thoughtfulness
Communication	Clarity
Cultural competence	Intelligence
Ability to apply principles related to	Clear personal/professional boundaries
sound and energy	Willingness to adhere to policies

Artists who are adept at performing in healthcare settings are those who can deliver a high quality performance while being completely responsive to the environment and the people in it. A study of seventeen hospital performers by Preti and Welsh (2013) identified a primary skill among the performers as the ability to decode a situation very efficiently. Artists must be able to observe the environment keenly, adapt the performance plan accordingly, and gauge appropriate elements for the performance, such as content, volume, energy, and duration.

In a healthcare setting, the "fourth wall" – the lights that separate the performer from the audience – are removed. Performers can see their audience, are often very close to them, and must be interested in and responsive to this audience. Without the fourth wall, artists can engage with people through their art in highly intimate and meaningful ways. Often during or after performances, patients will share what the performance meant to them or how it changed them. This is a tremendous gift for artists, and those that recognize and seek this sort of connection have the potential to succeed as performing artists in healthcare.

Assessing an artist's motivation for performing in a healthcare setting is crucial. Especially if payment is provided, it is helpful to take time to explore the artist's interests and motivations and to align performance opportunities with these interests. Preti and Welsh's (2013) study identified the primary motivation among the performers interviewed as a desire to make a positive impact on people's lives, and also identified a secondary motivation as getting performance experience. Program managers should be conscious of this potentially common motivation and consider whether the performer presents with enough experience and skill to work safely and effectively in the healthcare environment. A hospital should not be perceived as a "stepping stone" to the stage, in that it requires less skill. Performance quality in a healthcare setting is crucial. As has been noted, performances that are not positively perceived can increase stress and even compromise patient safety.

Earlier, the disparateness of healthcare and arts cultures was noted. Another distinction between healthcare and arts cultures is that healthcare cultures are full of rigid protocols and rules, while arts culture thrives on freedom and creativity. Artists selected to perform in healthcare settings must be able to operate in a healthcare environment in accordance with the many procedures that may seem cumbersome or limiting. Program leaders should look for how easily a potential artist can manage the hoops necessary to perform in a healthcare setting. If an artist is resistant to filling out forms or completing orientation or other required procedures prior to performing in a hospital, it is possible that they also will be unable to adhere to patient safety guidelines and be responsive to the needs of the environment. Program managers should also plan for regular time for ongoing observation, supervision, and reflective dialogue with artists to ensure that artists are maintaining performance quality as well as their own wellbeing.

Selecting performance venues in healthcare facilities

The primary consideration for planning performances in public areas should always be how the environment of care can continue to function as needed during a performance, and how the performance can be presented in a way that provides positive, but not negative, distraction.

In planning public area performances, administrators must contend with many considerations and practical guidelines. Most importantly, the primary purpose of a potential performance space must be clearly understood. Is it a designated waiting area? If so, what are the needs of the people who use the space? Would people have an easy option for being in another space if they don't want to be exposed to the performance? If so, is it an inconvenience or risk for them to change locations? Beyond these basic questions, program leaders need to consider who needs to be in the space and who needs to pass through the space. It is essential that people have a choice about whether to be exposed to a performance or not. We must remember that even a good thing can be a bad thing if it happens at the wrong time. A great performance can cause stress if it happens in the wrong place or at the wrong time.

Ideal public performance spaces are those that are large and not designated as waiting areas or primary pathways. Many hospitals have large, lofty atrium-like spaces that serve as excellent performance venues. These spaces allow people the option to come close, linger at the edges, or pass through without discomfort. This range of choice is important to provide in a complex healthcare environment, where stress levels tend to be high. Program organizers and performers must take every measure to ensure that everyone exposed to the performance has consented or has the opportunity to leave easily, and is likely to experience the performance as a positive distraction. Program leaders should consult with facilities management leaders to understand the purposes and needs of potential performance spaces and to design performance programs that enhance, rather than just complicate, the environment.

In addition to collaborating with facilities managers, performance planners should consider consulting with departments such as Volunteer Services, Patient

Safety, Security, Environmental Services, Public Relations, and Infection Control. These collaborations can enhance not only the organization and quality of a program, but can also ensure that patient safety, privacy, and the functional needs of the environment are protected.

Preparing and supporting artists

Healthcare facilities are intense and emotional places. People in them are dealing with some of life's greatest challenges and visitors often experience unexpected emotional responses, which can be triggered by memories, fears, and even empathy and compassion. For this reason, it is critical that performers are well prepared and well supported throughout their experience. Artists should have experiences that are meaningful and enriching, and not traumatizing. This can be accomplished with good preparation and support, which allows artists to function safely in the healthcare environment, present performances that provide positive impacts, and leave feeling enriched by the experience.

Preparation time with artists should include not only orientation processes, such as HIPAA (patient privacy), infection control, and other training as is undertaken with anyone working in the environment of care, but time for discussion. In this discussion, staff who will be supporting the artists should invite the artists to talk about their interests and motivations for performing in a healthcare setting, what they expect from the experience, and what previous experience they have – personally or professionally – in healthcare settings. This discussion should not feel intrusive or like therapy, but should be achieved in a professional manner in the context of preparation. The program organizer should also talk about the areas in which performances will take place, the patients and staff who might attend, and what those individuals may be going through. It is a good idea to describe any medical equipment patients may be using, as well as any other sights or sensory inputs that the artist might experience. In general, it is best to help the artist anticipate anything that is unique to the healthcare environment.

The artist should also be prepared to manage the unique protocols related to infection control, especially if they are playing an instrument. Clinical care units will have specific protocols related to bringing any objects into patient rooms that must be adhered to. In some cases, musical instruments may not be appropriate to use in these units. Managers should discuss performance plans with unit staff and with the hospital's infection control department to determine appropriate protocols for performing artists in these units.

A program organizer should also be present during performances, and should assure artists that they are there to support them. This support will help artists feel less vulnerable and more confident in the environment, especially if it is new. Staff should be available to assist artists with technical needs, watch for their emotional wellbeing, liaison with other staff, and should manage all functions related to set up and clean up, PR, consent for photos, coordinating volunteers, and managing evaluations. Performers should also be given permission to modify a performance plan if they are feeling emotionally overwhelmed or reach their capacity in any way. In a healthcare setting, "the show must go on" is not an appropriate guiding principle. The show should go on if it is in the best interest of everyone involved, including the performers. Performers should also be given an opportunity to reflect on their experience following performances. With this type of preparation and support, performers will likely be eager to continue to work in this environment.

Artistic excellence and quality

More research is needed to explore the importance of artistic excellence and other qualities in healthcare-based performing arts programs. However, professionals in the field have developed a general understanding that overall artistic "excellence" or "quality" is of lesser importance in one-to-one interactions between artists and patients – in the privacy of a patient's room, where creative engagement is the focus – and of greater importance in public areas where exposure is more difficult to moderate. Performing arts, like visual arts installations, that are presented in public areas must be of the highest quality possible to increase the likelihood that they will positively affect the majority of viewers and listeners, regardless of preference. While artistic excellence cannot be objectively defined, general standards related to artistry and technical quality of performances must be set by the program manager to fit the audience, setting, and local cultures.

Individual responses to arts performances are highly subjective. In studies of music, preference has been shown to be advantageous in eliciting positive responses, such as stress and anxiety reduction, immune function, and mood enhancement (Clark et al., 2006; Ebneshahidi & Mohseni, 2008; Jiang, Zhou, Rickson, & Jiang, 2013). These studies, however, look at music as an individualized intervention, and not at music performances in public spaces. While it is generally agreed upon that responding to preference is an ideal, performers in public spaces cannot query an audience to determine preference. Even if they could, the results would be highly varied. Artists performing in public areas should select a repertoire that has the highest likelihood to be generally pleasing, that best suits the environment and the needs of the people in it, and that can be performed at the highest level of quality possible.

In healthcare settings, quality encompasses several factors. One factor is the appropriateness of the performance to the setting, the people in it, and the particular moment in time. In order to achieve this type of quality, the artist must decode the many clues to the needs of the people in the space on a moment-to-moment basis. This is no easy task, and requires all of the skills and attributes that have been described previously. Quality also refers to how something measures up to other similar things. So, when a performance strikes an audience member as outstanding as compared to other performances, the response will likely be more positive, regardless of whether the style or genre of the performance fits with their general preference. In order to be perceived as positive, a performance should also fit with or exceed the expectations of audience members. In this regard, the way a performance is marketed makes a difference. The environment also sets an expectation for audience members. In a more casual setting, one expects less, and vice versa.

Conclusion

Performing arts program managers have a significant task in managing the many issues that have been discussed in this chapter, including merging the disparate cultures of the arts and healthcare, selecting the right artists and supporting them in having meaningful and impactful experiences, and maintaining a level of artistic quality that optimizes benefits, protects the safety of patients, and enhances the environment of care. Many programs are succeeding in this undertaking and providing best practice models that can be replicated. As performing arts programs become more commonplace in healthcare settings, two very significant goals can be achieved: increasing access to artistic excellence for all citizens, especially those for whom access is limited, and making healthcare environments more welcoming and conducive to healing.

References

About us. (2015). *Penn State Hershey Children's Hospital*. Retrieved from http://www.pennstatehershey.org/web/childrens/home/aboutus

American Society of Health-System Pharmacists. (1993). ASHP guidelines on preventing medication errors in hospitals. *American Journal of Health-System Pharmacy, 50*(2), 305–314.

Bygren, L. O., Konlaan, B. B., & Johansson, S. E. (1996). Attendance at cultural events, reading books or periodicals, and making music or singing in a choir as determinants for survival: Swedish interview survey of living conditions. *BMJ: British Medical Journal, 313*(7072), 1577.

Castora-Binkley, M., Noelker, L., Prohaska, T., & Satariano, W. (2010). Impact of arts participation on health outcomes for older adults. *Journal of Aging, Humanities, and the Arts, 4*(4), 352–367.

Clark, M., Isaacks-Downton, G., Wells, N., Redlin-Frazier, S., Eck, C., Hepworth, J. T., & Chakravarthy, B. (2006). Use of preferred music to reduce emotional distress and symptom activity during radiation therapy. *Journal of Music Therapy, 43*(3), 247–265.

Cuypers, K. F., Knudtsen, M. S., Sandgren, M., Krokstad, S., Wikström, B. M., & Theorell, T. (2011). Cultural activities and public health: Research in Norway and Sweden. An overview. *Arts & Health, 3*(1), 6–26.

Davies, C. R., Rosenberg, M., Knuiman, M., Ferguson, R., Pikora, T., & Slatter, N. (2012). Defining arts engagement for population-based health research: Art forms, activities and level of engagement. *Arts & Health, 4*(3), 203–216.

Ebneshahidi, A., & Mohseni, M. (2008). The effect of patient-selected music on early postoperative pain, anxiety, and hemodynamic profile in cesarean section surgery. *The Journal of Alternative and Complementary Medicine, 14*(7), 827–831.

Fenn, C., Bridgwood, A., Dust, K., Hutton, L., Jobson, M., & Skinner, M. (2004). *Arts in England: Attendance, participation and attitudes in 2003*. London: Arts Council England. Retrieved from http://www.artscouncil.org.uk/publication_archive/arts-in-england-2003-attendance-participation-and-attitudes/

Fitzpatrick, T. R., McCabe, J., Gitelson, R., & Andereck, K. (2006). Factors that influence perceived social and health benefits of attendance at senior centers. *Activities, Adaptation & Aging, 30*(1), 23–45.

Jiang, J., Zhou, L., Rickson, D., & Jiang, C. (2013). The effects of sedative and stimulative music on stress reduction depend on music preference. *The Arts in Psychotherapy, 40*(2), 201–205.

Johansson, S. E., Konlaan, B. B., & Bygren, L. O. (2001). Sustaining habits of attending cultural events and maintenance of health: a longitudinal study. *Health Promotion International, 16*(3), 229–234.

Kannampallil, T. G., Schauer, G. F., Cohen, T., & Patel, V. L. (2011). Considering complexity in healthcare systems. *Journal of Biomedical Informatics, 44*(6), 943–947.

Leckey, J. (2011). The therapeutic effectiveness of creative activities on mental well-being: a systematic review of the literature. *Journal of Psychiatric and Mental Health Nursing, 18*(6), 501–509.

Live performances at your facility. (2013). *Healing Arts Initiative*. Retrieved from http://hainyc.org/who-we-serve-what-we-do/health-and-social-service-agencies/live-performances-at-your-facility/

O'Neill, M. (2010). Cultural attendance and public mental health—from research to practice. *Journal of Public Mental Health, 9*(4), 22–29.

Preti, C., & Welch, G. F. (2012). The incidental impact of music on hospital staff: An Italian case study. *Arts & Health, 4*(2), 135–147.

Preti, C., & Welch, G. F. (2013). The inherent challenges in creative musical performance in a paediatric hospital setting. *Psychology of Music, 41*(5), 647–664.

Putland, C. (2008). Lost in translation: The question of evidence linking community-based arts and health promotion. *Journal of Health Psychology, 13*(2), 265–276.

Renton, A., Phillips, G., Daykin, N., Yu, G., Taylor, K., & Petticrew, M. (2012). Think of your art-eries: Arts participation, behavioural cardiovascular risk factors and mental well-being in deprived communities in London. *Public Health, 126*, S57–S64.

Sears, K., Scobie, A., & MacKinnon, N. J. (2012). Patient-related risk factors for self-reported medication errors in hospital and community settings in 8 countries. *Canadian Pharmacists Journal/Revue des Pharmaciens du Canada, 145*(2), 88–93.

Staricoff, R.L., Duncan, J., Wright, M, Loppert, S., & Scott, J. (2001). A study of the effects of the visual and performing arts in healthcare. *Hospital Development, 32*, 25–28.

State of the Field Committee. (2009). *State of the field report: Arts in healthcare 2009*. Retrieved from http://www.arts.ufl.edu/cam/documents/stateOfTheField.pdf

Tang, Y. Y., Ma, Y., Wang, J., Fan, Y., Feng, S., Lu, Q., & Posner, M. I. (2007). Short-term meditation training improves attention and self-regulation. *Proceedings of the National Academy of Sciences, 104*(43), 17152–17156.

Tuisku, K., Pulkki-Råback, L., Ahola, K., Hakanen, J., & Virtanen, M. (2012). Cultural leisure activities and well-being at work: A study among health care professionals. *Journal of Applied Arts & Health, 2*(3), 273–287.

Wilkinson, A. V., Waters, A. J., Bygren, L. O., & Tarlov, A. R. (2007). Are variations in rates of attending cultural activities associated with population health in the United States? *BMC Public Health, 7*(1), 226.

Windsor, J. (2005). *Your health and the arts: A study of the association between arts engagement and health* (Research report 37). London: Arts Council England. Retrieved from http://www.artscouncil.org.uk/publication_archive/your-health-and-the-arts-a-study-of-the-association-between-arts-engagement-and-health/

9

BEDSIDE ARTS ACTIVITIES

Judy Rollins

Group arts experiences routinely occur in many hospital settings. However, increasingly today's hospital artists-in-residence (AIRs) are finding that to meet the needs of their patient population, a greater percentage of their time is being spent conducting activities directly at the bedside. On average, hospitalized patients are sicker than they were even a few decades ago. Patients are hospitalized now primarily for complicated conditions; some of these individuals might not have survived in the past. Although some patients are treated in ward settings, the trend resulting from this high level of illness acuity coupled with a valid concern for infection control is the lone patient in the single-occupancy room.

This chapter discusses the work of bedside artists-in-residence, who they are, and what they do to meet the needs of patients who cannot or prefer not to leave their rooms for arts activities. Considerations for working effectively in this intimate setting are explored.

The artist at bedside

Artists who offer participatory experiences at bedside are one type of "artist-in-residence" or AIR. (Note: Please see Chapter 1 for a description of and a comparison between arts in healthcare, expressive arts therapies, and creative arts therapies.) These professional artists are skilled facilitators in any of the arts disciplines and, in some instances, more than one. Their role is to bring the arts to patients, visitors, caregivers, and the physical environment as a way of humanizing and enhancing the healthcare experience (Sonke-Henderson & Brandman, 2007). As professionals, they are paid for their services. An AIR may work as an individual employed by or under contract with a hospital, as a member of an artists-in-residence program within a hospital, or as a member of a community arts organization that contracts with a hospital.

Qualifications

Hospitals look for a variety of qualifications when selecting artists for this important role. In addition to characteristics such as flexibility, a sense of humor, openness, empathy, and compassion, artists need additional qualities to create both art and relationships, such as

- desire to connect with people and give back to the community,
- passion for sharing and teaching art and art-making,
- sensitivity to and respect for diverse cultures, biologies, physicalities, and ethnicities,
- understanding and respect for the power of the arts,
- understanding of personal limitations,
- capacity to listen and be sincerely supportive,
- well-defined personal and professional boundaries,
- ability to collaborate, and
- no physical or mental condition that would endanger self or others in a hospital (Herbert, Deschner, & Glazer, 2006; Rollins & Mahan, 2010).

Hospitals typically require artists to have a limited health screening, which usually includes a PPD test for tuberculosis and proof of either having had or immunization against certain childhood diseases such as measles, mumps, rubella, and chicken pox. There are mandatory immunizations, such as an annual flu shot. The hospital will conduct a background check and contact references. AIRs receive the hospital's general orientation, often through the hospital's volunteer department. Some hospitals require AIRs to take annual mandatory competency tests relevant to working in a hospital environment (e.g., fire and safety, infection control, critical incident, sheltering in place).

Artist preparation

General hospital orientation is insufficient preparation for the artist working at bedside. Moss and O'Neill (2009) point out the critical need for artists to be adequately prepared to work with vulnerable people in healthcare settings: "The needs of the patients are paramount and artists need to supplement their artistic sills with a range of skills common to health professionals of all disciplines" (p. 101). Other reasons for training may focus on the concerns of hospital staff members, family members, and even the artists themselves (Rollins, 2008; Rollins & Mahan, 2010). Lacking adequate preparation, artists with even the very best of intentions run the risk of hurting patients emotionally or perhaps even physically. Consultation exercises in Ireland found that artists were keen to be on an equal footing with their colleagues in healthcare settings and to undergo training that would equip them to work more effectively in this specialized area (Arts Council of Ireland, 2004).

A number of countries (e.g., Ireland, UK, US) have agreed that professional training for artists is needed (Arts Council of England and Department of Health, 2007; Arts Council of Ireland, 2004; Sonke, Rollins, Brandman, & Graham-Pole,

2009). Artists are receiving preparation through hospital training programs that go beyond the hospital's required orientation (e.g., Studio G Pediatric Artists-in-Residence Program at MedStar Georgetown University Hospital, Washington, DC), training by community arts organizations (e.g., Smith Center for Healing and the Arts, Washington, DC; The Creative Center, New York), or coursework at universities that lead to academic degrees or professional qualifications (e.g., Centre for Arts and Humanities in Health and Medicine, Durham, England; Manchester Metropolitan University, Manchester, England; University of Florida, Gainesville, Florida). However, at this time, a number of artists are engaging in self-study or on-the-job training.

The artist's specialized training varies from the preparation of other clinical professions, including creative arts therapists whose goals and relationships to the clinical environment differ (Sonke-Henderson & Brandman, 2007). Although artists are often part of the clinical care team (i.e., meeting with medical staff to discuss patient care issues and plans), they do not have clinical privileges and typically do not enter notes into patient records or provide services that are directly billable.

Three examples of training program content are described in Table 9.1. The first represents a hospital training program; the second, a community arts organization program; and the third, a university-based program. Other elements of preparation often include shadowing seasoned AIRs or completing a supervised internship. Depending upon work frequency, it typically requires about six months for the artist to feel comfortable working in the healthcare setting (Rollins & Mahan, 2010). Some programs incorporate ongoing continuing professional development opportunities and support.

AIRs working with special populations may be required to have additional qualifications and training. For example, ArtStream's Allies in the Arts Artists-in-Residence Program that serves wounded service members, their families, and hospital staff at Walter Reed National Military Medical Center in Bethesda, Maryland, requires the following (Rollins & King, in press):

1 general arts in healthcare coursework and internship (includes emphasis on being careful to work within an AIR's skill set and respecting the boundaries between AIR practice and that of creative arts therapists),
2 two-year minimum of experience working as an AIR in a hospital setting,
3 special orientation for working in military settings:

- overview of military life,
- deployment,
- transitioning home,
- family/children issues, and
- signature injuries: traumatic brain injury (TBI), post traumatic stress disorder (PTSD), depression

4 Red Cross orientation and related requirements, and
5 mental health first aid training.

TABLE 9.1 Hospital, Community Arts Organization, and University Training Program Examples

Training Program	Training Content
Studio G Pediatric Artists-in-Residence Training Program MedStar Georgetown University Hospital Washington, DC USA Hospital *12 hours + internship*	Children's hospitalization Children's perceptions of illness and hospitalization Meeting children's psychosocial/developmental needs Using the arts to meet psychosocial and developmental needs of children in hospitals Psychosocial assessment Family needs of children who are hospitalized Communicating with children in hospitals and their families Relationships with children and families The artist's routine Safety considerations Infection control Cultural issues Death and dying Stimulating creativity Art activity/adaptations Review of internship
Artists in Healthcare Training Program The Creative Center New York, NY USA Community Arts Organization *1 week*	Body systems for artists The unique culture of hospitals Cultural diversity in a healthcare setting Medical and professional protocols for artists The portable studio: Process, projects, and materials management Best practices in art-making: Visual, performing, and literary arts The artist and the community Hospice and palliative care Looking at and talking about art Caring for the caregiver: Art for families and healthcare staff Patient perspectives Artists logs/reflecting journaling
Arts in Healthcare Summer Intensive University of Florida Gainesville, FL USA University *2 weeks + online*	An historical perspective of the relationship between the arts and healing A theoretical understanding of the relationship between the arts and healing Introductory training and practical experience in the visual arts, movement/dance, music, writing, and theatre process Information and instruction regarding patient safety, healthcare culture, and other practical healthcare concerns Information and instruction regarding implementing, administrating, and funding arts in healthcare programming Experiential work with the arts in a medical setting An understanding of and experience with his/her own creative process An overview of existing career options and programs that integrate the artist into healthcare

The hospital bedside environment

Bedside environments vary between and within hospitals and have changed in many significant ways since Florence Nightingale's time. The bedside environment has important implications for artists planning and implementing arts activities at bedside.

Room occupancy

The artist at bedside will likely be working primarily in single-bed rooms. In recent decades there has been much debate internationally about the single-bed versus the multi-bed patient room. Although multi-bed rooms can offer companionship (which a patient might or might not view as desirable), the consensus among experts in Europe and North America is that single rooms are important in preventing and controlling healthcare-associated infections. Proponents of the single-bed room cite additional benefits for patients, such as 1) an increase in privacy, dignity, and confidentiality; 2) more patient control over the room environment; and 3) better sleep because there is less noise. Increasingly, the trend is leading toward the single-bed room. The United States and Scotland recommend one hundred percent single rooms (Pennington & Isles, 2013), and the United Kingdom's National Health Service has advised that fifty- to one hundred percent of all patient rooms should be single-occupancy in newly built hospitals (Dowdeswell, Erskine, & Heasman, 2004).

Artists will often find family members or visitors present who might wish to participate in the arts experience. In addition to the factors discussed, the single-bed room also facilitates family involvement (Rollins, 2009). Responding to the crowding that can sometimes occur in the one-bed space, hospitals are beginning to build larger single-bed rooms, some furnished with daybeds to accommodate overnight sleeping for a parent, spouse, or other family member. As many hospitals subscribe to the philosophy of family-centered care, artists honor this concept by inviting all people present in the room to participate.

Territoriality

Artists who work at bedside keep the concept of territoriality in mind as they go about their work. Humans have territories, ranging from primary territory to public territory. Territory is different from personal space; personal space is "carried around" with individuals as they move, whereas territory is associated with a particular physical environment. For the individual who is hospitalized, primary territory is the patient's room (Shepley, 2005).

Territoriality is a pattern of behavior and attributes based on perceived, attempted, or actual control of a quantifiable physical space, one's territory. Territoriality differs from privacy in that it addresses domain and ownership rather than a sense of personal separation. An important aspect of territoriality is that it is only in relation to other people that individuals mark and defend their claims (Brown, Lawrence, & Robinson, 2005). Territorial behaviors are not simply about expressing ownership over an object (e.g., this is *mine*) but are centrally concerned with establishing, communicating, and maintaining one's relationship with that object relative to others in the social environment (e.g., this is mine and *not yours*).

Territoriality affects relationships between people, including the relationship between the patient and the artist conducting arts experiences at bedside. Shepley (2005) discusses three ways in which a territory may be disturbed: 1) *invasion*, 2) *violation*, and 3) *contamination*. See Table 9.2 for definitions and examples.

Realizing that they are invading the patient's territory, artists knock on the door (or say "knock, knock" if a curtain), wait for a response, and ask permission before entering the room. With violation in mind, they ask permission before moving any items within the room. And finally, they carefully survey the room before leaving to ensure that nothing inappropriate has been left behind to contaminate the patient's territory.

Clear territories help us know who controls a space and who is in charge in that space (Augustin, 2009). With a constant stream of hospital staff and other individuals entering their room, it is understandable that patients would feel that boundaries are unclear and that they have very little control over their territory. Although few studies have been conducted on territorial behavior in healthcare settings, an early study with adult patients found that when intrusions of territory take place, patients experience anxiety (Allekian, 1973).

Bedside displays

Items on display at a patient's bedside can play an important role for artists working at bedside. The content may provide valuable information about the individual's identity and interests. Hospital rooms are no longer the stark, colorless settings of the past. Although monitors and other sophisticated equipment are often present,

TABLE 9.2 Territory Disruptions

Concept	Definition	Example
Invasion	When a territory is physically entered by an outsider	When artists enter the patient's room
Violation	When a territory is purposely modified by an outsider	When artists move something, such as the patient's lunch tray, to make space for art supplies
Contamination	When something inappropriate is left behind	When artists forget to retrieve a personal item, such as a sweater from the patient's chair, when leaving the room at the completion of the session

among these items can often be found a variety of visual displays that reflect different aspects of the patient's life. Lewis, Kerridge, and Jordens (2009) refer to such items as a bedside display. Such displays are also a method individuals use to mark their territory (Shepley, 2005). Although bedside displays may be mounted in rooms of patients at any age, they are more common at the bedsides of children. Displays might contain a variety of items, combining text, objects, and two-dimensional images such as drawings, paintings, or photographs. In addition to the patient, contributors to the display often include family members, visitors, and hospital staff.

Research findings indicate that these bedside displays accomplish much more than decoration alone and should be understood as aesthetic interventions that serve a wide range of communicative purposes (Jordens, Lewis, & Kerridge, 2009). In interviews with patients and mothers of young children in an Australian pediatric hospital, Jordens and colleagues found that the most frequently reported purpose of the displays was to facilitate spoken interaction between patients and nurses, with visitors, other patients, medical students, and doctors mentioned as interlocutors as well. Conversations triggered by the displays were viewed as a means for children to 1) interact with adults directly rather than having their parents answering questions, 2) establish their identity, and 3) continue conversations beyond mere pleasantries.

Planning bedside arts activities

With thoughtful planning, most arts activities that are common in other settings can be facilitated in some form at bedside. Factors to consider include novelty of the experience, patient-centered approach, space, safety and infection control, and adaptive materials and processes.

Novelty

Research tells us that people who are hospitalized are more likely to engage in arts activities that offer new or interesting experiences (Stoner & Sahni, 2006). Ermyn King, ArtStream's Allies in the Arts artist in residence, has developed many interesting projects for wounded services members and their families. Figure 9.1 depicts an example of an amulet bag, which is small pouch that hold objects such as gems, simple stones, coins, tokens with words, or prayers, that are intended to bring good luck or protection to its owner.

The bags are generally worn at heart level. As they make their bags and select the objects, participants talk about the reasons for their choices and their stories come forth. Another activity she offers is Chinese brush painting, which is a new and interesting experience for many people (see Figure 9.2).

She demonstrates brush painting technique and offers choices of painting a scene or copying a Kanji character that has personal meaning. Once placed in a

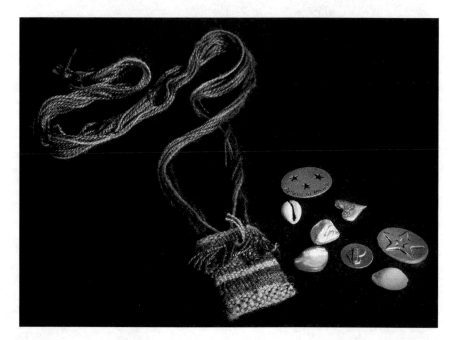

FIGURE 9.1 Amulet Bag

FIGURE 9.2 Chinese Brush Painting

simple, inexpensive frame, the painting becomes a beautiful addition to a patient's bedside display or a gift for a family member or friend.

Patient-centered approach

Artists arrive on the unit and receive information about patients. This information could include referrals, a list of patients that might be most receptive to or in need of an arts experience, and names of patients that should not be disturbed. Although artists may be told a patient's age, especially when the patient is a child, patient diagnosis is typically withheld.

With this information in hand, the artist goes room to room offering arts activities based on his or her area of expertise and the patient's interests and abilities, a patient-centered approach. Once only used in rehabilitation, a person- or patient-centered approach is now reshaping practice throughout healthcare (Rollins, 2013). Patient-centered care is respectful of and responsive to individual preferences, needs, and values, and ensures that the individual's preferences and values guide all decisions.

Having the opportunity to participate in an arts activity can provide the patient with a great number of choices, and artists ensure that the patient is aware of them. One choice may be to decline participation. Although artists new to working at the bedside may be disappointed and perhaps take the decision personally, they understand that they have given the patient an opportunity to say no and to have that no honored, perhaps the only time that day. In a hospital setting where so little is within the patient's control, this gift can have great meaning.

Space

Although the trend in hospital design is toward larger single-occupancy rooms, limited space for art supplies and for moving about remains a consideration. In planning activities, artists consider the work surface available. For example, the average overbed table is approximately 36" × 16". Beside the bed is a bedside table, which may or may not be available to the artist.

Art carts filled with art supplies and equipment may be brought from room to room. The cart can store musical instruments, props for drama, journals for writing, and other supplies beyond visual art materials. Some art carts are designed to enable the space on the top to be used as a work area. For painting, drawing, printmaking, collage, and other visual arts activities, artists can make bed easels by clipping paper to a Masonite board using binder clips and then leaning the board against the overbed table for support.

Dancers quickly learn to adjust to the space available (see Figure 9.3). Technology has helped reduce space requirements for the recorded music dancers often use. The large boombox has now been replaced by music on laptops, iPads, or even tiny smartphones.

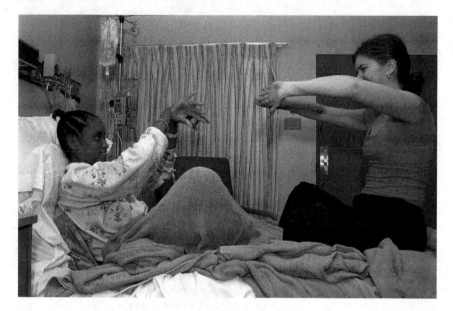

FIGURE 9.3 Dancing at Bedside

Safety and infection control

A number of resources are available recommending appropriate, safe art materials for use at bedside. The Art & Creative Materials Institute, Inc., an international association of over 200 art, craft, and creative material manufacturers, seeks to promote safety in art and creative products through its certification program. Information about products can be found on the Institute's website (www.acminet. org). *The Artist's Complete Health and Safety Guide* (Rossol, 2001) is another excellent resource to guide artists in the selection of safe materials and methods to use with a vulnerable patient population.

Seemingly innocent materials may hold potential for harm for certain individuals. For example, a patient whose immune system is compromised from chemotherapy might need to avoid a project with exposure to soil or other materials where bacteria may be present. AIRs may be required to gown up in protective garb to enter a patient's room. Well-trained AIRs understand isolation protocols, know to ask a nurse or another medical professional if they are uncertain about the appropriateness of a certain material, and always have on hand new, unopened materials for use by these patients. Other isolation protocols require AIRs to bring in art supplies to remain in the room so as not to be exposed to other patients.

Adaptive materials and processes

In the hospital setting, patients may be temporarily or permanently unable to participate in an arts activity without adaptations. AIRs who develop methods to work with the common circumstances of their patient population will be better able to promote participation for patients who could benefit most from the experience. Adaptation could be something as simple as slipping sponge hair rollers over a brush handle or pencil for a patient with grasping difficulties.

In other situations, special equipment can make an enormous difference for a patient. For example, arm amputations are common among service members wounded in current US conflicts. Many of these young men and women previously played guitar. A digital guitar that can be strummed with a stump brings music back into their lives and provides a sense of empowerment and hope for the future.

Facilitating activities at bedside

The Shands Arts in Medicine Program at the University of Florida developed a helpful metaphor for the facilitation of the arts at bedside. The metaphor, which is called the "Four Bridges," is not a method to be applied, but simply an observation of the progression of what often occurs in this process (Sonke-Henderson & Brandman, 2007).

The first bridge: moving into relationship

The artist-in-residence facilitates a creative process for patients through relationship. Thus, the art of conversation is an extremely important skill for the AIR. Sonke-Henderson and Brandman (2007) point out that conversation is one of the great pleasures of the role. Efficiency of communication is very important for hospital staff and highly valued in the hospital environment. However, this kind of communication can be highly depersonalizing and alienating for patients. "Artists have the unique opportunity to talk with patients and, even more importantly, to listen" (Sonke-Henderson & Brandman, 2007, p. 75).

Through listening, the AIR gains a better understanding of the patient, and simply engaging in conversation and being listened to can be enormously comforting and nourishing for a patient. The artist is available for further creative interaction; however, if the process does not move beyond conversation, it does not make the process any more or less successful. A successful artist/patient interaction is whatever is useful and meaningful for the patient.

Rapport with the artist helps build a patient's confidence to create. Cultivating rapport often begins with conversation or storytelling. The relationship may develop quickly or over an extended period of time, but should never be rushed. Bedside displays are good conversation starters. An observant artist also is quick to note patients' body language for clues regarding what parts of conversations or stories seem to excite or interest them, information that could provide the basis for a creative activity. Engaging in an arts activity together or with the patient watching the artist create are other ways to build relationship. Patients are relieved of the pressure of conversation and often find it very relaxing to watch a piece of art emerge (Sonke-Henderson & Brandman, 2007).

The second bridge: moving into creativity

Adults, especially, may be reluctant to create, but because rapport has been established, patients may cross the second bridge into creativity with relative comfort. When the patient is ready to begin, the artist generally guides the process. "This is the 'Hey, I've got an idea, follow me . . .'" part of the process (Sonke-Henderson & Brandman, 2007, p. 78).

The artist then leads with ideas that have personal meaning to the patient by using memories, images, and even physical gestures the patient provided in the first bridge's conversation. This part of the process is often very therapeutic in and of itself. Even without creating something uniquely personal or metaphorical, the act of dancing, singing, reading poetry together, or painting can be tremendously joyful, physically invigorating, and inspiring. The journey may end with the second bridge, but it can be continued or maintained over time (Sonke-Henderson & Brandman, 2007).

The third bridge: moving into the patients' creative process

Although some patients will direct the creative experience immediately, most look to the artist for leadership. The third bridge represents the transition of leadership from the artist to the patient. The artist can often recognize a visible shift in the patient that signals this transition. Sonke-Henderson and Brandman (2007) offer the following example: "Within a movement activity, the patient may alter her gaze from outward (following the artist's lead) to inward (following her internal imagery or impulse) or might initiate this shift by sharing images, memories, or feelings that arise from the movement" (p. 79).

Supporting patients in developing their creative process follows. In the dance example above, Sonke-Henderson and Brandman (2007) suggest that the artist might gently mirror or echo the patient's movement, physically support the patient, or improvise from the patient's images or movement motifs in a way that helps her maintain her focus. Insights ranging from interesting to life altering are discovered during this stage of the creative journey. Further, for patients, it is empowering to have their work affirmed by another.

Although possibly tempting, the artist resists attempting to interpret or assign meaning to a patient's images or creative process. Sometimes patients choose to explore the meaning within their work. When this occurs, the artist listens and honors their thoughts: "Artists support the patient in his or her creative journey, knowing that the process itself has therapeutic value and that it may also yield important discoveries, but do not guide the patient toward interpretation, therapeutic exploration, or catharsis. If this occurs, the artist supports as any fellow human being might, and if additional psychological support is needed, garners the assistance of mental health staff" (Sonke-Henderson & Brandman, 2007, p. 80).

Expression may be direct or indirect. For example, while some patients may create art on their own, others may be reluctant or physically or mentally unable to do so. Still others may simply prefer to be passive. In these instances, an artist may paint an image for a patient, dance a patient's dance, or act a patient's story. These often considered passive experiences are nonetheless active, engaging, and often transformative (Sonke-Henderson & Brandman, 2007). By becoming an instrument of expression for patients, the artist fosters the expression of their experiences, ideas, and hopes.

The fourth bridge: moving toward closure

The fourth bridge represents transition from the creative space back to a focus on the present. At times closure can be challenging. Having something to leave with the patient for the future (e.g., art supplies, a journal, a list of resources) can ease the transition. Dancers often give the patient the gift of a small movement motif, preferably something that the patient is physically able to do, that comes from the session's shared experience (Sonke-Henderson & Brandman, 2007).

Documentation

Artists typically do not write notes on the patient record. However, most AIRs complete a session report or write entries in a program log book or journal, which in most cases is reviewed by an AIR program director or a healthcare professional. Documentation serves several purposes. In addition to offering a mechanism for accountability, documentation provides valuable information about the patient's interests and process for the artists who follow. It also can capture simple statistics, an evaluation of the patient's response, and rich qualitative data for program evaluation, which can be used for program improvement and funding requests.

Further, documentation often offers fresh insight to healthcare professionals about the patient. For this reason, nurses or other staff with access to the patient record may note information an artist has recorded or reported for others on the healthcare team to read. Copies of a patient's poem or drawing can sometimes be found within a patient's record, helping to further humanize the patient for the staff.

Conclusion

Increasingly, artists are providing their services directly to the patient at bedside. The intimate environment affords an opportunity to focus on one patient at a time using a patient-centered approach. With creativity, appropriate training, and support, artists can use a full palette of art modalities to safely and effectively meet the needs of hospitalized patients at bedside.

References

Allekian, C. (1973). Intrusions of territory and personal space. *Nursing Research, 22*(3), 236–241.

Arts Council England and Department of Health. (2007). *A prospectus for arts and health.* London: Arts Council England and Department of Health.

Arts Council of Ireland. (2004). *Arts and health conference proceedings and 'how to' workshop notes.* Dublin: The Council.

Augustin, S. (2009). *Place advantage: Applied psychology for interior architecture.* Hoboken, NJ: John Wiley & Sons.

Brown, G., Lawrence, T., & Robinson, S. (2005). Territoriality in organizations. *Academy of Management Review, 30,* 577–595.

Dowdeswell B., Erskine, J., & Heasman, M. (2004). *Determinants influencing single room provision: A report for NHS Estates by the European Health Property Network.* Retrieved from www.pcpd.scot.nhs.uk/PDFs/EUHPN_Report.pdf

Herbert, G., Deschner, J., & Glazer, R. (Eds.). (2006). Artists-in-Residence: The Creative Center's approach to arts in healthcare. Billings, MT: Artcraft Printers.

Jordens, C., Lewis, P., & Kerridge, I. (2009). Decoration or communication? A qualitative study of images displayed around the bedsides of hospitalized children. *Communication & Medicine, 6*(1), 61–71.

Lewis, P., Kerridge, I., & Jordens, C. (2009). Creating space: Hospital bedside displays as facilitators of communication between children and nurses. *Journal of Child Health Care, 13*(2), 93–100.

Moss, H., & O'Neill, D. (2009). What training do artists need to work in healthcare settings? *Medical Humanities, 35*(2), 101–105.

Pennington, H., & Isles, C. (2013). Should hospitals provide all patients with single rooms? *British Medical Journal, 347,* f5695.

Rollins, J. (2008). Arts for children in hospitals: Helping to put the 'art' back in medicine. In B. Warren (Ed.), *Using the creative arts in healthcare and therapy* (3rd ed.) (pp. 181–195). London: Routledge.

Rollins, J. (2009). The influence of two hospitals' designs and policies on social interaction and privacy as coping factors with children with cancer and their families. *Journal of Pediatric Oncology Nursing, 26*(6), 340–353.

Rollins, J. (2013). *Bringing the arts to life: A guide to the arts and long-term care.* Washington, DC: Global Alliance for Arts & Health.

Rollins, J., & King, E. (in press). Promoting coping for children of hospitalized service members with combat injuries through creative arts engagement. *Arts & Health: An International Journal for Research, Policy and Practice.*

Rollins, J., & Mahan, C. (2010). *From artist to artist-in-residence: Preparing artists to work in pediatric healthcare settings* (2nd ed.). Washington, DC: Rollins & Associates.

Rossol, M. (2001). *The artist's complete health and safety guide* (3rd ed.). New York: Alworth Press.

Shepley, M. (2005). The health-care environment. In J. Rollins, R. Bolig, & C. Mahan (Eds.), *Meeting children's psychosocial needs across the health-care continuum* (pp. 313–349). Austin, TX: ProEd.

Sonke-Henderson, J., & Brandman, R. (2007). The hospital artist in residence programs: Narratives of healing. In I. Serlin (Ed.), *Whole person healthcare volume three: The arts and health* (pp. 67–86). Westport, CT: Praeger Publishers.

Sonke, J., Rollins, J., Brandman, R., & Graham-Pole, J. (2009). The state of the arts in healthcare in the United States. *Arts in Health: An International Journal of Research, Policy, and Practice, 1*(2), 107–135.

Stoner, S., & Sahni, S. (2006, April). *How do we know we made a difference?* Paper presented at the Society for the Arts in Healthcare Annual Conference, Chicago, IL.

10

EVALUATING THE ARTS IN HEALTHCARE PROGRAM

Building a story about the program's activities, paths to improvement, and achievements

Jana Kay Slater

This chapter describes the strategy used to evaluate an arts-based health education program developed for patients with dementia and their caregivers.[1] An interprofessional team consisting of a neuropsychologist, professional artists, and research psychologist developed the program design and evaluation strategy. Together, the team conceptualized and developed the health education program through its full program life cycle – from initial planning through sustained operation. Unobtrusive evaluation strategies were integrated into program implementation. Multiple types of evaluation data were collected and analyzed by the team; results were put to immediate use in improving program implementation. In the end, evaluation findings and recommendations will serve as authentic evidence for justifying program continuation and expansion.

Case study vignette: a typical program session

Every seat around a long conference table is occupied by an older adult, some in their sixties and others in their seventies and eighties. At the front of the room is a neuropsychologist who specializes in dementia. Two professional teaching artists flank him on either side. Running down the center of the conference table is a plethora of arts-related materials: paints, markers, papier-mâché boxes, dried flowers, pages from calendars, paintbrushes.

The twelve participants voluntarily signed up for this innovative program and have come in pairs – an individual who has been diagnosed with some form of dementia and his or her caregiver. As the first class of the four-week health education program begins, most eyes turn to the neuropsychologist, who will be talking this week about strategies for managing and coping with declining memory. There is hope and fatigue in the eyes of the caregivers, and some degree of confusion and lack of focus in the eyes of most of the patients.

The psychologist completes his thirty-minute educational talk with concrete recommendations about the use of a memory box. A memory box is a special container in which to place frequently lost items such as keys and wallets. He then introduces the two teaching artists who will lead the participants in an activity during which each participant pair will co-construct their own memory box to take home with them. Papier-mâché boxes are distributed and participants begin to handle the art supplies that run the length of the table. After brief instruction provided by the professional teaching artists, caregiver and patient teams begin working together on the construction of their memory box.

The artists mill around as participants work on their boxes, providing helpful tips for making the box design meaningful and gently encouraging reluctant participants. The neuropsychologist wanders and engages participants in conversation. "What sorts of things do you plan to put in this box?" "What strategies do you use to deal with frustration when items are lost?" A resident physician interacts with participants as well, providing a compassionate ear and reiterating the educational messages delivered by the neuropsychologist. As they work, participants chat casually with one another, swapping stories about their past and current lives, exchanging coping ideas, making connections, all while working intently on the creation of the personal memory box. Laughter erupts occasionally. Everyone in the room watches as the neuropsychologist models an effective strategy for diffusing frustration when one woman with dementia lashes out at her spouse, creating a moment of tension in the room. At the end of ninety minutes, the neuropsychologist lets participants know the topics that will be covered in the next class and encourages everyone to make lists of questions and concerns over the course of the week that he can address next time.

A practical perspective on program evaluation

Evaluation is a process of systematically collecting information to make judgments and decisions about value or worth. It is a close cousin to research – evaluation uses the same data collection strategies and conducts the same types of analyses as research, but the aim of research is to prove a hypothesis while the aim of evaluation is to improve a program (Stuffelbeam, 1983). The literature on program evaluation has been growing steadily since the 1960s, with academics, program practitioners, organizational theorists, and others making contributions that focus on important aspects of theory, practice, and utilization. Most of these writers strive to further the practice of evaluation by suggesting different ways to conduct evaluations, making the case for slight variations that purportedly can make a difference in the accuracy or usefulness of an evaluation. Key historical and contemporary approaches that have shaped evaluation have been described by Alkin and Christie (2004). For academics and professional evaluators who work on national-level studies, there can be important differences between the various evaluation theories, purposes, approaches, strategies, methods, and uses. But is an in-depth understanding of differences between various approaches to evaluation important for program directors and coordinators of community-level programs? Not so much. In reflecting back on the development of evaluation as a field, Ernie House (2014) remembers that in the 1970s, there were already more than fifty different evaluation models yet really only a few basic approaches. The fundamental bones of the various approaches are similar. They address basic and not-so-basic evaluation questions such as: Has the program been implemented as planned? What progress has been made in reaching its objectives? What specific changes can be made to strengthen program effectiveness? What is the impact of the program? And the ultimate question – What is the value of this program?

Not surprisingly, many local program directors and coordinators view evaluation with a wary eye. The confusing abundance of models, debates about the merits and shortcomings of various approaches, and complicated academic jargon contributes to the sense that evaluation is complex and elitist. Indeed, there is a pervasive belief that only professional evaluators have the wherewithal to conduct an evaluation. This may be true for national-level multi-site programs, but it is not true for the evaluation of local community-based local programs. Trending now in program development and evaluation is the engagement of interprofessional teams, comprised of local people who care about the program, to work together to make it the best program possible. Given a straightforward, practical framework for evaluation, arts in healthcare interprofessional teams can have the capacity to incorporate evaluation strategies into the everyday functioning of their programs – to continually improve program implementation and maximize its positive effects. A purpose of this chapter is to illustrate how familiarity with basic concepts, careful preparation, and systematic thinking (along with well-timed expert consultations as needed) are the most essential ingredients for planning and conducting meaningful and useful program evaluations.

Using the dementia health education program described above as a case study, this chapter illustrates an interprofessional team approach and process for developing and evaluating an arts in healthcare program.

The planning phase

Samaritan Health Services, based in Corvallis, Oregon, has had an arts and health initiative for more than ten years. Professional artists work one-on-one with patients and family members at the bedside, musicians perform on wards and in public areas, and the environment is enhanced by commissioned art and award-winning healing gardens. Patients and family members are able to participate in artist-led activities during one-time events (e.g., mural creation) or multi-class series (art group for cancer survivors). As a regional health system comprised of five hospitals, seventy outpatient clinics, and a long-term care facility, bringing the arts up to scale in all locations is an ongoing challenge.

Over the past decade, the arts had become an integral part of the culture of this largely rural health system, but never before had a health professional initiated and partnered with professional artists to develop and provide a unique art-enhanced patient-centered service in a group setting. The impetus for this innovative arts-based program came out of a discussion between a research psychologist, neuro-psychologist, and artist. The neuropsychologist was looking for a more effective way to deliver health education information to his patients. At that time, he educated his patients about dementia during office visits. Sometimes he would see caregivers and patients only once, and had to provide as much information as he could during a one-hour visit. This was, he believed, inadequate time to deliver all the information that people need for managing dementia. Additionally, emotions can run high during healthcare office visits, making it difficult to process information. And as a neuropsychologist, he knew that older adults process and retain information better when it is repeated several times and in multiple modalities. Further, when making presentations about dementia in community settings, he found the rooms were often filled to capacity. With this firsthand information regarding the need for health education about dementia, he convened an inter-professional team to brainstorm: How could health education information about dementia be provided in a group setting using teaching strategies that maximize retention in older adults? The interprofessional team worked together to flesh out the arts-based health education program design and evaluation.

During the first few meetings, the team grappled with big picture questions – what type of a program would be most effective and what resources will be needed to accomplish this? It was surprisingly difficult to reach agreement; each member of the team had a different perspective and priorities. Reaching consensus took several meetings, but in the end the team agreed upon overall goals and objectives for the health education program and its evaluation.

> **Goal**: Develop, implement, and evaluate an arts-based health education program for patients with dementia and their caregivers, the aims of which are health improvement for modifiable health factors and improvement in quality of life.
>
> **Objective 1**: Establish and convene monthly an interprofessional team to develop and evaluate the arts-based health education program for patients with dementia and their caregivers.
>
> **Objective 2**: Develop program materials (description of program model, evidence-based course curriculum, instructional manual for associated art activities) in sufficient detail to allow replication in other communities and for other conditions by (specified date).
>
> **Objective 3**: Over a twelve-month period, deliver two health education sessions **with** the arts component for dementia patients and caregivers (four classes each session), serving at least twenty-four people.
>
> **Objective 4**: Over a twelve-month period, deliver two health education sessions **without** the arts component for dementia patients and caregivers (four classes each session), serving at least twenty-four people.
>
> **Objective 5**: Establish evaluation as an integral part of the program: use findings to provide ongoing feedback for continuous quality improvement,

document health outcomes, and determine the program's value for participants and the healthcare system.

It should be noted that "interprofessional team" and "evaluation" were listed as specific objectives as a way of keeping these components high on the radar, as optimizing team functioning and tracking evaluation activities were considered essential to the program's success. An additional desire of the team (but not listed as a specific objective) was to engage medical students and resident physicians in the program, in some manner, to introduce the next generation of providers to the concept of arts in healthcare and to the idea of presenting health education information in a group setting.

Very quickly, the team realized that the arts-based health education program could eventually serve as a foundation for an expanded menu of arts-based health education programs that address other chronic diseases and conditions. With this in mind, the team made development of an evidence-based replicable program model a priority. Evaluation was viewed as equally important. Although Samaritan Health Services had a wide range of existing arts and health activities, this program was a first-time-ever attempt to add an arts component to health education provided by a health provider. How would this new idea work? When a health provider is delivering health education information, will adding an arts component result in better outcomes for participants than traditional lecture-only health education? The evaluation would need to compare outcomes in classes that included the arts component with outcomes in classes that did not include the arts component. The neuropsychologist also wanted to measure differences in outcomes between group-based health education (with and without arts) and his standard method of delivering the information during patient office visits.

It was helpful for the team to create a schematic that provided a basic framework for the program and how it would be evaluated. The evaluation would measure differences in participant outcomes when health education information is delivered in any of three approaches: (1) group-based health education **with** coordinated arts activities, (2) group-based health education **without** the arts activities, and (3) patient office visits. The schematic in Table 10.1 illustrates the three health information delivery strategies and the timing for the collection of information.

The team agreed that the evaluation should be designed around the real-life delivery of the health education information. Although random assignment is a cornerstone for research, the interprofessional team decided against randomly assigning caregiver-patient teams to one of the three delivery approaches. Participation in an arts-based health education program like the dementia program will always be voluntary. The team was interested in learning about the relative effectiveness of the three approaches for delivering information about dementia when participants chose the delivery modality that makes sense for them personally. Some participants will prefer the arts-based group classes, some will prefer

TABLE 10.1 Schematic Description of the Timing for Collecting Evaluation Information

	Health education **with** arts activities		Health education **without** arts activities		Health education during office visit(s)	
	Before	*After*	*Before*	*After*	*Before*	*After*
Surveys and Tests (quantitative data)	X	X	X	X	X	X
Interviews and Focus Groups (qualitative data)		X		X		X
Monitoring and Tracking (sign-in sheets, tracking forms)	Ongoing					

lecture-only classes, and some will prefer to meet with the neuropsychologist one-on-one during regular patient appointments.

The team also opted for a comprehensive mixed-methods evaluation strategy. Team members wanted information that would strengthen program implementation and also information that would demonstrate the degree to which participation increased outcomes, such as knowledge and skills for managing dementia. Quantitative and qualitative types of data would need to be gathered using multiple data collection strategies (e.g., surveys, interviews, observation, standardized tests) and representing multiple perspectives (e.g., patients, artists, family members).

Making evaluation an integral and seamless part of the program was another priority for the team. *Process evaluation* (sometimes called *formative evaluation*) refers to evaluation activities designed to learn about program implementation, that is, how the program operates and how well it has been delivered. Process evaluation information would be collected continuously during the program's delivery through standard tracking and monitoring methods (e.g., sign-in sheets, class observation, feedback from participants, artists, and psychologist). The team committed to monitor process data monthly to detect potential problems early and intervene quickly. Narrative stories would be gathered from participants through class conversations, interviews, and focus groups. Narrative stories can reveal problems in program implementation and also illustrate program effectiveness.

Outcome evaluation (sometimes called *summative evaluation*) refers to evaluation activities designed to learn about program effectiveness, that is, how well it has succeeded in improving the lives of its participants. Outcome evaluation information relating to program effectiveness would be collected via published instruments, which were selected by the neuropsychologist (e.g., instruments to measure quality of life, knowledge, and skills). The team opted for a pre–post design because they wanted to measure change between two time periods – before and after receiving the program. Participants who chose either group-based health education strategy would be asked to commit to attending four classes (twice a month, for two months). Participants who preferred to receive information during patient office visits would be asked to provide evaluation information before (pre) meeting with the neuropsychologist and again two months later (post) via telephone conversation with the neuropsychologist. Annually, all data would be analyzed with particular attention on outcomes (differences between pretest and posttest data) in order to make evaluative judgments about the relative merits of the three delivery methods.

The logic model

Objective two called for the development of a detailed and comprehensive description of the program. Sara Lawrence-Lightfoot (1997) refers to this step as developing a "portrait" of a program, an apt description for an arts-based program. This description has also been called a program theory or a logic model. Whatever it is called, developing a clear description of the program is essential for telling the story of how it will be implemented and what it will accomplish. This team opted to develop a program logic model. The standard components of the logic model approach for describing a program includes the following sections: inputs, activities, outputs, outcomes, and impact (W. K. Kellogg Foundation, 2004). A good resource when developing and using a logic model has been developed by the Centers for Disease Control and Prevention (http://www.cdc.gov/dhdsp/programs/nhdsp program/evaluation guides/docs/logic model.pdf). A logic model has this structure:

Inputs → Activities → Outputs → Outcomes → Impact

The components of the logic model are explained below, along with the rationale for the logic model that was developed for the dementia health education program.

Inputs

Imagine that you are making a case for your program to your hospital Chief Executive Officer. You explain why it makes sense to move forward by listing all of the existing resources and strengths that will contribute to the success of the program. These are program "inputs." Here's what the team came up with for the arts-based dementia program:

- **Established Arts and Health Initiative:** Samaritan Health Services has more than ten years of experience and success in implementing and sustaining environmental, visual, and participatory bedside arts to enhance the healthcare experience for patients, family members, staff, and community members.
- **Strong interprofessional team:** The interprofessional team consists of a neuropsychologist, professional teaching artists, and a research psychologist.

- **Experienced and engaged artists:** Samaritan Health Services already contracts with twenty trained professional teaching artists who are working in various capacities within the organization.
- **Enthusiastic health providers:** Within Samaritan Health Services, there exists an enthusiastic cadre of health providers and allied healthcare professionals who have embraced the value of arts-based health programming – psychologists, primary care providers, resident physicians, oncologists, social workers, medical students, and others.
- **Billable provider services:** The proposed program is economically sustainable because providers and allied health professionals are able to bill for services provided in group settings.
- **Aligned with organizational healthcare reform priorities:** The arts-based health education model, delivered in the group setting, is aligned with Samaritan Health Services' strong commitment to achieve healthcare reform's triple aim of "Better Care, Better Health, Lower Costs."
- **Sustainability:** Once the arts-based health education program has been developed and evaluated, it can be sustained through provider fees, support from the hospital foundation, and anticipated grant funding from multiple sources.

Activities and outputs

For this part of the arts-based health education program story, the team constructed a list of key activities that would be carried out during program implementation and who would be responsible for each activity. Think of this as an implementation to-do list that includes details about each activity (what is involved, when it will be completed, and who is responsible). Activities are generally listed in the order in which they will occur. For our program, the key responsible persons were all interprofessional team members (T), the Project Director (PD), an artist who was also serving as the Program Coordinator (PC), and the Evaluator (E). The neuropsychologist served as the Project Director and the research psychologist served as the evaluator. It should be noted here that although it is beneficial to have someone trained in the discipline of evaluation on an interprofessional team, it is not essential. By their very nature, interprofessional teams are comprised of individuals with a broad range of skills and interests. Usually someone on the team possesses analytical skills and this individual would be the natural choice as the person responsible for aggregating data. The entire team then looks at the aggregated data and other sources of information to draw evaluative judgments about what is and is not working well. Professional evaluators can be engaged as consultants to help a team develop goals and measurable objectives, set up the logic model, establish the evaluation design, and create the measurement instruments. Once these resources are in place, an interprofessional team will be able to conduct and sustain evaluation activities independently. The professional evaluator can then be used on an as-needed basis, should the need for additional assistance arise.

Outputs are the concrete indicators that each activity was completed as planned. They are usually defined as counts (e.g., number of people or sessions) or completed products. Funders and administrators are fond of outputs because they provide unambiguous evidence that you completed the activities in your program plan. Monitoring and tracking progress can be as simple as checking off each activity after it is completed and documenting its output. When viewed through a slightly different lens, this same information is an important part of the process evaluation. The team developed the following list of activities and output indicators (see Table 10.2). Sources of documentation for the outputs is indicated in parentheses.

Outcomes and impact

Outcomes refer to changes that can reasonably be attributed to the program. These changes can occur in people (e.g., caregivers, patients, artists, providers), communities (e.g., increased access to arts-based health education programs), and organizations (e.g., decreased costs, improved community relations, increased market share). Outcomes can be measured immediately after a program has ended (short-term outcome) and at a later date to see if they have been sustained over time (intermediate or long-term outcome). The term "impacts" refers to global changes that are long lasting. The team generated the following comprehensive list of desired outcomes and impacts.

Outcomes for caregivers and patients

- Increased health literacy (increased knowledge and understanding of dementia, increased ability to address sensitive issues and express needs to provider)
- Improved quality of life
- Improved general health
- Increased self-efficacy for managing dementia

Outcomes for providers, residents, medical students, and artists

- Improved communication with patients and caregivers
- Increased compassion for patients and caregivers
- Increased job satisfaction

Outcomes for the organization

- Increased patient satisfaction survey ratings
- Increased patient ratings of quality of care
- Increased ability to provide a range of high-quality services delivered in a group setting at a lower cost
- Increased visibility in communities through positive publicity about innovative patient-centered services

TABLE 10.2 Activities and Outputs Included in the Logic Model

Activities	Outputs
Obtain signed contracts with Program Coordinator and Evaluator *by specified date* (PD)	Signed contracts are on file (actual contracts)
Recruit medical students and residents to participate in class sessions *by specified date* (PD)	# medical students # resident physicians participating in sessions (sign-in forms)
Establish billing procedures for providers *by specified date* (PD)	Billing procedures are established (written procedures)
Convene interprofessional team monthly to develop and guide all aspects of program development, implementation, and evaluation *by specified date* (PD)	# times the team met over a twelve-month period (meeting minutes)
Complete tracking forms and obtain selected standardized outcomes measures *by specified date* (E)	Tracking forms were completed and standardized instruments were obtained (actual forms and instruments)
Submit proposal to Institutional Review Board *by specified date* (E)	IRB reviews and approves the proposal (IRB approval form)
Secure locations for the health education classes, coordinate with artists, arrange for coffee and snacks *by specified date* (PC)	Locations for classes were reserved, artists scheduled, snacks purchased (session tracking forms)
Healthcare providers inform caregivers and dementia patients about opportunities to receive dementia health education via: (1) health education classes with arts, (2) health education classes without arts, and (3) one-on-one office visit(s), *by specified date* (T)	# primary care providers and # psychologists who agreed to promote the program among their patients (provider engagement tracking form and participant sign-in sheet that indicates PCP)
Schedule, enroll, and conduct two health education sessions with the arts (four classes each session) *by specified date* (PC)	# participants enrolled # participants completing each class (sign-in sheets)
Schedule, enroll, and conduct two health education sessions without the arts (four classes each session) *by specified date* (PC)	# participants enrolled # participants completing each class (sign-in sheets)
Communicate and use evaluation findings for continuous quality improvement and to document outcomes *by specified date* (T)	# meetings of team where evaluation findings were reviewed (meeting minutes)
Continue to submit at least two grants for further development, replication, and research *by specified date* (T)	Two grant proposals were developed and submitted (completed proposals)
Sustain arts-based dementia health education sessions, providing important services for the local community, *ongoing* (T)	Two additional arts-based health education classes scheduled in neighboring community (sign-in sheets)

- Established platform for development of a diverse range of cost-effective behavioral health interventions developed in a group setting (e.g., ADHD management, grief counseling services, chronic disease self-management)

Impacts

- Communication between patients, caregivers, and providers is strengthened due to increased health literacy
- Patients with dementia and caregivers experience improved physical health, quality of life, and self-efficacy
- Communities, especially rural communities, have increased access to programs aimed at improving health literacy through innovative group-based arts-enhanced health education workshops
- Providers, residents, and medical students build new skills and capacity for compassion, which are essential professional attributes for providing patient-centered care
- Satisfied patients recommend the healthcare system to their friends
- Healthcare providers and allied healthcare professionals have new strategies for delivering evidence-based programs for achieving the healthcare reform goal of "better health, better care, lower cost"
- The next generation of healthcare providers (residents and medical students) learn about the benefits of working in interprofessional teams on innovative behavioral health programs

A logic model is typically an elegant snapshot of a program story, from input to impact. General concepts are captured in the schematic model, which is accompanied by an explanatory narrative like that provided above. Logic models can be developed artistically or in a linear fashion (e.g., see https://www.mcknight.org/system/asset/document/213/McKArtsLogicModel.pdf). A quick internet search using keywords of logic model and the arts will lead to many examples of different logic model designs.

Focusing the evaluation

The team agreed that the evaluation would serve several purposes: accountability for funders, program improvement, and justification to Samaritan Health Services for continuing and expanding the arts-based health education program.

Accountability: During the planning phase, the team developed a detailed program design with integrated evaluation and submitted a grant application to support the program implementation. They accomplished this and received an internal grant to support the development of the program. Quite reasonably, the funder expected the Program Director to be accountable for the monies received and requested a final written report showing that the program had been implemented as proposed (e.g., activities and associated outputs) and providing evidence as to whether or not participants benefitted from program participation (e.g., outcomes such as improved health literacy and self-efficacy).

Program improvement: The first year of implementation would be the pilot test of the program. The team wanted to collect and use evaluation data for program improvement – to guide decisions about which aspects of the program to retain and which to jettison.

Justification for continuing the program: The team also wanted the evaluation to be sufficiently rigorous to provide credible justification to Samaritan Health Services for sustaining and expanding the program. Most healthcare organizations are challenged by budget reductions, and Chief Executive Officers and Boards of Directors must make difficult decisions about which programs to retain and which to drop. The team wanted to be able to demonstrate program outcomes and provide evidence that arts-based health education is cost effective as well.

In working together to further focus the evaluation, the team experienced a classic evaluation conundrum: they wanted to conduct an evaluation of such magnitude that it would have dwarfed the program itself. Restricting the scope of an evaluation so that it addresses just a few key evaluation questions can be challenging. As this team discovered, it's easy to go overboard on evaluation. The team had already generated a list of all imaginable outcomes and impacts (see above). However, this brainstorming activity had to be followed by a priority-setting process, in which the most important evaluation questions were identified. It's not a good idea (and, basically, not possible) to try to evaluate all possible outcomes and impacts at the same time.

Fortunately, this program was designed to be sustainable over an extended period of time, offered on a seasonal basis year after year. Because of the ongoing nature of the program, the team opted to implement a "rolling evaluation" (Festen & Philbin, 2007), where two or three evaluation questions are selected as the focus each year. For the first year evaluation, the team chose to look at short-term outcomes for caregivers and patients only. Future evaluations may look at outcomes for providers, residents, medical students, and artists, outcomes for the organization, and long-term impact. An overly ambitious evaluation is a burden for everyone. Evaluation activities are more likely to be carried out when they are unobtrusive and a seamless part of the program. Program participants don't have to become frustrated by completing multiple surveys, and program coordinators don't need to be swamped by paperwork.

Thus, the team resisted the natural tendency to try to answer all evaluation questions as soon as the program was out of the gate. In the first year, they formulated a few key process evaluation questions to address basic issues of program implementation and collected selected short-term outcome data for participants. Understanding the ingredients of successful program implementation would help them strengthen the program in its second year. The first-year evaluation questions were intentionally broad and exploratory:

Which program activities worked well and which needed to be modified?
Which aspects of the health education curriculum and arts activities did participants find most useful and enjoyable?

Of the three information delivery methods, which had the most positive effects on participants as measured by responses regarding the quality of life and other selected instruments?

The team also managed to surmount a barrier common to many arts and health program evaluations, which is the difficulty of translating empirical outcomes into meaningful information. Some people argue that the most important aspects of arts and health programs can't be measured. For example, how is it possible to measure the experience of caregivers of dementia patients who have felt a lift from their despair and isolation while working with an artist? Indeed, with some ingenuity, there are ways to gather information about beneficial outcomes such as this. For example, survey questions can ask caregivers to rate their feelings of isolation both before and after participating in an arts and health program. At the same time, narrative stories can be gathered via journals or through interviews from caregivers about their experiences of isolation before and after participation. Photos of the sessions and the art created by participants can be useful indicators of program effectiveness. In fact, the use of arts-based data collection and analysis methods that use produced art as evaluation data is an emerging field. In *Singing our Praises: Case Studies in the Art of Evaluation,* Suzanne Callahan (2004) describes innovative examples of arts-based data collection methods and strategies that have been used successfully in the arts. These types of data include literary writing, music, dance, poetry, paintings, drawings, and other forms of art.

A meaningful evaluation will synthesize all data types – numbers, stories, photos – into an authentic portrait of a program and make evaluative recommendations about the value of program components and the overall program, now and into the future.

Finally, the program evaluation design was submitted to the Institutional Review Board (IRB) for review prior to its launch. Most hospitals and all academic institutions have an IRB that provides oversight for research activities, to ensure that participants are not put at risk for harm and that the study is conducted in accordance with federal, institutional, and ethical guidelines. Although program evaluation may not fall under the definition of a study that requires IRB review, it is prudent to let the IRB make the determination as to whether your evaluation design warrants a full board review.

Using evaluation results

There's no reason to conduct an evaluation if the results aren't used for strengthening the program and supporting its continuation. The team-based strategy of ongoing review and monitoring during program implementation worked well for this group. Monthly reviews of data revealed several pitfalls in implementation that could have been problematic had the team not quickly intervened and modified areas of weakness. For example, it was important to offer the program during the day rather than in the evening, particularly during the winter months. Similarly, enrollment was low in the winter months because so many retired people travel to warmer climates; the best seasons to offer this program are spring, summer, and fall. Initially, the plan was to offer the arts-based program to spousal caregivers and patients only, but requests from non-spousal caregivers (e.g., adult children, other family members, and private caregivers) quickly prompted the team to open sessions to all types of dedicated caregivers. It was also important to provide an incentive to encourage participants to attend all four classes in a session, so that all information could be delivered and the cumulative benefits of participating in the arts activities could be experienced. At the end of the last class, each pair of participants received a copy of *The 36 Hour Day: A Family Guide to Caring for People Who Have Alzheimer Disease, Related Dementias, and Memory Loss* by Nancy Mace and Peter Rabins. Other incentives considered by the team included a gas card or gift certificate to local grocery stores.

At the time of this writing, outcome data are not yet available. When they are, the team will present these evaluation findings to hospital administrators. In the meantime, however, participant feedback and other process evaluation data reveal a tremendous interest in our communities for the arts-based health education programs. Based on this early feedback, work is underway to modify and replicate this arts-based health education program in other health areas related to chronic conditions and diseases.

Helpful resources

In the past decade, a number of practical books have stripped evaluation down to its essence in an attempt to make it more accessible (e.g., see Boulmetis & Dutwin, 2005; Davidson, 2005; Festen & Philbin, 2007; Melton, Slater, & Constantine, 2004). These are excellent resources to draw upon when designing your program and its evaluation. There are abundant resources online as well. A few examples include:

> CDC Evaluation Guide: Developing and Using a Logic Model. http://www.cdc.gov/dhdsp/programs/nhdsp_program/evaluation_guides/docs/logic_model.pdf
> CDC Introduction to Program Evaluation for Public Health Programs: A Self-Study Guide. http://www.cdc.gov/eval/guide/index.htm
> CDC Writing SMART Objectives. http://www.cdc.gov/dhdsp/programs/nhdsp_program/evaluation_guides/smart_objectives.htm
> The Community Toolbox (University of Kansas). http://ctb.ku.edu/en/evaluating-initiative
> Evaluating your Community-Based Program (American Academy of Pediatrics). http://www2.aap.org/commpeds/htpcp/resources.html
> Georgia Council for the Arts. Getting Started with Evaluation: A Guide for Arts Organizations. http://www.nasaa-arts.org/Member-Files/Evaluation_Guide.pdf

W.K. Kellogg Foundation Evaluation Handbook. http://www.wkkf.org/resource-directory/resource/2010/w-k-kellogg-foundation-evaluation-handbook

W.K. Kellogg Foundation Logic Model Guide. http://www.wkkf.org/resource-directory/resource/2006/02/wk-kellogg-foundation-logic-model-development-guide

Note

1 This project was supported by a grant from the John C. Erkkila, MD, Endowment for Health and Human Performance.

References

Alkin, M., & Christie, C. (2004). An evaluation theory tree. In M. Alkin (Ed.), *Evaluation roots: Tracing theorists' views and influences* (pp. 12–66). Thousand Oaks: Sage Publications.

Boulmetis, J., & Dutwin, P. (2005). *The ABCs of evaluation: Timeless techniques for program and project managers* (2nd ed.). San Francisco: Jossey-Bass.

Callahan, S. (2004). *Singing our praises: Case studies in the art of evaluation.* Washington, DC: Association of Performing Arts Presenters.

Davidson, E. J. (2005). *Evaluation methodology basics: The nuts and bolts of sounds evaluation.* Thousand Oaks: Sage Publications.

Davidson, E. J. (2014). How "beauty" can bring trust and justice to life. *New Directions for Evaluation, 142*, 31–44.

Festen, M., & Philbin, M. (2007). *Level best: How small and grassroots nonprofits can tackle evaluation and talk results.* San Francisco: Jossey-Bass.

Fetterman, D. (2005). A window into the heart and soul of empowerment evaluation: Looking through the lens of empowerment evaluation principles. In D. Fetterman & A. Wandersman (Eds.), *Empowerment evaluation principles in practice* (pp. 1–26). New York: The Guilford Press.

Fraser, K., & al Saya, F. (2011). Arts-based methods in health research: A systematic review of the literature. *Arts & Health: An International Journal for Research, Policy and Practice, 3*(2), 110–145.

Griffith, J., & Montrosse-Moorhead, B. (2014). The value in validity. *New Directions for Evaluation, 142*, 17–30.

House, E. (2014). Origins of the ideas in *Evaluating with validity. New Directions for Evaluation, 142*, 9–16.

Lawrence-Lightfoot, S. (1997). A view of the whole. In S. Lawrence-Lightfoot & J. Davis (Eds.), *The art and science of portraiture* (pp. 1–17). San Francisco: Jossey-Bass.

Melton, M., Slater, J., & Constantine, W. (2004). Strategies for smaller foundations. In M. Braverman, N. Constantine, & J. Slater (Eds.), *Foundations and evaluation: Contexts and practices for effective philanthropy* (pp. 201–222). San Francisco: Jossey-Bass.

Stufflebeam, D. L. (1983). The CIPP Model for program evaluation. In G. F. Madaus, M. Scriven, & D. L. Stufflebeam (Eds.), *Evaluation Models: Viewpoints on Educational and Human Services Evaluation* (pp. 117–141). Boston: Kluwer Nijhof.

W. K. Kellogg Foundation. (2004). *Logic model development guide.* Battle Creek, MI: W. K. Kellogg Foundation. Retrieved from http://www.wkkf.org/knowledge-center/Resources-Page.aspx

PART 4

Managing arts in healthcare programs for special populations

11

HOW TO START AN ARTS PROGRAM FOR MILITARY POPULATIONS

Naj Wikoff

FIGURE 11.1 National Guard Spouse Susan Olsen Making Prayer Flags at a Creative Healing Connections Retreat for Military Spouses

The arts offer effective toolkits and processes for healing military experience, and have done so throughout human history. Yet, they are not used easily or embraced with open arms by many who could benefit most from them. Developing a practical framework for using the arts to support psychological, social, and spiritual healing for American active-duty and veteran military personnel and their families requires appreciation of the differences between military and civilian culture, the particulars of past and present-day military and veteran experience, and the sometimes profound changes undergone by service personnel who join the military and return as veterans. This chapter offers a context-based view of the realities of today's active-duty and veteran military personnel, with practical suggestions for making the arts available and valued in this milieu.

Examples of successful arts programs for military populations are provided throughout this chapter, drawing in particular on the experience of the author's leadership of Creative Healing Connections, a nonprofit organization expanding its arts- and nature-based retreats for women living with cancer to serve women military personnel living with military sexual trauma, as well as to serve military spouses, families, and caregivers. The author is also a founding member of the National Initiative for Arts & Health in the Military.

Overview of the US active duty military and veteran population

Active duty military and veteran personnel make up a small percentage of the US population. Moreover, the number of veterans is declining as WWII and, increasingly, Korean and Vietnam War veterans reach the end of their life span. In 2012, there were slightly more than 3.6 million members of the military (including Air Force, Navy Marine, Army, Coast Guard, and DOD reserve components), according to a 2014 Defense Data Center report (Defense Data Center, 2014, p. iii). This report states that 2.7 million of these individuals were, at the time of the study, active-duty personnel making up 0.86 percent of the US population, and that 22 million of these individuals were veterans, making up 7 percent of the US population. The total number of veterans is projected to decline to fourteen million by 2040, while the number of active duty military is projected to reduce to pre-WWII levels (Alexander & Shalal, 2014).

Eleven percent of total military personnel and thirty-three to fifty percent of the deployed experience combat (McGrath, 2013, pp. 40–83). In recent Gulf Wars, even those deployed in non-combat positions work in highly stressful conditions. Field support personnel, for example, are vulnerable to IEDs (improvised explosive devices), enemy fire, and persistent threat of terrorism, where it is often impossible to differentiate combatants from civilians by dress. The Gulf Wars were characterized by growing numbers of deployments with increased demands. At the beginning of the Gulf Wars, members of the National Guard were deployed without having signed up for combat; fighting national disasters and addressing urban unrest had been their service expectations. Deployment was emotionally and financially difficult on them and their families, who lived far from military bases able to provide support services.

The military culture

Military values set standards of service conduct as well as the expectations that members of the military have of their families and civilian (non active-duty) military personnel. Rules are clear and apply to all; leaders make decisions. Individualism and autonomy, valued in business and civilian life, run counter to military culture, where the individual may be sacrificed for the collective good. As an outcome, many in the military dislike being called "heroes" or "heroines" as, for them, these standards are those of "their job."

In contrast, the arts and life in the arts have their own codes of discipline; they are not governed by set rules. Rather, they often favor individual or small-group thinking and expression. A process is often more prized than an outcome. Thus, the arts provide members of the military with new sets of circumstances and opportunities to gain skills for crossing back into civilian life. The difference in values, however, can impede the partnering efforts required to bring the arts to them in the first place. Buy-in from command often smooths a process of mutual accommodation. Command membership, however, tends to shift: many leaders are rotated in or out every three years.

The hero's journey

According to Dr. Edward Tick (2008), most combatants see their work as being in the service of traditional "warrior" values: protecting one's country and its ideals, one's family, community, and fellow combatants. If they kill or risk being killed, they need overwhelming justifications for doing so. "Throughout history, the only reason for fighting that has survived moral scrutiny is direct attack with real, immediate threat to one's people. PTSD (Post-Traumatic Stress Disorder) is, in part, the tortured conscience of good people who did their best under conditions that would dehumanize anyone" (Tick, 2008, p. 1).

It is easier to use the arts in the military if, first, one considers the experience of those holding traditional warrior values who find themselves thrust into demanding situations. Joseph Campbell did so, and developed a motif that he called "the Hero's Journey" (Campbell, Cousineau, & Brown, 1990). Campbell felt that all myths devolve from this motif, made up episodes: call to adventure, investment with supernatural aid, crossing of a threshold, dwelling in the belly of a whale, coming upon a goddess, atonement with a father, and return.

Overlaying Campbell's hero's journey on military experience, a call to adventure might be the recruit leaving behind their social life and self to take on new rules and mores: civilian clothes traded in for a uniform, haircut, new expectations, speech, and behaviors.

Campbell's life-changing experience, the death of an old and birth of a new self, takes place "in the belly of the whale." Military personnel tell civilians that they cannot understand these experiences; that only someone who has been through them can, such as witnessing collateral damage, death of an innocent person, senseless loss of a friend, taking a life. What is remembered as life-changing may take place in a flash, yet impacts a person for life. These experiences test abilities and expose weaknesses and fears. They may include elements of profound exhaustion, exaltation, humiliation, loss of limb, great intensity, or boredom. Occurring either in or out of combat, these experiences forge deep bonds with others who have served.

What is conceptualized as a celebratory return in Campbell's metaphor is in many ways the most difficult experience for a veteran of military service: leaving the mythical land, its mores, rules, rituals, and camaraderie for civilian life. The world has gone on. Families have made adjustments to survive. The return is a paradox, requiring as it does reentry to a changed world. Vietnam veterans were shunned; today, military personnel are thanked for their service. But then what?

Challenges facing military personnel

Women entered the Gulf Wars military in increasing numbers on or near the front lines where they were exposed to enemy fire as well as, tragically, sexual trauma – at times at the hands of their own comrades or ranking personnel. The Veterans Administration describes Military Sexual Trauma (MST) as psychological trauma resulting from sexual assault or battery or sexual harassment. In 2012, seventy-three percent of women military personnel reported sexual harassment, and one third of women military personnel reported sexual abuse. Such abuse is not confined to women; half of all military sexual abuses have been reported by men. On average, thirty-eight men a day are sexually assaulted within the ranks of the US military (Department of Defense, 2013).

In 2014, Veterans Affairs' National Center for PTSD reported that thirty percent of Vietnam veterans, twelve percent of First Gulf War veterans, and eleven–twenty percent of later Gulf War veterans experience PTSD. Traumatic Brain Injury (TBI) is often found in combination with PTSD. Carina Storrs (2013) reports that "around 25% of the nearly 700,000 US troops deployed in 2013 experienced a range of physical and mental ailments during or shortly after their tour that persist to this day" (p. 1). These health challenges include widespread pain, fatigue, mood and memory disorders, as well as gastrointestinal, respiratory, and skin problems. The Department of Veterans Affairs (VA) states that thirty percent of Operations Enduring Freedom, Iraqi Freedom, and New Dawn (2001–2012) veterans treated by the VA have PTSD.

Reintegration

"War poisons the spirit, and warriors return tainted," says Dr. Edward Tick (2008), explaining that traditional cultures as varied as the Buddhist, ancient Israeli, Native American, and Zulu provided returning warriors with significant purification rituals before they could reenter their communities, believing that non-purified warriors could be dangerous to themselves and to community life. Tick suggests that "the absence of these rituals in modern society helps explain why suicide, homicide, and other destructive acts are common amongst veterans" (p. 1).

A manual for reintegrating veterans highlights five challenges: overcoming alienation, transitioning from simplicity to complexity, replacing war with another form of high, moving beyond war to find meaning in life, and coming to peace with self, God, and fellow humans (Jewish Board, 2011, p. 9). Returned service men or women can feel vulnerable and lost in civilian life. Some awaken to nightmares; many feel frustrated and angry about what they see to be as social frivolities. Some can't get or keep a job, slip into alcoholism or abusive behavior, even take their own lives. Veterans make up eleven to twelve percent of the homeless (U.S. Department of Housing, 2013, p. 38).

Strong family support – before, during, and after deployment – is one of the best assets for a returning service person. However, many military spouses say that the best time to marry a serviceperson is after they have served: only then can one know the person one is marrying. For the waiting spouse, the loved one has been so changed by their experience that reconnection may be impossible. A high percentage of military marriages fail, in particular once the serviceperson leaves the military.

Military families are already stressed by frequent moves, with a spouse or parent absent for significant periods of time. These absences are all the more challenging when time away has been in a war zone. The stressors of single parenting, often combined with the demands of work, feelings of isolation, and financial challenges, are highlighted by the return of a spouse/parent who may be gravely

FIGURE 11.2 A Father and Son Sharing Their Feelings through a Creative Healing Connections Workshop

disfigured and may experience emotional challenges. Fifty-six percent of active-duty service members are married. Fifty percent of their children are under the age of seven. "Studies consistently find that, as the cumulative stress model would predict, the longer and more often a parent is deployed, the greater the psychological, health, and behavior risk for the child" (Lester & Flake, 2013, p. 130).

"The post-deployment period represents a stage during which family fitness is especially important, while the service member experiences the positive and negative stress associated with reintegration" (Yosick et al., 2012, p. 23). As a strong family unit is of significant benefit to the deployed and returned service man or woman, arts activities to strengthen family wellbeing can contribute to healthy reintegration.

Ritual

Ritual matters. Throughout history, healers have used ritual as a primary tool for setting the stage for healing, including the use of ritual to open and close sessions and activities. "Rituals serve to alter the meaning of an experience by naming and circumscribing unknown elements of that experience and by enabling patients' belief in a treatment and their expectancy of healing from that treatment" (Welch, 2003, p. 21).

One simple ritual is to declare a space safe: "What is said here stays here." Another is sitting in circles when in groups. Rules can be rituals, such as, "Rank is left at the door." Dimmed lights, relaxation techniques, shared refreshments, asking participants what they hope to achieve, and reflecting back to them so that they feel heard, all create a mood for and an expectation of healing. Cleansing can take the form of hand washing, a sweat lodge, a swim in a lake, canoeing at night under stars, or sitting on a river bank. Participants can create bundles of twigs in which to burn small pieces of paper on which they have written their angers or hurts.

Many may suffer not only physical and emotional wounds of war, but its moral wounds, wondering if their war was justified (Maguen & Litz, 2012). The "spiritual return" envisaged by traditional American warrior societies included ritual atonement for damage done and retribution made through new forms of service. With some creativity, it is possible to use the arts to these ends.

Arts and the military

The arts and the military came together in earliest recorded history when battle scenes were depicted on caves, walls, and ceramic vessels. Most of Western literature of the heroic period depicts the emotional, physical, and spiritual costs of war. Goya's *Disasters of War* and Picasso's *Guernica* are more recent, well-known visual depictions of war.

There is a long history of the arts used in the service of both heroism and propaganda. For troops bivouacked at Valley Forge in the bitter winter of 1777–78,

General Washington commissioned a performance of Joseph Addison's play, *Cato*, about a historical figure who resisted Julius Caesar. The play itself is quoted as the source of Patrick Henry's ultimatum, "Give me liberty or give me death," and Nathan Hales's, "I only regret that I have but one life to lose for my country" (Miller, 2011, p. 1).

When the United States declared war on Germany in 1917, the then Surgeon General Major General William Crawford Gorgas called for the establishment of arts and occupational therapy programs in the hospitals established for his wounded and mentally disturbed soldiers and sailors. Contemporary research on the therapeutic benefits of the arts was conducted from then on through World War II, leading to the establishment of many of the arts therapies as we know them today.

After World War II, use of the arts for healing declined in both military and civilian hospitals. On the military side, arts in healthcare interventions were rekindled to address the many problems of Vietnam veterans, initially through grassroots efforts in community settings and shelters. At the same time, the arts were increasingly accepted in civilian care, in particular at many of the nation's leading medical centers. With the arts increasingly utilized in civilian care, the arts have again become reintegrated into formal military care paradigms, in particular for those serving in the Gulf Wars. Interest in the arts increased in part due to the Veterans Administration system being flooded with an aging generation of Vietnam veterans still living with untreated or poorly treated psycho-social outcomes of war. Interest also increased due to today's troops sustaining wounds that, heretofore, they would not have survived – resulting in many of today's veterans living with high rates of PTSD, TBI, and MST.

The difference the arts make in healthcare settings has caught the eye of many in leadership positions: National Guard chaplains, base commanders, VA Medical Center directors, and, recently, Rear Admiral Alton L. Stocks, SHCE, USN, commander of Walter Reed National Military Medical Center (WRNMMC). A new dialogue about arts and health in the military commenced, led by representatives of Americans for the Arts, the Society for the Arts in Healthcare, the National Endowment for the Arts, The Kennedy Center, Creative Healing Connections, Smith Center for Healing and the Arts, the National Center for Creative Aging, and others, including many individual arts practitioners.

Two weeks after it opened in 2011, WRNMMC in Bethesda, now the largest military medical center in the US, serving over a million patients a year, hosted the first National Summit on Arts & Health in the Military (SAHM). In 2012, The Kennedy Center hosted the Arts & Health in the Military Roundtable. In 2013, a second SAHM was held at Walter Reed and gave rise to the white paper, *Arts, Health and Well-Being Across the Military Continuum*, published in 2013 by Americans for the Arts. In an introduction to the white paper, Bob Lynch, President and CEO of Americans for the Arts writes: "We reach for the arts to tell our story at every solemn and joyous occasion we have in our military and in our secular lives" (Americans for the Arts, 2013, p. 6). The third SAHM, to focus on research, will be held at the National Institutes of Health in Bethesda in 2015. The continuity of the SAHM convenings is a good indication of the arts' return to a position to support the healing and reintegration of service men and women, their loved ones, and their caregivers throughout the span of military service.

A growing body of research shows that the arts play an important role in healing the stress-related conditions affecting military personnel. These findings buttress the efforts being made to bridge the gap between military and civilian services. The full spectrum of the arts can be used to support the healing journey, but familiarity with this body of research provides clues to what any arts practitioner can accomplish in any given situation. The white paper *Arts, Health and Well-Being across the Military Continuum* provides an introduction to the practicalities of applying research: determining what's needed, what can work, what can be accomplished.

Creating bridges

In an interview with the author, Major Robert Gilbert, then chaplain for Fort Drum's Warrior Transition Battalion, said: "To connect with the military, you need a Rabbi" (personal communication, December 18, 2009), suggesting that a faith-based facilitator would be needed to bridge the military-civilian divide. Similarly, Gay Hanna, executive director of the National Center for Creative Aging, urges arts in healthcare program initiators to "find a strong advocate from within" (personal communication, December 21, 2014).

Indeed, the process of entering the arena of arts and health in the military can be daunting. Judy Rollins, a leader in this area of arts in healthcare programming, gives an idea of requirements on the ground:

> Security is a major issue. Expect background clearances, fingerprinting, and other security measures. Requirements often tighten with each new threat to our nation's security. Building relationships with hospital leaders is important. If they are active duty personnel, they are likely to be transferred or deployed, which means that establishing new relationships is routine. Certain arts programming may require submitting a proffer letter or memorandum of understanding for legal approval. It helps to have a champion within the facility and *lots* of patience. There are many hoops to jump through, but being able to do this work makes it all worth the effort.
>
> (personal communication, January 5, 2015)

Bridge-builders may be chaplains, doctors, nurses, or any VA medical center staffer. Chaplains are unique in the military. They understand the value of a story, of being heard, and they have permission to talk with those of any rank.

Troops themselves can build the bridges. "People come here and say I can't write a story or a song, but the teachers get around that: they get each of us to write a bit of it!" says Connie, a veteran who participated in a Creative Healing Connections retreat for women veterans (personal communication, August 8, 2013). "I tell the women in my VA, you've got to come: people arrive here as strangers and leave as family." Military clients will tell their friends and colleagues about their experiences with arts programs, will advocate programs they like to their VA health liaison, and speak about their experiences at conferences. Simply put, the military go places no civilian can. When they support an arts program, moats are crossed, and walls are scaled.

Connecting

Service members often seem unwilling to confide; in part, this can be because they find it easiest to be among those who share experiences similar to theirs and because, even there, opening up is contrary to their shared culture. They can also fear expressions of weakness getting into their records and blocking military advancement. Therefore, it is critical to provide participants with ways of increasing the safety of present-time self-expression by grounding themselves in present reality with breathing, imagery, or movement, and even by dimming lights and playing relaxing music.

Trained therapeutic artists and arts therapists offer service members listening time, modes and media of individual and collective expression, and the independence from command structure that makes them non-threatening. Arts practitioners who can make themselves vulnerable often make it easier for service members to be open with them and with their comrades present. Once "conversation" has begun, many veterans, for example, are eager or grateful for opportunities to participate. On the other hand, a good therapeutic arts practitioner presents a firm structure by knowing and respecting their limits in choices of programming and services offered. It is unethical to act as a therapist without being a trained counselor. Often, directing someone to a professional is the best help one can give. It is also not in the best interests of patients to keep critical confidences they share from head nurses or medical supervisors. A client's concerns, behaviors, and breakthroughs are best discussed in a team where interdisciplinary expertise, a support structure, and a safety net are available.

The military is wary of "Miss Americas," warns Major Robert Gilbert, referring to people who connect on their own agendas, never to be seen again (personal communication, December 18, 2009). Service people open up to people who listen, walk their talk, and are in it for the long haul. Veterans notice attendance at the annual Memorial and Veteran's Day activities and engagement with other agencies that support veterans. They have a gut feeling about people who care. Thus it is critical that arts practitioners emulate the behaviors that they wish to elicit.

Pain is often part of the healing process. Grief is an essential part of many healing processes. Tears can be shed and people may at times need to be held. Arts practitioners who don't go out of their way to cause or avoid grief, but provide safe space, quiet, and the opportunity for healing, closure, and next steps, are providing "discipline" in the special modality of the arts. Their ability to "hold" shared emotion restores dignity.

Art forms can be tailored to the setting, people, and circumstances, the better to elicit involvement and active participation. On the other hand, when a participant says that they can't draw, sing, write, or dance, it can be a good tactic to politely ignore the statement. A competent arts practitioner is much more interested in finding the way for such people to share a narrative, by beginning to express themselves in any manner they can. Arts practitioners may find that many in the military are terrific at avoiding what they don't want to do and able to come up with quite imaginative reasons or ruses. It is possible to ignore all that, with humor. Nearly always, someone is willing to take the first step, make the first mark on paper. The rest soon follow. Group process shows people that their experience is shared. Colleagues of different ranks and in other services have similar experiences. Someone may be going through something far worse. Or they may have gained something along the way that is of help to others.

It is important to give clients dignity and credence. More beneficial than "I understand" is "I don't understand. I've never experienced what you've been through. What was it like for you?" By asking for a client's help in understanding what their experience was or is like, a practitioner becomes less interested in what happened and more in how it felt, where the client is now as a consequence, and what they would like to achieve by some future date.

The arts allow for placing a tolerable amount of a painful experience or emotion on paper, in words, or in movement. The pain is now at arms' length and it can be seen more freely, spoken of, related to. Progressively, it will have less power over those whose lives it has engulfed. The burden of soul wounds is lightened by compassion for what is kept hidden. And the arts have always served to share what otherwise would not be seen. No single drawing will heal, but the person who has made it has taken a first step. Arts practitioners should want to see every client walk away from a group process with one new friend, a person who "has their back" in the new world, as they have theirs. The next step, follow-through, will be critical. Participants are known to return to arts retreats annually, making of them a ritual, and to take up art forms, making them their practice.

Training artists and creative arts therapists

Professional artists and creative arts therapists who want to work with active duty and military populations benefit from learning about the military experience – combatant and non-combatant – by reading the scholarly articles of medical and mental health practitioners and veterans, speaking with veterans, and viewing films, documentaries, plays, exhibitions, and other creative media about the military experience.

VA and other major medical centers as well as the Red Cross provide volunteers training in basic patient work protocols. It is useful to be familiar with the websites and knowledgeable about the agencies that support the military and their families, both nationally and in one's area. It is wise to seek out exchange with colleagues having years of supervised experience in medical centers, hospices, rehabilitation facilities, or community-based programs that serve military populations. It is an asset to have artists or arts therapists who are themselves veterans, have faced turning points, or who have come through major challenges as mentors or on one's team.

Professional artists and art therapists are equally well suited to work with military populations, each bringing different yet complementary gifts to the table. An ideal team has both. Above all, a good healer is un-presupposing, a good listener, present to their clients, generous with their humor, and has a good heart. Rigidity and dogmatism are not helpful. Those well-accepted in the field draw on interdisciplinary knowledge to conceptualize their work: they are familiar with current research on trauma, the body, and the brain, learn all they can about the experiences of PTSD, MST, and TBI, and are aware of current studies on the effectiveness of arts therapy methods. The Trauma Center at the Justice Resource Institute of Boston is one good resource. Bessel Van der Kolk, MD, one of its founders, authored the first integrative text on PTSD and has since published research showing theatre role-play, yoga, and movement (dance therapy) to be effective interventions for PTSD (Trauma Center, 2007; Interlandi, 2014, p. 1). Knowing the science behind such findings helps practitioners justify arts interventions.

Arts professionals working with highly stressed populations, as may be encountered in the military, benefit from taking care of each other. It is all very well that, as professionals, they are able to manage and orient the emotions of their clients, but the reality is that some of the pain and heartbreak will stick to them. Practitioners need the support of others: they need to be heard, cared for, and refreshed. They too can benefit from opportunities to individually and collectively use the arts to these ends.

Using the arts for the military

The first step to start a program, be it in a Department of Defense or VA medical facility or a community setting, is to determine who is to be served, what will be accomplished, and how benefit will be measured. As programs often have a "start-up" quality, they often involve a lot of creativity and vision. Here are few examples:

A soldier-drummer at Walter Reed Medical Center had lost a leg to a roadside bomb but hoped to perform again. He inspired pianist-composer Arthur Bloom to develop a technical solution that allowed him to do so. Bloom went on to found Musicorps, a group of musicians, instrument makers, and computer programmers who modify musical instruments and music performance techniques to support wounded warriors as they develop new skills and express themselves through music.

Fran Yardley, storyteller and then director of Creative Healing Connections, which uses the arts, complementary therapies, and nature to support healing for women with cancer, read about the high numbers of women veterans sexually assaulted in military service. As a result, Creative Healing Connections piloted a 2009 program for women veterans. Since then, it has hosted yearly retreats for active-duty and veteran servicewomen and, with other agencies, offered male veteran, military spouse and family, and caregiver programming using storytelling, songwriting, the visual arts, prayer-flag making, drumming, ritual, yoga, wilderness access, and other arts and complementary modalities.

Retired Lieutenant Colonel Ron Capps founded the Veterans Writing Project (VWP) in 2011 to provide free writing workshops and seminars for veterans and their families based on the benefits he experienced from writing about his own military experience, his struggle with PTSD, a failed marriage, and difficulty keeping a job. Recruiting other veteran writers, and establishing partnerships with organizations such as the Writers Guild and the Wounded Warriors Project, VWP offers programs in locales across the country.

SongwritingWith:Soldiers, founded by musician Darden Smith, teaches active-duty and veteran military personnel to write songs about military experience and the transition home. Its free sessions and retreats led by professional songwriters are designed to build bridges between military and civilian communities. Participants receive a CD and photo/lyric book of the songs they write. With the participants as co-authors, all songs are registered with the American Society of Composers, Authors, and Publishers (ASCAP).

"You Are a Work of Art" is an initiative designed for military nurses by Art-Stream, a community-based arts organization in Silver Spring, MD. Partnering with

FIGURE 11.3 SongwritingWith:Soldiers, Darden Smith Writing a Song with Veteran Chuck Hawthorne

Photographer: Matt Sturtevant for SongwritingWith:Soldiers

WRNMMC nurses and ArtStream artists, Judy Rollins leads off-base arts-and-healing workshops and on-base pop-up sessions designed to address the military-life stressors faced by Department of Defense nurses, including short-notice deployment to war zones from hospitals such as Walter Reed. The programming demonstrates how nurses can use the arts for self-care wherever they are stationed.

A list of organizations using the arts for the military together with reference material can be found at the National Initiative for Arts & Health in the Military tab on the Americans for the Arts website at http://www.americansforthearts.org/by-program/reports-and-data/legislation-policy/the-national-initiative-for-arts-health-in-the-military. The section on practice in the Americans for the Arts' white paper *Arts, Health and Well-being Across the Military Continuum*, referenced above, shares advice and showcases profiles of arts activities in military, VA, and community settings. It is important to note that the vast majority of veterans live in communities across the United States. One can start locally, by working with American Legions, Veteran of Foreign Wars Posts, and local veteran support agencies. The need is great in communities across the country.

Connecting the community

A wounded warrior returns feeling frightened that a fellow citizen will set off a bomb by turning on their cell phone. Both citizen understanding of them and their understanding of what has happened to them are essential – as are services that don't keep service people waiting a year for an appointment. Educating the general public about the military experience and the moral dilemmas of military life can be a key to healing. While returning troops appreciate being thanked for their services, being thanked can be a dilemma. Many wonder: What am I being thanked for? Destroying the lives of people who have done me no harm? Blowing up a hospital because I got the intel wrong? Destroying someone's olive grove in a far-away world to protect a way of life that I can't reintegrate with? Am I being thanked for accepting to undergo experiences that led to mental illness, estrangement from family and children?

The arts can help the general public understand military experience: feature films *Hurt Locker* and *Taking Chance*; documentaries *Restrepo, Brats*, and the *Invisible War*; plays *ReEntry* and *Theatre of War*; touring exhibitions such as *Unclassified: The Military Kid Art Show*; and Garry Trudeau's comic strip, with its principle Vietnam veteran character, attest to this. Screenings and readings from works such as these, followed by question and answer sessions with an author, organizer, or veteran, help the general public develop a rounded view of the impact of military service. The play *ReEntry* is based on stories elicited by playwrights Emily Ackerman and K. J. Sanchez from Marines and their families. *Theatre of War* presents readings of Sophocles's *Ajax* and *Philoctetes* to civilian and military audiences. The exhibition *Unclassified: The Military Kid Art Show*, organized by Brats Without Borders and the Military Kid Art Project, illustrates the impact of military life on children.

Conclusion

There is no single, cut-and-paste formula for starting up an arts and health program for active-duty or veteran military personnel. VA medical centers and military posts are more restrictive of programming than are civilian medical centers and healing institutions. And these, in turn, are more restrictive than community settings. Every setting, though, provides opportunities to connect with those who serve or have served in the military, along with their families and caregivers. It is important to always keep in mind that many pay or have paid a hard price for service: those deployed, those on base, those at home, and those who provide care.

Caring intensely for its own, "leaving none behind," the military can resist civilian participation. Yet the military cannot do the work of transitioning home alone; it needs civilian partners. Thus, although it takes patience to engage fully with military clients, the benefits to the community are worth the effort.

As throughout the ages, the arts can provide dignity, recognition, companionship, reduction of pain, and self-expression as a legacy to others. Opportunities to share the arts can profoundly touch those learning what the arts are as well as those able to lead that experience. Arts practitioners are changed by working with the military, finding the journey to establish connections, build bridges, be inspired by possibilities, develop programming, and reach clients, though at times frustrating, well worth their efforts in the end.

References

Alexander, D., & Shalal, A. (2014, February 24). Budget cuts to slash U.S. Army to smallest since before World War Two. *Reuters*. Retrieved from http://www.reuters.com/article/2014/02/24/us-usa-defense-budget-idUSBREA1N1IO20140224

Americans for the Arts. (2013). *Arts, wealth and well-being across the military continuum: A white paper and framing a national plan for action*. Retrieved from http://www.americansforthearts.org/sites/default/files/pdf/2013/by_program/legislation_and_policy/art_and_military/ArtsHealthwellbeingWhitePaper.pdf

Campbell, J., Cousineau, P., & Brown, S.L. (1990). *The hero's journey: Joseph Campbell on his life and work (The Collected Works of Joseph Campbell)*. New York: New World Library.

Defense Data Center for the Office of the Deputy Assistant Secretary of Defense. (2014). *2012 demographics: Profile of the military community*. Retrieved from http://www.militaryonesource.mil/12038/MOS/Reports/2012_Demographics_Report.pdf

Department of Defense. (2013). *Fiscal year 2013 annual report on sexual assault in the military*. Retrieved from http://www.sapr.mil/public/docs/reports/FY13_DoD_SAPRO_Annual_Report_on_Sexual_Assault.pdf

Interlandi, J. (2014, May 25). A revolutionary approach to treating PTSD. *New York Times Health Issue*. Retrieved from http://www.nytimes.com/2014/05/25/magazine/a-revolutionary-approach-to-treating-ptsd.html

Jewish Board of Family and Children's Services. (2011). *Home again: Veterans and families initiative*. (2011). Retrieved from http://www.mhaofnyc.org/wp-content/uploads/2014/07/September-2011-Military-Cultural-Competency-for-Providers-Adriana-Rodriguez-LCSW-and-Rebecca-Wynn-JBFCS-Home-Again-Veterans-and-Families-Initiative.pdf

Lester, P., & Flake, E. (2013). How wartime military service affects children and families. *The Future of Children, 23*(2), 121–141.

Maguen, S., & Litz, B. (2012). Moral injury in veterans of war. *PTSD Research Quarterly,* *23*(1), 1050–1835.

McDaniel, Lt. Colonel M. L. (2009). Occupational therapists before World War II (1917–40). *U.S. Army Medical Department, Office of Medical History.* Retrieved from: http:// history.amedd.army.mil/corps/medical_spec/chapteriv.html

McGrath, J. J. (2013). *The other end of the spear: The tooth-to-tail ratio (T3R) in modern military operations* (The Long War Series occasional paper 23). Fort Leavenworth, KS: Combat Studies Institute Press. Retrieved from http://www.cgsc.edu/carl/download/csipubs/ mcgrath_op23.pdf

Miller, J. L. (2011, July). On life, liberty and other quotable matters. *Wall Street Journal,* p. 1. Retrieved from http://www.wsj.com/articles/SB100014240527023043144045764117 21705429718

Office of Public Health, Veterans Health Administration. (2012). *Report on VA Facility Specific Operation Enduring Freedom, Operation Iraqi Freedom, and Operation New Dawn Veterans Coded with Potential PTSD – Revised.* Retrieved from http://www.publichealth. va.gov/docs/epidemiology/ptsd-report-fy2012-qtr3.pdf

Storrs, C. (2013, March). Brain changes could contribute to Gulf War illness: Study. *Health.* Retrieved from http://news.health.com/2013/03/21/brain-changes-could-contribute-to-gulf-war-illness-study/

Tick, E. (2008, May 19). Heal the warrior, heal the country. *Yes Magazine.* Retrieved from http://www.yesmagazine.org/issues/a-just-foreign-policy/heal-the-warrior-heal-the-country

Trauma Center at Justice Resource Institute. (2007). About Dr. Bessel van der Kolk. Retrieved from http://www.traumacenter.org/about/about_bessel.php

U.S. Department of Housing and Urban Development. (2013). *Annual Homeless Assessment Report to Congress.* Retrieved from: https://www.hudexchange.info/resources/docu ments/ahar-2013-part1.pdf

U.S. Department of Veterans Affairs. (2014). PTSD: National Center for PTSD. Retrieved from http://www.ptsd.va.gov/public/PTSD-overview/basics/how-common-is-ptsd.asp

Welch, J. S. (2003). Ritual in western medicine and its role in placebo healing. *Journal of Religion and Health, 42*(1), 3–96.

Yosick, T., Bates, M., Moore, M., Crowe, C., Phillips, J., & Davidson, J. (2012, February). *A review of post-deployment reintegration: Evidence, challenges, and strategies for program development.* Arlington, VA: Defense Centers of Excellence for Psychological Health & Traumatic Brain Injury. Retrieved from http://www.dcoe.mil/content/Navigation/ Documents/Review_of_Post-Deployment_Reintegration.pdf

12

THE ARTS IN PEDIATRIC HEALTHCARE SETTINGS

Judy Rollins

A growing number of pediatric hospitals are opening their doors to artists and creative arts therapists. This chapter begins with a discussion of what hospitalization is like for children, viewed through the developmental framework of childhood. Acknowledging family-centered care as best practice, issues for family members also are examined. A theoretical basis for using the arts is explored, citing examples. A preparation process for creating a psychosocially sound pediatric arts program is described, including the important role of child life services in hospitals and how it relates to arts programming. The chapter concludes with challenges unique to pediatric settings.

Children and hospitalization

Hospitalization is a stressful experience for anyone, but research indicates that it is especially difficult for the developing child (Pearson, 2005). Children are rarely permitted to refuse treatments, medications, and procedures, and "things" are constantly being done to them. Strangers ask them to hold still for painful procedures that they may not understand, leaving them feeling powerless and confused. Placed in passive roles with limited opportunities to make meaningful choices, children's emotions are often intense and confusing (Rollins, 2005a).

The hospital environment seethes with the unfamiliar. Sights, such as strange cords or wires on walls, may look like monsters at night. There is a constant parade of strangers; an older study reveals that children typically see more than fifty strangers during their first twenty-four hours of hospitalization (Johnson, 1975), a figure that likely remains fairly accurate today.

The child is exposed to many other strange sights, sounds, smells, and tastes – any of which can be frightening if the child does not know what they are. Loud noises can lead to disengagement from the environment. Extreme noise can promote a sense of helplessness and powerlessness. Hearing a child crying softly in another room can be frightening for other children as they wonder why the child is crying, what the child did to cause it to happen, and most importantly, "Are they going to do the same thing to me?"

The effect of smells is often underestimated. Smell reaches more directly into our memory and emotions than any of the other senses. Unpleasant odors can increase heart and respiration rates, and medicinal smells can produce anxiety (Rollins, 2008). Medication and illness may alter the sense of taste, which is related to smell, so food may taste bad. Further, children may be required to take nasty tasting medicines or preparation mixtures for procedures.

Touch is also a consideration. Although being touched is often comforting, being touched can be a source of discomfort and confusion, especially when children are examined in areas of their bodies they have been told never to let strangers touch.

With bodily intrusion and exposure being common experiences, children's dignity is a topic of concern (Reed, Smith, Fletcher, & Bradding, 2003). No consensus exists regarding the age at which dignity becomes an issue for children. However, research confirms that children's privacy and dignity are not always respected in the hospital (Popovich, 2007). For some children, this lack of respect may be the most difficult hospital stressor of all.

Salmela, Salantera, and Aronen (2009) studied hospitalized children ages four to six years and found that ninety percent of the children were afraid of at least one aspect of being hospitalized. Common fears involved nursing interventions, being a patient, and fears related to the child's developmental level. Children also mentioned fears caused by the unfamiliar environment or lack of information; child-staff relations; and the physical, social, and symbolic environment. Coyne (2006) reported that older children ages seven to fourteen years identified a range of fears and concerns, including separation from family, unfamiliar environment, investigations and treatments, and loss of self-determination.

Children do not leave behind stressors from everyday life when they come through the hospital door. Whether a pending parental divorce, difficulty in school, or a neighborhood bully, these stressors, too, will have an impact on the child's experience, sometimes more so than hospital-related stressors.

A developmental approach

The child's developmental stage offers the most practical guide to his or her response to hospitalization. Table 12.1 summarizes developmental stage-related issues of concern and possible responses.

Because separation from parents is a huge issue for young children, infants and toddlers are two of the age groups at highest risk for negative effects of

TABLE 12.1 Understanding Children Who Are Hospitalized: A Developmental Perspective

Hospitalization Issues	Possible Troublesome Responses
Infant (0–1 year)	
Separation	Failure to bond
Lack of stimulation	Distrust
Pain	Anxiety
	Delayed skills development
Toddler (1–3 years)	
Separation	Regression (including loss of newly
Fear of bodily injury and pain	learned skills)
Frightening fantasies	Uncooperativeness
Immobility or restriction	Protest (verbal and physical)
Forced regression	Despair
Loss of routine and rituals	Negativism
	Temper tantrums
	Resistance
Preschooler (3–6 years)	
Separation	Regression
Fear of loss of control, sense of own power	Anger toward primary caregiver
Fear of bodily mutilation or penetration by	Acting out
surgery or injections, castration	Protest (less aggressive than toddler)
	Despair and detachment
	Physical and verbal aggression
	Dependency
	Withdrawal
School-ager (6–12 years)	
Separation	Regression
Fear of loss of control	Inability to complete some tasks
Fear of loss of mastery	Uncooperativeness
Fear of bodily mutilation	Withdrawal
Fear of bodily injury and pain, especially intrusive	Depression
procedures in genital area	Displaced anger and hostility
Fear of illness itself, disability, and death	Frustration
Adolescent (12–18 years)	
Dependence on adults	Uncooperativeness
Separation from family and peers	Withdrawal
Fear of bodily injury and pain	Anxiety
Fear of loss of identity	Depression
Concern about body image and sexuality	
Concern about peer group status after	
hospitalization	

Note: Adapted from Rollins, J., & Mahan, C. (2010). *From artist to artist-in-residence: Preparing artists to work in pediatric healthcare settings* (2nd ed.). Washington, DC: Rollins & Associates.

hospitalization (Hart & Rollins, 2011). Separation is compounded by restriction on newly acquired independence for the toddler and preschool child. Regression is common. For example, the previously toilet-trained toddler may have "accidents." Children may not reach their pre-hospital level of development until well after discharge. Young children's egocentricity adds to their vulnerability. Viewing themselves as both the center and the cause of events, they may consider hospitalization and its troublesome aspects punishment for a bad deed or thought.

School-aged children usually understand why hospitalization is necessary and thus tend to be better able to cope. However, they are often concerned with losing the control they worked so hard to achieve. Thus, they find procedures that interfere with control of their bodies (e.g., anesthesia) as threatening. Hospitalization casts adolescents back to unwanted dependence. They are separated from their friends, a critical source of their social life and sense of self-worth. They worry about plans for the future, fitting in, threats to their physical integrity and body image, and being left out of the mainstream of life.

Regardless of age, all children can experience homesickness. Not all children are homesick for their parents; a child may miss home cooking or the family pet most. In a study of hospitalized children, eighty-eight percent of the children reported some homesick feelings (Thurber, Patterson, & Mount, 2007). A successful strategy for combating homesickness is doing something fun with someone. The arts offer many opportunities to implement this strategy.

Family needs of hospitalized children

Understanding the perspectives of family members provides the basis for developing evidence-based, effective arts programming. Although "family" is whomever the child considers family, the needs of parents, siblings, and grandparents are commonly considered when a child is hospitalized.

Parents

According to Hockenberry and Wilson (2007), parents' initial response is usually disbelief, especially if the illness or injury is sudden or serious. They often search for reasons for the child's condition, frequently blaming themselves or projecting their anger at other people. Regardless of severity, parents usually question their adequacy as caregivers and review any actions they could have taken or omissions they might have made that could have prevented, or caused, the illness or injury. Hospitalization intensifies guilt because parents feel helpless in being unable to alleviate their child's physical and emotional pain.

Parents respond to these stressors in different ways. They may be protective of their child, depressed, or angry. Additionally, it has become standard practice for parents to stay at their child's bedside overnight, which offers benefits for both the child and parent. However, sleep is often disrupted, leaving the parent tired and sleepy during the day.

Siblings

A brother's or sister's hospitalization can have a significant impact on his or her siblings. Siblings face changes in family and daily functioning, including alterations to the well sibling's relationship with other family members; feelings of displacement, loneliness, confusion, and isolation; lack of communication; and concern for their own health. Siblings may feel responsible for their brother or sister's hospitalization, and jealous of the attention and gifts the child receives.

Transplants are standard therapy for many life-threatening conditions, and often siblings are donors. Some siblings report that they were offered no real choice in the matter, and that the procedure's psychological aspects outweighed the physical aspects (MacLeod, Whitsett, Mash, & Pelletier, 2003). They may feel isolated, angry, depressed, anxious, and experience low self-esteem (Packman, Beck, VanZurphen, Long, & Spengler, 2003).

As with the hospitalized child, the sibling's developmental stage provides a practical guide to his or her response. Preschoolers may withdraw or become irritable; older siblings tend to act out (Rollins & Mahan, 2010). Siblings might stammer, have nightmares, wet the bed, and complain of headaches and stomachaches. Because of the overwhelming demands of caring for the hospitalized child, parents sometimes neglect addressing their other children's legitimate health needs.

Grandparents

Grandparents can make a significant contribution to their grandchild's hospitalization, providing both emotional and instrumental support. Today, with many mothers in the workforce, grandparents often are at the child's bedside. Research indicates that, much like their sons and daughters, they, too, are frightened and worried. Grandparents experience a "double grief" or "double concern;" they are sad and worried about their child's emotional pain as well as their grandchild's physical and emotional pain (Hall, 2004a, 2004b).

Theoretical basis

Arts participation can address many realities of hospitalization and illness, and engaging in expressive activities can be therapeutic. Although artists can facilitate these opportunities, they must take care to not cross boundaries into creative arts therapy. Creative arts therapists (CATs) are highly trained arts and health professionals who use the wide range of arts modalities and creative processes to enhance self-awareness; foster health communication and expression; promote the integration of physical, emotional, cognitive, and social functioning; and facilitate behavioral and personal change (National Coalition of Creative Arts Therapies Associations, n.d.). Preparation for other professions (e.g., social work, nursing, child life) includes content that qualifies its members to also use the arts to achieve therapeutic goals.

Pain and discomfort

Illness typically involves some pain or discomfort. Children can distance and distract themselves from pain through music, drawing, painting, storytelling, poetry, dance, and other art forms. A landmark study suggests a relationship between arts experiences and the release of endorphins – the body's own pain reliever (Goldstein, 1980). Also, oxygen saturation rates decrease when children are in pain or distress. Longhi and Picket (2008) found that thirty minutes with a professional musician who sang and played the guitar increased children's oxygen saturation rates. Through a device clipped to the child's finger, rates are continuously monitored. Artists can read the monitor to evaluate the impact of their activities.

The Gate Control Theory (Melzack & Wall, 1965) offers a framework for understanding the use of the arts in helping children cope with pain. According to this theory, pain impulses are moderated by a gating mechanism in the spinal cord that opens to allow nerve impulses to reach the brain or closes to decrease or prevent impulse transmission. Anticipation, anxiety, and excitement may open the gate and thus increase the perception of pain. However, non-pain and pleasant stimuli (e.g., imagery, distraction, music) tend to close the gate and block the transmission and perception of painful stimuli.

Reduced opportunities to make decisions

Hospitalization reduces choice. According to learned helplessness theory, a continuing series of uncontrollable events can lead to the expectation that no responses in one's repertoire will control future outcomes (Maier & Seligman, 1976). The "compliance" sometimes seen in hospitalized children may reflect their response to this lack of control.

The opportunity to make decisions gives children a much-needed sense of control over something in their lives. The arts provide numerous opportunities to make decisions (e.g., what to paint; what musical instrument to play; the ending to a story, poem, or song; a movement for a dance).

Children can, and often do, choose not to participate in an arts activity. This decision, too, can have immense value; it may be the only real choice the child has had honored that day (Rollins & Mahan, 2010).

Passive role

Children are poked, prodded, led, doctored, and nursed from the moment they enter the hospital. Engaging in the arts takes children from a passive role to an active one for a time (see Figure 12.1).

Children who are actively creating are children in charge. Whether squishing clay, pounding nails, or singing at the top of their lungs, for that moment they are in control, the masters of their universe (Rollins, 2005a).

Emotions

Hospitalized children experience a variety of emotions. Being asked to hold still for a painful procedure, dealing with nausea, getting injections, or missing prom are tremendous stressors that can leave children feeling angry and often confused. Young children may wonder why their parents, their protectors, are letting these awful things happen to them. They may target their anger at people as well as at events, often expressed in misbehavior or refusal to cooperate.

Children, particularly younger ones, may lack the language skills to express their feelings verbally and find it easier to do so through the arts. Facilitated by creative arts therapists or other qualified healthcare professionals, children can process these feelings. Dealt with openly and honestly, difficult feelings lose some of their

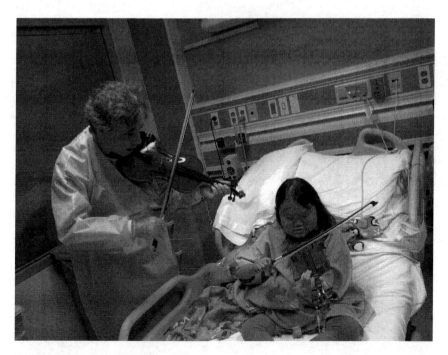

FIGURE 12.1 Making Music Together

strength. Even older children may find it easier to express their feelings through the arts, especially when dealing with a difficult issue. For example, a twelve-year old girl with a brain tumor rendered the drawing in Figure 12.2.

She explained that this is her when she was told that she had cancer, and that she was afraid of dying then and was again now. At the end of the long road with no treatment options left, she sensed that she was dying and, in fact, was, but no one had

FIGURE 12.2 "This is How I looked; I was a Frightened Girl."

spoken with her about it. Her parents were reluctant to tell her and did not want her physician to do so. Her drawing convinced everyone that it was the appropriate time to have that conversation (Rollins, 2005b).

Research findings support the notion that self-expression can reduce stress. Yount, Rachlin, and Siegel (2013) measured cortisol, a physiological biomarker that rises with stress, collected from children's saliva samples before and after an expressive art therapy session. They reported a measurable trend of decreased salivary cortisol following the ninety-minute session.

A relatively new research focus is the economic benefit of using the arts to reduce children's anxiety and distress. For example, in a study of procedural-support music therapy, Walworth (2005) reported a one hundred percent success rate of eliminating the need for sedation for pediatric patients receiving echocardiograms (ECGs). Cost analysis on the ninety-two ECG patients revealed a savings of $76.15 per patient.

Although hospitals are filled with situations that provoke negative emotions, not all of the emotions children experience while hospitalized are unpleasant. Engaging in the arts can bring children great joy and contentment, taking them to a different place, if only for a moment. The arts are there for children to use to express these good feelings, too.

Physical limitations

Hospitalized children may be physically limited, some temporarily (e.g., arm immobilized for an intravenous line, skeletal traction), others permanently. Also, certain conditions, such as cystic fibrosis or cancer, lower children's energy levels and thus limit their activity. Adaptations often can be made to enable children's participation. Methods or equipment the child uses to hold a spoon to eat can sometimes be used to hold a paintbrush. The arts experience can be redefined; children may dance using only their arms, head, or even simply their eyes. The essence of an arts experience is the good feeling that results from self-expression, which is acting at whatever level possible.

Artist by proxy is another method that enables children's participation. Peter Paul Rubens used the practice when his gout made it difficult to work on the small scale needed for preparatory drawings for his prints (Galenson, 2006). Children unable to physically participate in an activity can make important creative decisions (e.g., choice of colors, dance movements), with the artist as their instrument. It is quite an empowering experience for a child to choreograph a dance.

Research confirms the benefits of artist by proxy. Hospitalized children (ages six–nineteen years) participated in a forty-five to sixty minute artist by proxy session based on *The Moon Balloon* book (Rollins, Drescher, & Kelleher, 2011). Children chose balloons that represented different feelings and the artist drew the balloons with the child's requested images inside. The artist continually asked the child to describe details to generate richness and enhance interaction (e.g., "What color is your dog?"), and after drawing, asked for verification (see Figure 12.3).

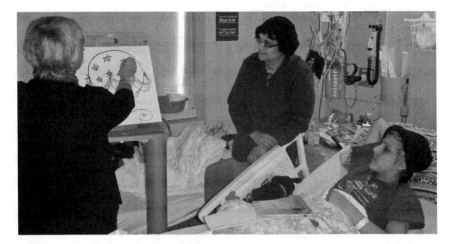

FIGURE 12.3 Moon Balloon Artists by Proxy Session

The session improved children's perceptions of their present quality of life and provided an effective method for children to express their thoughts about the hospital, illness, and unrelated issues.

Some children (e.g., children pre–post transplant), although able to move about, may be physically confined in their room for infection control or protection. Children report feeling shut in and needing to maintain contact with the outside world (Hart & Rollins, 2011). Artists can design arts experiences that help these children feel less isolated and part of the hospital community. Children can create a portion of a larger art piece, such as a painting or a quilt. Poets can go room-to-room asking children to write a line for a poem on a certain topic, compile them, and return to each room with a copy of the completed poem. Dancers can go room-to-room requesting movement suggestions for a dance, and return to dance the full dance for each child. Some hospitals use in-house television or radio networks to broadcast arts experiences that encourage children's engagement and provide a sense of community.

Healthcare atmosphere

The healthcare atmosphere does little to foster the normal experiences of childhood. Engaging in expressive activities such as art and play is normal, the essential work of childhood. Further, children often share these experiences with family members and friends. Parents report that watching their children enjoying normal childhood activities gives them a real sense of hope for the future.

Children who possess a variety of coping mechanisms will be the most successful in adapting to the many stressors hospitalization presents. Christie and Moore (2005) acknowledge that humor is one of those strategies. Benefits are both psychological and physiological (Franzini, 2002; Klein, 2003). Two art forms that use humor are magic and clowning. Hospital magicians use tricks that incorporate two fundamental principles of comedy: surprise and humorous self-deprecation on the part of the comedian (Hart & Walton, 2010). Magicians teach children tricks, which can increase concentration and improve motor, cognitive, and perceptual capabilities (Healing of Magic, 2008); decrease recovery time; and increase children's enjoyment in the rehabilitation process (Fisher & Fisher, 2007).

Clown doctors are specially trained professional artists who interact with patients, families, and staff. Working in pairs, clown doctors employ music, improvised play, and the artistry of traditional clowns (e.g., mime, dance, juggling, magic, pratfalls). Clown doctors avoid the traditional clown face paint that frightens some children, wearing only a red nose, which can quickly be removed if they need to break character. Mansson, Elfving, Petersson, Wahl, and Tunnell (2013) found that hospital clowns aid in children's wellbeing and recovery.

Art can be used to soften the harshness of the hospital environment. To add the familiar, art themes often are related to the hospital's locale. For example, acknowledging its place as the hometown of the Beatles, Alder Hey Children's Hospital in Liverpool, England transformed its magnetic resonance imaging (MRI) machine into a yellow submarine. At Children's Hospital of Philadelphia, child life specialists are exploring ways to use the professional artwork in the ceilings of sedation rooms to help children cope with procedures (Rollins, 2011). Initial assessment of children's distress indicates that the use of these images may reduce children's anxiety.

Learning and growing

Self-expressive activities provide opportunities for children to work through, reflect, and find meaning in their experiences. Children can communicate their understanding of their condition and treatment to healthcare professionals and parents, who then have the opportunity to discuss children's concerns and misconceptions. Some children enjoy creating art using medical equipment and supplies, such as painting with syringes. Handling items that may be used in their care and treatment makes the items more familiar and thus less scary. However, children should always have the choice of traditional art supplies.

Contact with the arts while hospitalized can be the beginning of a lifetime of enjoyment for a child. Artists encourage such interests by providing resources and professional materials, tools, and equipment whenever possible to help nurture budding interests.

Working in pediatric healthcare settings

Some arts practitioners are salaried hospital employees; others are contract employees working full-time, part-time, or on an hourly basis. Important considerations for effective pediatric arts programming include the place within the hospital in which arts programming resides, artist preparation, and attention to the realities of working with hospitalized children.

Finding a home for arts programming

With a goal of providing opportunities for creative expression, most pediatric hospital arts programming appropriately fits within child life services (e.g., Children's Hospital of Philadelphia's "Child Life, Education and Creative Arts Therapy"; MedStar Georgetown University Hospital's "Child Life, Education and Arts"). Although a number of hospital services – social work, chaplaincy, nursing – address children's psychosocial needs, the provision of child life services is considered a quality benchmark of an integrated patient- and family-centered healthcare system and an indicator of excellence in pediatric care (American Academy of Pediatrics, 2014).

With an educational background in human growth and development, education, psychology, or a related field of study, child life specialists promote effective coping through play, preparation, education, and self-expression activities; provide emotional support for families; and encourage optimum development of children facing a broad range of challenging experiences (Child Life Council, 2014). The child life specialist is a wonderful resource for assistance in training artists and providing ongoing learning opportunities, supervision, and support. In rehabilitation hospitals, arts programming may be within recreation therapy. Some child life specialists and recreation therapists are also certified arts therapists (CATs).

Preparation

Artists need special preparation to work in pediatric settings. Without training, would artists understand that broad smiles might appear threatening to preschool and young school-aged children, or the importance of a child in isolation briefly seeing their face before donning a mask to enter the room?

Founded in 1993 in partnership with the Child Life Program, the Studio G Artists in Residence Program at MedStar Georgetown University Hospital in Washington, DC, uses a four-step process for creating a psychosocially sound pediatric arts program (Rollins & Mahan, 2010):

1   *Artist recruitment and selection* – The personal characteristics, talents, knowledge, and skills to look for (see Box 12.1).
2   *Artist training* – An intense, twelve-hour training to provide a foundation of knowledge, skill, and trust on which to build.
3   *Supervised internship* – A minimum of three three-hour sessions under the supervision of the Studio G coordinator and the child life coordinator.
4   *Ongoing education and support* – Formal and informal team meetings to provide opportunities for problem solving, continued learning, mutual support, and growth.

BOX 12.1 CRITERIA FOR ARTIST SELECTION

1 *A genuine interest in children, a caring attitude, and sensitivity to cultural and ethnic values.* Without an appreciation for the uniqueness of each child, the trust needed to establish a helpful and enjoyable relationship with children will be absent.

2 *Knowledge and experience in a chosen art form.* Artists who are confident in their ability can communicate that confidence to children and help them be successful. Although it is desirable that the artist has knowledge and experience in other art forms, sometimes it is fun for children and the artist to explore new possibilities together.

3 *A respect for the child's creative process and products.* Respect for the uniqueness of the individual includes respect for each individual's creative process and products of that process. Artists must want to facilitate rather than interfere with that process.

4 *An appreciation and respect for the power of the arts and an understanding of personal limitations.* Art is a powerful communicator, one that carries both a tremendous potential and an equally great responsibility. Artists who lack clinical training in one of the creative arts or expressive therapies can provide children with genuinely helpful and in many ways "therapeutic" art experiences, but should not use such experiences to delve deeply into understanding or remediation of internal psychological problems (Rubin, 1984).

5 *Flexibility.* Artists need to be able to adapt to a variety of children and situations that may change during the course of an activity with an individual child or group of children.

6 *A sense of humor.* Artists who can laugh at themselves and humorous situations convey a sense of warmth that facilitates trusting relationships with children.

7 *The ability to collaborate with others.* Helping children through hospitalization is a team effort. Artists need to be able to work effectively with hospital staff, volunteers, and family members for the most successful outcome.

8 *No health condition that could result in harm to the children or to the artist.* Hospitals require a health screening for persons who will have regular contact with children. Artists with certain chronic health conditions need to be aware of the possibility that their health may be compromised by exposure to children with particular diseases or conditions.

Note: Adapted from Rollins, J., & Mahan, C. (2010). *From artist to artist-in-residence: Preparing artists to work in pediatric healthcare settings* (2nd ed.). Washington, DC: Rollins & Associates.

See References for a link to download the training manual, *From Artist to Artist in Residence: Preparing Artists to Work in Pediatric Healthcare Settings*, free of charge.

Realities of working with hospitalized children

Challenging situations occur when working with an ill or injured individual of any age, but some may be more common or difficult when working with children. Two to consider are relationships with children and families, and death and dying.

Relationships with children and families

Many artists say that the joys of working in pediatrics stem from the relationships that they establish with children and their families. In considering the nature of these relationships, it is helpful to explore some of the differences in working with adult and pediatric patients. The physical boundaries are not the same. In pediatric settings, children are often held, kissed, and nurtured. Under most circumstances, the same does not hold true among strangers in adult healthcare settings. Artists, as well as healthcare professionals, sometimes struggle because, although the physical boundaries are taken away in pediatrics, it is expected that emotional boundaries remain clear. The struggle intensifies when parents are unavailable.

Children with life-threatening conditions have identified the connected relationship – where the professional sees the child as a person first and as a patient second – as one of the most important factors in helping them cope with the healthcare experience (Rollins, 2009). A connected relationship is an easy role for the artist to fill. However, artists need to avoid an overinvolved relationship of favoritism that could be harmful to other children. Often it is difficult to recognize when one has crossed the line, so it is important that colleagues are alert and willing to intervene.

Death and dying

Artists working with children who are dying have many opportunities to help the child and family develop legacy projects (e.g., memory boxes, prints); provide comfort through music, stories, and dance; and otherwise make a child and family's final days together more meaningful. Families sometimes request a hospital musician to provide music for their child's funeral service. Most hospitals hold an annual memorial service for children who have died, and ask musicians and other artists to participate in the program.

A process needs to be in place for notifying artists of a child's death. The sad news is made more difficult when artists arrive at the hospital, ask about the child, and hear that the child has died. The death of a child is different from that of an adult. A child's death breaks the natural order of life where the old die and the young carry on. Losing a child is likely the most difficult event a parent will ever experience: "When you lose a parent, you lose your past; when you lose a child, you lose your future" (Rollins & Mahan, 2010, p. 77). Thus, witnessing the parents' pain can be excruciating. Artists may be invited to attend bereavement debriefing sessions with hospital staff. Although difficult work, most artists regard it a privilege to be with children and their families during this sacred time.

Conclusion

Children in hospitals are first of all children. With play and self-expression the normal work of childhood, the arts have a natural home in pediatric settings. Participating in arts experiences can help children cope with the stressors of hospitalization and illness, while supporting their development as they learn and grow.

References

American Academy of Pediatrics. (2014). Policy statement: Child life services. *Pediatrics, 133*(5), e1471–e1478. Retrieved from http://pediatrics.aappublications.org/content/133/5/e1471.full

Child Life Council. (2014). What is a child life specialist? *The Child Life Profession.* Retrieved from http://www.childlife.org/the%20child%20life%20profession/

Christie, W., & Moore, C. (2005). The impact of humor on patients with cancer. *Clinical Journal of Oncology Nursing, 9*(2), 211–218.

Coyne, I. (2006). Children's experiences of hospitalization. *Journal of Child Health Care, 10*(4), 326–336.

Fisher, D., & Fisher, C. (2007). Magic touch: Rehabbracadabra. *ADVANCE for Occupational Therapy Practitioners, 23*(15), 14–18.

Franzini, L. (2002). *Kids who laugh.* Garden City Park, NY: Square One Publishers.

Galenson, D. (2006). *Painting by proxy: The conceptual artist as manufacturer.* Cambridge, MA: National Bureau of Economic Research.

Goldstein, A. (1980). Thrills in response to music and other stimuli. *Physiological Psychology, 8,* 126–129.

Hall, E. (2004a). A double concern: Grandmothers' experiences when a small grandchild is critically ill. *Journal of Pediatric Nursing, 19*(1), 61–69.

Hall, E. (2004b). A double concern: Danish grandfathers' experiences when a small grandchild is critically ill. *Intensive and Critical Care Nursing, 20,* 14–21.

Hart, R., & Rollins, J. (2011). *Therapeutic activities for children and teens coping with health issues.* Hoboken, NJ: John Wiley & Sons.

Hart, R., & Walton, M. (2010). Magic as a therapeutic intervention to promote coping in hospitalized pediatric patients. *Pediatric Nursing, 36*(1), 11–16.

Healing of Magic. (2008). *Information for the therapists.* Retrieved from www. magictherapy. com/therapists

Hockenberry, M., & Wilson, D. (2007). *Wong's nursing care of infants and children* (8th ed.). St Louis: Mosby Elsevier.

Johnson, B. (Producer). (1975). *To prepare a child* [Film]. Washington, DC: Children's National Medical Center.

Klein, A. (Ed.). (2003). *Humor in children's lives: A guidebook for practitioners.* Westport, CT: Praeger.

Longhi, E., & Pickett, N. (2008). Music and well-being in long-term hospitalized children. *Psychology of Music, 36*(2), 247–256.

MacLeod, K., Witsett, S., Mash, E., & Pelletier, W. (2003). Pediatric sibling donors of successful and unsuccessful hematopoietic stem cell transplants (HSCT): A qualitative study of their psychosocial experience. *Journal of Pediatric Psychology, 28*(4), 223–230.

Maier, S., & Seligman, M. (1976). Learned helplessness: Theory and evidence. *Journal of Experimental Psychology: General, 105,* 3–46.

Mansson, M., Elfving, R., Petersson, C., Wahl, J., & Tunnell, S. (2013). Use of clowns to aid recovery in hospitalized children. *Nursing Children and Young People, 25*(10), 26–30.

Melzack, R., & Wall, P. D. (1965). Pain mechanisms: A new theory. *Science, 150,* 971–979.

National Coalition of Creative Arts Therapies Associations. (n.d.). *About NCCATA.* Retrieved from www/nccata.org

Packman, W., Beck, V., VanZutphen, K., Long, J., & Spengler, G. (2003). The human figure drawing with donor and nondonor siblings of pediatric bone marrow transplant patients. *Art Therapy: Journal of the American Art Therapy Association, 20*(2), 83–91.

Pearson, L. (2005). Children's hospitalization and other health-care encounters. In J. Rollins, R. Bolig, & C. Mahan (Eds.), *Meeting children's psychosocial needs across the health-care continuum* (pp. 1–41). Austin, TX: ProEd.

Popovich, D. (2007). Preserving dignity in the young hospitalized child. *Nursing Forum, 38*(2), 12–17.

Reed, P., Smith, P., Fletcher, M., & Bradding, A. (2003). Promoting the dignity of the child in hospital. *Nursing Ethics, 10*(1), 67–76.

Rollins, J. (2005a). The arts in children's health-care settings. In J. Rollins, R. Bolig, & C. Mahan (Eds.), *Meeting children's psychosocial needs across the health-care continuum* (pp. 119–174). Austin, TX: ProEd.

Rollins, J. (2005b). Tell me about it: Drawing as a communication tool for children with cancer. *Journal of Pediatric Oncology Nursing, 22*(4), 203–221.

Rollins, J. (2008), Arts for children in hospitals: Helping put the "art" back in medicine. In B. Warren (Ed.), *Using the creative arts in therapy and healthcare* (3rd ed.) (pp. 181–195). East Sussex, UK: Routledge.

Rollins, J. (2009). What a hospital should be. In W. Turgeon (Ed.), *Creativity and the child: Interdisciplinary perspectives* (pp. 201–211). Oxford, England: Inter-Disciplinary Press. Retrieved from http://www.interdisciplinary.net/wp-content/uploads/2009/12/CE-09.pdf

Rollins, J. (2011). Arousing curiosity: When hospital art transcends. *Health Environments Research & Design Journal, 4*(3), 72–94.

Rollins, J., Drescher, J., & Kelleher, M. (2011). Exploring the ability of a drawing by proxy intervention to improve quality of life for hospitalized children. *Arts & Health: An International Journal for Research, Politics and Practice, 4*(1), 55–69.

Rollins, J., & Mahan, C. (2010). *From artist to artist-in-residence: Preparing artists to work in pediatric healthcare settings* (2nd ed.). Washington, DC: Rollins & Associates. Retrieved from http://www.rollinsandassoc.com/PDFs/ArtistInResidence.pdf

Rubin, J. (1984). *Child art therapy* (2nd ed.). New York: Van Nostrand Reinhold Company.

Salmela, M., Salantera, S., & Aronen, E. (2009). Child-reported hospital fears in 4 to 6-year-old children. *Pediatric Nursing, 35*(5), 269–276, 303.

Thurber, C., Patterson, D., & Mount, K. (2007). Homesickness and children's adjustment to hospitalization: Toward a preliminary model. *Children's Healthcare, 36*(1), 1–28.

Walworth, D. (2005). Procedural-support music therapy in the healthcare setting: A cost-effectiveness analysis. *Journal of Pediatric Nursing, 20*(4), 276–284.

Yount, G., Rachlin, K., & Siegel, J. (2013). Expressive arts therapy for hospitalized children: A pilot study measuring cortisol levels. *Pediatric Reports, 5*(2), 28–30.

13

ARTS, HEALTH, AND AGING

Gay Powell Hanna

As one grows old, life and art become one and the same.

—Pablo Picasso

From the point of view of an artist like Pablo Picasso, living is the vehicle for the making of art – in fact, longer life gives time for the creation of masterful art (Galenson, 2006). More time to live means more time to practice, to understand, and to gain insight, making one better able to create something new of value – and this is true not just for artists, but for everyone. This chapter will explore the creative process and its central role in aging vitally as well as in coping with chronic illness and caregiving.

Whether the creation is an original Picasso, Jonas Salk's discovery of the polio vaccine, or a successful variation of one's favorite family recipe, it contributes to the individual's self-esteem and society's capacity to move forward (McCarthy, Ondaatje, Zakaras, & Brooks, 2004). C. G. Jung believed creativity to be one of the most important human instincts. Creativity allows the relativizing of the ego that is so important in Jung's ideas about individuation. The ego participates in a larger reality through creative expression; the creative process demands surrender of oneself so that one can merge with the transpersonal dimension. There is an important connection between one's creativity and one's spirituality. It is certainly a process that makes one feel engaged and productive and enables one to learn new things (Hanna, 2014).

The creative age

While problems certainly accompany aging, what has been universally denied is the potential around aging. The ultimate expression of potential is creativity.
—Gene Cohen, M. D. (cited in Hanna & Perlstein, 2008, p. 1)

Awakening the human potential in the second half of life, Gene Cohen (2005) insists, is about being creative in using life experiences to invent new ways of living. This enables one to continue to be generative and to contribute to one's own life and the lives of those across generations.

We can distinguish between "Creativity" (with a capital C) and "creativity" (with a small c). "Big C creativity" includes contributions to society at large that change its knowledge base and revise structures through discoveries. It includes major works of art and scientific discoveries that enable society to move forward. From the invention of the printing press to that of the data chip, creativity comes in all shapes and sizes, but in all cases the human experience is amplified to reach new levels of consciousness (Cohen, 2005, pp. 167–182). David Galenson, author of *Old Masters and Young Geniuses: The Two Life Cycles of Artistic Creativity* (2006), describes two kinds of creative genius: the youthful burst of prodigies like Mozart and the slow and methodical work of a master like Beethoven. Galenson found that the majority of creations come later in life. Through living and experimenting, the artist or scientist gains insights and information that lead to major breakthroughs or advances.

"Little c creativity" is accomplished by exploring and finding potential in new ways of carrying out the everyday activities of work and pleasure. New methods of gardening, cooking, and arts and crafts are often developed from family traditions or stimulated by community settings through social engagement. Many cultures hand down methods of creative expression that define their overall society based on customs related to family, faith, and work – such as the totems of the Native Americans of the Northwest or the grass baskets of the South. Improvements in skills and individual interpretation result in new creations to be shared and treasured.

Creative expression compounds and amplifies itself, sparking increased self-knowledge and self-esteem. The potential of creative expression does not diminish with age but rather can be enhanced by it, through the exploration of personal preferences and environmental opportunities. Like Jung, Cohen (2005) describes later life as a time for self-reflection, evaluation, and liberation. The question, "If not now, when?," Cohen (2005) says, is the impetus for trying something creative. He explains that age brings freedom – an older person asks, "What can anyone do to me in any case, if I try and fail?" (p. 52).

There are three key entry points to engagement in creative expression or activities. An older person can become engaged in creativity for the first time late in life. Alternatively, some older people become engaged in the arts as children or young adults, have to stop because of other demands on their time and energies, and then later in life begin again. Finally, there are older people who have been able to maintain creative pursuits all their lives.

Above ground

> "How are you doing today?" the researcher asks.
> The 97-year-old artist responds, "Well, I'm above ground."
>
> —Joan Jeffri (2007, p. 4)

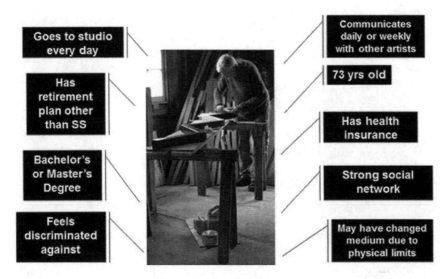

Goes to studio every day

Has retirement plan other than SS

Bachelor's or Master's Degree

Feels discriminated against

Communicates daily or weekly with other artists

73 yrs old

Has health insurance

Strong social network

May have changed medium due to physical limits

FIGURE 13.1 Profile of an Older Artist

In the research study "Above Ground: Information on Artists III: Special Focus on New York City Aging Artists," Joan Jeffri (2007) writes, "Artists who have learned how to adapt their whole lives have a great deal to offer as a model for society, especially as the workforce changes to accommodate multiple careers and as the baby boomers enter the retirement generation" (p. 4). This study interviewed 213 visual artists, 146 of them professionals between the ages of 62 and 97, in all five boroughs of New York City and across cultures, with interviews in English, Spanish, and Chinese. It found remarkable evidence that a life spent making art leads to satisfaction with oneself and one's career choice. Despite a low average income (approximately $30,000 annually) and discrimination because of age, gender, and sometimes artistic discipline, these older people displayed remarkable resilience. They communicated with their artist peers at least weekly and sold works continually. They found ways to adapt their art-making when their physical abilities weakened. For instance, if a chosen medium (such as stone carving) became too difficult to continue, the artist might turn to ceramics as a less demanding way to create sculpture. To give up making art was not an option. When asked about retirement, the older artists responded that, for them, to retire from making art would be to retire from life itself.

A framework for accessing creative potential in later life: policy, research, and practice

In March 2011, the National Endowment for the Arts (NEA), in partnership with the US Department of Health and Human Services, convened leaders from the public and private sectors to explore the relationship between the arts, health, and wellbeing. Rocco Landesman, the NEA chair at the time, opened the summit asking, "How do the arts help build us as a people and as individuals? We share a fundamental mission – how to improve the quality of life. The arts are central to human development" (National Endowment for the Arts, 2011, p. 3). Human development encompasses a complex web of factors affecting the health and wellbeing of individuals across the lifespan. Together, these factors yield cognitive and behavioral outcomes that can shape the social and economic circumstances of individuals, their levels of creativity and productivity, and their overall quality of life (p. 7). This summit focused on three developmental areas: early childhood, youth, and older adulthood. The section entitled "The Arts and Older Adults" made the case for arts participation because of its optimization of health outcomes through creative expression and cognitive enhancement (including imagination and arts processes related to Alzheimer's disease and neurocognitive disorders) and through the building of community and strong social networks (pp. 24–28).

As a result of the summit, an intergovernmental task force developed and produced a subsequent workshop by the National Academies on the Arts and Aging, "The Arts and Aging: Building the Science," convened in September 2012. This workshop focused on research gaps and the opportunities for exploring the relationship of the arts to the health and wellbeing of older people. Presentations illustrated exciting possibilities for the therapeutic use of the arts as interventions to improve cognitive function and memory, as well as general self-esteem and wellbeing, and to reduce stress and other common symptoms of Alzheimer's disease and other neurocognitive disorders (such as aggression, agitation, and apathy). Some interventions were found to promote psychosocial benefits as well. Interventions reviewed in the five papers presented at the workshop included music, theater, dance, and visual arts, with a strong focus on environmental design, especially the use of universal design to accommodate various physical and cognitive disabilities (Kent & Li, 2013).

Early studies are being replicated and expanded to further confirm findings that community arts programs have a significant positive impact on the health and wellbeing of older people. A key study (Cohen et al., 2006) looked at choral group participants and a control group of equally active nonparticipants, with a mean age of 80. Compared to the control group, the health of participants significantly improved during a three-year period: less medication was used, less depression was recorded, and greater social interaction occurred. Based on these results, possible savings in Medicare expenditures in billions of dollars were projected. A national task force is continuing with the aim of encouraging further research and policy changes, resulting in increased funding for these efforts despite the restrictive economic environment in the governmental sector. A meta-analysis conducted by Noice, Noice, and Kramer (2014) concluded that, in studies addressing the health benefits of arts participation by older adults, significant positive results are continuing to emerge.

Creativity in later life for health and wellbeing, lifelong learning, and place-making

From the grassroots activism of the 1970s, when Robert Butler wrote *Why Survive? Growing Old in America* (1975), to the macro governmental systems of the twenty-first century with an asset-based focus on the benefits of creativity in later life, accessibility to the arts and other creative opportunities are evolving into communities of practice. Creativity supports increased health and wellbeing, lifelong learning, and community engagement, and professionals in arts education have unprecedented opportunities to grow the field by developing support services in these three areas. This section of the chapter identifies ways in which creative expression can positively and significantly impact older people, their families, and their communities. The areas of practice are not mutually exclusive, but rather each builds upon and reinforces the others, in a structure that resembles Maslow's hierarchy of needs.

Health and wellbeing

Health and wellness in later life certainly requires staying active by living a robust physical, social, and spiritual life. Later life is a time of reflection that, according to Erik Erikson, should bring the resolution of past failures and a celebration of accomplishments, helping to integrate one's life story (Erikson, Erikson, & Kivnick, 1966). This is crucial to successful aging through, in Jung's term, the arch of life (Corbett, 2012).

Physical health becomes more dependent on nurture in later life. The casual engagement in physical activities by youth gives way to the imperative of the body-mind connections of later years. Through creative activities, the mind, body, and spirit can be renewed and refreshed, as shown in research such as Cohen et al. (2006). One can dance, sing, recite poetry, or act in a play, tapping all the senses and engaging the body in movement. The brain processes new information and solves new problems, while the spirit's reflections provide content for meaningful expressions that build self-knowledge and a legacy to share with others.

Community-based programs, such as those involved in field-tested studies – including Elders Share the Arts (Brooklyn, New York), Encore Creativity for Older Adults (Greater Washington, DC), and the Institute on Aging's Center for Elders and Youth in the Arts (San Francisco) – are accessible to older adults with differing abilities and economic status and encourage vibrant, healthy living in later life. Programs like these are being developed around the country, but they are still the exception.

Older adults who have significantly compromised cognitive abilities because of chronic diseases such as Alzheimer's can access the arts through highly innovative programs, such as TimeSlips, Songwriting Works, Alzheimer's Poetry Project, and the MoMA Alzheimer's Project. These programs focus on imagination rather than memory to create common experiences between people with cognitive disability and their families, caregivers, and the community at large, enabling them to retain meaning and purpose in later life.

Lifelong learning

As Cohen writes in *The Mature Mind* (2005), the misconceptions about later-life learning have been part of the view of aging as relentless decline. With the discovery at the end of the twentieth century of late-in-life neurogenesis, what we thought to be true about the inability of older people to learn new things has been scientifically refuted, but these stereotypes still persist in society. As mentioned earlier, artists and scientists who have made creative pursuits their life profession have always defied the aging stereotypes by producing the majority of their best work in later life. Because mind, body, and spiritual connections are involved in creative expression, solving the mysteries of bringing new identities into existence, the brain is fully stimulated to regenerate itself and grow. It does not matter if it is a "Big C" or a "little c" creation – the positive benefits are the same.

The major challenge to providing lifelong learning is finding ways for people to access community programming. While opportunities exist, there is no infrastructure through which one can easily find classes that cater to adults, much less creative programs for older adults in such fields as visual arts, music, dance, writing, and drama (Ivey & Tepper, 2008).

Higher education classes (credit and noncredit) exist but are not uniformly open to helping adults build new skills for new jobs or life enrichment. Osher Lifelong Learning Institutes, which include the arts, are being established across the country through university partnerships, and Oasis programs are offered in retirement or community centers. Classes based in arts organizations such as museums and theaters are finding a new market in lifelong learners. The number of summer camps for older adults, such as Chautauqua, is growing. One of the earliest educational services for older people, Elder Hostel, now called Road Scholar, is gaining attention and increased participation. Distance learning opportunities for those with cognitive impairments are being designed by major museums, such as the Cleveland Museum, where museum educators can work directly with caregivers to provide innovative programs based on the museum collection. Older distance learning programs, such as Dorot, use the telephone in a low-tech, high-touch way to bring quality enrichment programs to older people, especially those in underserved areas. Senior Center Without Walls brings many programs to older people in a virtual way as well.

The potential market is huge, but currently business plans mostly target those with economic means. As Corbett (2012) observes, successful aging in this country depends on social status and economic means.

Place-making

Health and wellness coupled with lifelong learning enhance more than the life of individuals and their families. If successful, these two protocols for aging with integrity produce wisdom, as noted by Corbett (2012) and Cohen (2005). This wisdom influences neighborhoods, communities, and society at large by creating social capital. The functional work of bringing wisdom into the community is creativity (Cohen, 2005 p. 201).

Social capital can be built through the late-in-life creative process, and this potential is largely untapped. This involves the mature genius of lifelong innovators, such as artists and scientists, as well as the contributions of late-in-life community volunteers, as Marc Freedman describes in his books *Encore* (2007) and *The Big Shift* (2011). Late-in-life wisdom can be applied creatively to solve intractable problems, such as school delinquency and food insecurity, and it can lead to the renewal of underutilized community resources, such as parks, libraries, and other public spaces. The services offered in community settings by innovative arts programs – such as Engage (Burbank, California), LifeTime Arts (Westchester, New York), Ruth's Table (San Francisco), and Iona Senior Services (Washington, DC) – are changing the way older people live independently, helping them find meaning and purpose. The Age Friendly Cities initiative (affiliated with the World Health Organization) is finding that the arts in communities break down isolation and increase social engagement across cultures and generations.

Hanna and Perlstein (2008, p. 3) write about older adults as keepers of culture, important members of society because they are repositories of living history. Wisdom and creativity are central to this kind of resource development. As we now have thirty more years to live than did our ancestors of the early twentieth century, the potential to gain from the active engagement of older people in community life has grown exponentially.

To sum up this section, creativity plays a central role in aging well. Creative engagement benefits the individual and society at large. It builds the infrastructure for an individual to gain self-knowledge and wisdom internally, as well as provides ways to tap the potential of the enlightened individual for the benefit of the community. Creativity comes in all forms, from the profound to the whimsical, and it can be used at will throughout the lifespan. But it is particularly important in later life – a time of reflection and rebalancing as one moves toward the end of the arch of life. Gaps exist in providing access to creative opportunities because of a lack of arts services for older adults, despite the potential market for programs promoting health and wellness, lifelong learning, and community engagement. The disparities between individuals based on social status and economic means constitute barriers for all successful aging initiatives, including the utilization of creative programs. However, given society's growing attention to the benefits of these activities in later life, creativity can flourish with little means but self-direction, time, and a safe, supportive environment.

The new science of old age

Will a greyer, quietly better future cause interest in football to wane as theatregoing enjoys a renaissance (Easterbrook, 2014, p. 62)? With lifespans increasing to 100-plus, will the future provide an opportunity for the arts to engage older

FIGURE 13.2 Beautiful Mind

people for longer periods of time? Indeed, this first century of the new millennium offers unparalleled opportunities in arts program development across the lifespan.

At the turn of the twentieth century, life expectancy was just 45 years, but by the beginning of the twenty-first century, it had reached 79 years for men and 81 for women. Even skeptics agree that babies born today have a high likelihood of living to 100. Therefore, in developing arts programs for older people, the horizon for management is extremely broad. Never before have artists, arts educators, and arts administrators been given such a large platform for curriculum development, as K–12 pedagogies now give way to instructing 50- to 100-year-old learners. However, there are new demands for program services supporting arts participation in later life. One must possess the knowledge and ability to produce adult education that is strongly learner-centered, pairing sophisticated instructions for skill-building with a thorough respect for the life experiences of the older learner. One must recognize that the older learner is motivated from within to engage in the arts and has a personal desire to make art in order to achieve life enhancement goals. *Creativity Matters: The Arts and Aging Toolkit* (Boyer, 2007), a publication available online, describes the step-by-step process of planning, developing, and evaluating arts programs for older people in all art forms.

Who are the older adults in this greyer society? First, they include people who have discretionary time and (usually) resources; their careers are settled, and their children are grown. Second, many are leaving their careers and are looking to find a new sense of meaning and purpose in arts engagement or reengagement. They might be considering a new career in the arts. Third, some have health issues; for them, the arts become life enriching and therapeutic, and attention must be given to family and professional caregivers.

Professional arts educators, teaching artists, artists in healthcare, and arts administrators are essential in providing quality services to support a wide spectrum of related services for all three of these groups. Indeed, the issue becomes one of workforce development, as we seek to satisfy the new demands of this greyer society on so many levels with an adequate supply of high-quality arts programs. Expanding program delivery across settings – from independent living in communities to end-of-life environments – requires new services in arts education, arts processes, and arts products.

The development of arts programs for older adults

How should arts programs be developed to support participation across distinct target populations, who have diverse interests and needs in differing stages of later life? Let's look at three groups of older adults. First, an arts manager should consider the person living independently at home in a naturally occurring community. This older person most likely is looking to learn more about the arts in terms of history, process, and production, and such people usually have time and resources to do so. Opportunities for arts engagement include community centers, libraries, senior centers, faith-based organizations, and institutions of higher education (including community colleges and online courses). Additional channels to serve this population include arts centers and discipline-based arts organizations, such as museums, symphony orchestras, and theaters. Most often, trained artists and volunteers provide services in such community settings. Professional development in lifelong learning for arts educators, artists, and arts administrators – as well as volunteer training – needs to be developed to meet demand. However, the infrastructure for this kind of professional development is not readily available. Vehicles for training are being developed and offered online and through professional associations, yet professionals are most often left to find ways to provide these important services on their own. One such vehicle is the NCCA Online Artist Training in Arts and Aging (National Center for Creative Aging, 2012). It offers professional development to providers of arts and other services, showing how to create comprehensive arts programs in community and healthcare settings to encourage participation in the arts by older people.

What is the business model to sustain new, expansive, life-long learning programming in community settings? For older people with discretionary income, a fee-based/earned income system is evolving. However, to keep arts accessible and inclusive for all members of the community, new public and private collaborations must be cultivated. The evidence base of model programs to encourage public and philanthropic investment is small but growing. Outcomes from the evidence to date show greater social engagement and mastery, which result in better health, lower risk, and lower cost for long-term care.

The second group of the older population referenced above includes those who are beginning to need assistance to perform daily activities. Arts engagement becomes particularly important for such people as they seek to keep from being isolated and to retain a sense of purpose. In naturally occurring retirement communities and "villages," a small amount of assistance with maintenance and transportation will keep older adults in their homes, and participating in the arts will provide a bridge to meet neighbors and keep mental processes engaged. In contrast, planning arts programs for people living at home with assistance requires program delivery in partnership with other service providers. Partnerships among social services, aging, health, and the arts are in the pioneering stage. Arts programs requiring implementation in partnership with other assisted living services need substantial onsite or distance learning professional development opportunities for the artists and administrators involved.

The third group includes older persons who decide to relocate into an assisted living facility, long-term care facility, or continuing care retirement community. In these settings, the opportunities for arts engagement focus on life enrichment and move toward clinical protocols and delivery systems, including expressive therapies. Community partnerships remain extremely valuable. Providing consistently high quality services in these settings is a management challenge. There is a lack of knowledge among health service providers for the elderly about how to work with artists and arts organizations that are trained to provide services to this population group. As a result, entertainers or non-arts activities often replace high quality and engaging arts participation opportunities. In assisted living communities, providers of arts services usually are life enrichment specialists and activities directors who may not have any training at all in the arts and humanities. However, with the growth in demand for assisted living and long-term care, the provision of participatory arts experiences is becoming recognized as a requirement for high-end facilities, especially as these institutions try to attract younger residents in their late 60s and early 70s. *Bringing the Arts to Life: A Guide to the Arts and Long Term Care* (Rollins, 2013) is a comprehensive resource for artists and other service providers seeking to better understand institutional senior living facilities and how to develop programs within them.

In arts programs for older adults in all three of these groups, learning in the arts through all media and disciplines should be made available for the creation of any kind of arts work, and program leaders should also recognize that the person's own life story becomes increasingly important in older age. Research (Butler, 1975; Cohen, 2005; Erikson et al., 1966) demonstrates that life review and reminiscence become a critical phase in a person's life, enabling one to accept life's failures and celebrate accomplishments. It is a time to be generative in terms of passing wisdom to the next generation. Practices serving older adults must recognize and respect the importance of this work, especially at the end of one's lifetime when building integrity is essential to avoid sinking into despair.

At the end of life, the arts can play an important part in giving comfort to older persons, their families, and their friends. It is important to have highly trained professional artists and volunteers provide these arts services. For this population group, training in hospice and palliative care is essential for the arts service provider, and it is crucial for these arts providers to be part of the clinical and spiritual team.

Finally, many opportunities and challenges exist in providing services to multiple generations and inter-generationally. Across the lifespan, arts programs have the potential to link generations to build social capital to support stronger communities. With people living longer lives, mentorship programs should be developed in each community to support arts education across the lifespan. In addition, opportunities for creative expression through technology offer new avenues for individuals and intergenerational program services. Interestingly, the NEA study, *The Arts and Human Development* (2011), reports that the younger generation and the older generation use technology more than the generations in between. It can be argued that intergenerational programs are where the future is most richly formed, where older people stay generative, where younger people are strengthened, where social capital is expanded, and where entire communities can be renewed and reinvented. This is where deep work can be accomplished to improve the health and wellbeing of generations to come. However, the development of intergenerational arts programs requires structure, attentive preparation, and engagement. The younger and older generations must be prepared to work with each other to dispel stereotypes on both sides. Projects are accomplished most effectively at a simple level first, then they can grow into sustained programs and services. Partnerships are key, as is the understanding of how to build inclusion in diverse settings and cultural contexts.

In summary, arts programs to engage older people need to be learner-centered in ways that go beyond pedagogy, including the recognition that mastery of new material will come by choice and by respecting life experience. Older adults requiring assistive and long-term care need to be served in partnership with social and healthcare services, while the focus on high standards for the creative experience is retained. Cross-cultural and intergenerational programs will be a major focus of this work, with the goal of providing both individual and societal benefits. New business models and educational models are required for success, as is research to build an evidence base that will encourage public and philanthropic investment. The field of arts and health for the aging population is on the cusp of dramatic growth, and professional development is crucial to effectively meet new demands (Hanna, Noelker, & Bienvenu, 2015).

Conclusion: next steps beyond bingo

The pleasure of passing time playing bingo is not to be completely dismissed. But there is a hugely expanding demographic of older adults who are enjoying decades of good health, and engaging in new ways of life, and this can include participation in the arts across all settings, from one's home to community centers and even while receiving healthcare. It is incumbent upon artists and arts organization to provide high quality, age-appropriate arts engagement services. To do so requires a reorientation in the workforce, moving from a focus on K–12 education to arts engagement across the entire lifespan. It is also necessary to expand the capacity of arts organizations to include new business models and marketing and to build bridges between related aging, community, and health services. In doing so, we will create an infrastructure composed of partnerships focusing on the potential of older people to live lives of meaning and purpose, not only for themselves but for their families and the community at large. The task ahead is large, and it should be addressed systematically through research and policy changes that encourage best practices in the arts in order to serve across the span of human development.

References

Boyer, J. M. (2007). *Creativity matters: The arts and aging toolkit.* New York, NY: National Guild of Community Schools of the Arts.

Butler, R. N. (1975). *Why survive? Being old in America.* Baltimore, MD: Harper and Row.

Cohen, G. (2005). *The mature mind.* New York, NY: Basic Books.

Cohen, G., Perlstein, S., Chapline, J., Kelly, J., Firth, K., & Simmens, S. (2006). The impact of professionally conducted cultural programs on the physical health, mental health, and social functioning of older adults. *The Gerontologist, 46*(6), 726–734.

Corbett, L. (2012, March 28). *Successful aging: Some Jungian contributions to development in later life.* Manuscript presented at Library of Congress, Washington, DC.

Easterbrook, G. (2014, October). What living to 100 will mean for you and society. *The Atlantic,* 60–72.

Erikson, E. H., Erikson, J. M., & Kivnick, H. Q. (1966). *Vital involvement in old age.* New York, NY: Norton.

Freedman, M. (2007). *Encore: Finding work that matters in the second half of life.* New York, NY: Public Affairs.

Freedman, M. (2011). *The big shift: Navigating the new stage beyond midlife.* New York, NY: Public Affairs.

Galenson, D. W. (2006). *Old masters and young geniuses: The two life cycles of artistic creativity.* Princeton, NJ: Princeton University Press.

Hanna, G. (2014). The central role of creativity in aging. In L. Sawin, L. Corbett, & M. Carbine (Eds.), *C. G. Jung and aging: Possibilities and potentials for the second half of life* (pp. 123–135). New Orleans, LA: Spring Journal Books.

Hanna, G., Noelker, L., & Bienvenu, B. (2015). The arts, health, and aging in America: 2005–2015. *The Gerontologist, 55*(2), 271–277.

Hanna, G., & Perlstein, S. (2008). *Creativity matters: Arts and aging in America.* Washington, DC: Americans for the Arts.

Ivey, B., & Tepper, S. J. (2008). *Engaging art: The next great transformation of America's cultural life.* New York, NY: Routledge.

Jeffri, J. (2007). *Above ground: Information on artists III: Special focus on New York City aging artists* (Research report by Research Center for Arts and Culture, Teachers College). New York, NY: Columbia University.

Kent, M., & Li, R. (2013). *The arts and aging: Building the science* (Paper prepared for the National Endowment for the Arts, Office of Research and Analysis). Retrieved from http://arts.gov/sites/default/files/Arts-and-Aging-Building-the-Science.pdf

McCarthy, K. F., Ondaatje, E. H., Zakaras, L, & Brooks, A. (2004). *Gifts of the muse.* Santa Monica, CA: RAND Corporation.

National Center for Creative Aging (NCCA) (2012). *NCCA online artist training in arts and aging.* Retrieved from http:www.creativeaging.org/programs-people/ncca-online-artist-training-arts-and-aging

National Endowment for the Arts (2011). *The arts and human development* (White paper). Washington, DC: NEA.

Noice, T., Noice, H., & Kramer, A. F. (2014). Participatory arts for older adults: A review of benefits and challenges. *The Gerontologist, 54,* 741–753.

Rollins, R. (2013). *Bringing the arts to life: A guide to the arts and long-term care.* Washington, DC: Global Alliance for Arts & Health.

14

THE USE OF MUSIC-THANATOLOGY WITH PALLIATIVE AND END-OF-LIFE POPULATIONS IN HEALTHCARE SETTINGS

Jane Franz and Sandy LaForge

Due to the aging "baby boomer" population in the United States, the "silver tsunami" is now crashing down upon us. Not only are there more older people in the workforce, there are also more people entering the "end of life" stage. The often-avoided, if not forbidden, subject of death is coming out of the closet in our society as the impact of the large, aging population affects everyone's daily life. The workforce in this country is struggling to meet the demands of the aging population. Healthcare systems are being inundated with more and more patients who need extended end-of-life care at a time when many hospitals, hospices, and care facilities are attempting to streamline and cut back on staffing to make ends meet. There is greater need than ever before for cost-effective, patient-centered services that directly serve the needs of those who are dying and their loved ones.

The medical field of palliative care, defined by the National Hospice and Palliative Care Organization (NHPCO) as "treatment that enhances comfort and improves the quality of an individual's life during the last phase of life" (cited in Connor, 2009, p. 2) is reflected in the dramatic rise of the hospice movement, both in the United States and abroad. Focused on alleviating pain and suffering, the modern hospice movement started in England in the 1950s with Dame Cicely Saunders, who subsequently introduced the concept of hospice in the United States in 1963.

> Hospice provides support and care for persons in the last phases of an incurable disease so that they may live as fully and as comfortably as possible. Hospice recognizes that the dying process is a part of the normal process of living and focuses on enhancing the quality of remaining life. Hospice affirms life and neither hastens nor postpones death. Hospice exists in the hope and belief that through appropriate care, and the promotion of a caring

community sensitive to their needs that individuals and their families may be free to attain a degree of satisfaction in preparation for death.

(NHPCO, cited in Connor, 2009, p. 2)

Even when cure is no longer possible, healing can always take place. Live, prescriptively delivered music can create an atmosphere where healing can occur, where patients and loved ones can enter more fully into living, even at the end of life. A specific arts-based intervention within palliative care is called *Music-Thanatology*. As defined on the website of the Music-Thanatology Association International (MTAI), "Music-thanatology is a musical/clinical modality that unites music and medicine in end-of-life care. The music-thanatologist utilizes harp and voice in prescriptively delivered music at the bedside to lovingly serve the physical, emotional, and spiritual needs of the dying and their loved ones."

Music-thanatology is at the forefront of recognized "best practices" programs in palliative care services that are available through the PeaceHealth Sacred Heart Medical Centers (SHMC) and Hospice, located in Eugene and Springfield, Oregon. Palliative care services allow patients and families to have more contact with trained, caring individuals as they journey through the medical system. These services increase the observation of patient and family needs, which often can surface unnoticed by staff if nurses are busy or uncomfortable interacting with patients who have been given the "palliative" care label, especially at the end of life (Chiplaskey, 2013).

PeaceHealth SHMC offers the oldest and largest music-thanatology program in the world to its patients and their families, across the spectrum of palliative care in hospital and hospice settings. At SHMC, music-thanatology is offered through an arts in healthcare program named *Strings of Compassion*. Palliative care at SHMC uses an integrative approach, offering supportive services alongside the clinical care; this often includes the use of music-thanatology visits (called *music vigils*). Professional music-thanatologists are employees who are members of interdisciplinary teams, working alongside doctors, nurses, social workers, and chaplains. Internationally, they serve in hospitals, hospices, nonprofit organizations, and independent contractor practices. This chapter introduces the field of music-thanatology and describes how this arts intervention can greatly enhance quality of life in palliative care settings.

What is music-thanatology?

"Since antiquity, music and medicine have a long tradition as allies in healing" (MTAI website). *Music-thanatology* is a contemporary field founded on this long tradition, developed over the past four decades based on the pioneering work of Therese Schroeder-Sheker through the Chalice of Repose Project. Today, two training programs exist and music-thanatologists are certified through the Music-Thanatology Association International (MTAI). Certified music-thanatologists[1] complete a master's level training program over two years, during which time they become proficient with harp and voice and the prescriptive delivery of music at the bedside. They are also trained clinically to be able to interact with physicians and nurses about patient diagnoses, symptoms, and prognoses.

According to the MTAI website:

> Prescriptive music is live music that responds to the physiological needs of the patient, moment by moment. By observing vital signs such as heart rate, respiration and temperature, the music-thanatologist provides music that is tailored to each specific situation. The goal of this work is to create an atmosphere of peace and release for patients and loved ones as they struggle with anticipatory grief and impending loss. The warmth of this living music can bring solace, dignity and grace to those approaching the ultimate journey at the end of life. This music can help to ease physical symptoms such as pain, restlessness, agitation, sleeplessness, and labored breathing. It offers an atmosphere of serenity and comfort that can be profoundly soothing for those present. Difficult emotions such as anger, fear, sadness, and grief can be relieved as listeners rest into a musical presence of beauty, intimacy and compassion.
>
> Music-thanatology is not intended to entertain or distract the patient. . . . Applause or comment is not necessary during the silence between the musical offerings. The patient and others present are simply invited to receive the music, which allows those present to enter into the unbinding process of letting go in his or her own very personal way. It affords families a chance to be with their loved one in a very intimate yet safe atmosphere where words are not necessary, and the words that are said can come from a deep place, aided by the music.

As medical technology becomes ever more advanced, medical practitioners recognize that there is often suffering that eludes even the most sophisticated symptom management. Many physicians and caregivers welcome music vigils as an integral form of care that offers an opportunity for relieving suffering. In addition, the music is also an expression of caring, beauty, and love that transcends and supports diverse affiliations of faith and culture (MTAI).

As explained by Richard Groves (2005) in *The American Book of Dying*:

> For people of all ages and cultures, music is a language that speaks strongly during times of transition. . . . A thousand years ago, the monks at Cluny, France, developed elegant caregiving practices using different modes of music. . . . Today, studies show the healing properties of certain instruments such as the harp. For many patients, the resonance from the strings often sets up a relationship between the sound and the listener, resulting in an enhanced quality of life for both patients and caregivers alike.

(p. 262)

The music vigil

The MTAI explains that the word "vigil" refers to watchfulness or a period of watchful attention. A music vigil is the time during which a music-thanatologist is present, offering live, prescriptively delivered music with harp and voice. In order to understand "prescriptively delivered music," it is helpful to compare the manner in which a physician may understand and use the word "prescriptive." When a patient presents to a doctor, the doctor assesses the situation (the patient's presentation) and may determine a "path" or "course" for the patient to follow, often in the form of a prescription for medicine or other therapies. The prescription is made to achieve a goal, usually some sort of cure or symptom management.

The music-thanatologist similarly assesses the patient's situation and then determines a musical path or course, a musical prescription. By intentionally using harp and voice, the music-thanatologist offers the prescriptive qualities of the elements of the music. The goal, in this case, is to create an atmosphere of peace and comfort so that the patient and their loved ones may process in whatever manner and at whatever level they choose, within a peaceful, beautiful, and supportive cradle of sound.

Musical elements such as rhythm, pacing, volume, and tone are tailored, or prescribed, live at the bedside. The delivery changes in attentive response to the patient. For example, the length and shape of the musical phrase can correspond to the rise and fall of the patient's breath. Fluctuations in dynamics may reflect variations from restless to calm, or from effort to ease. Rhythm may be an avenue to achieve a close synchronization, and the letting go of that rhythm may support the possibility of inner and outer movement. This is not to say that there is a particular formula to be followed, only that live music at the bedside provides a broad spectrum of choices for the trained practitioner to employ in seeking to accompany patients, families, and caregivers as they work through the end-of-life process.

The music used in the vigil setting is contemplative music, quiet and restful, even meditative. While the material used might draw from sources such as sacred song (Gregorian chant, hymns, prayer, and praise songs), lullabies, and other traditional forms, it is important to understand that these sources simply provide seed material which can then be tailored to suit the needs of the situation at hand. The prescriptive delivery of music is not dependent on specific repertoire. Instead, it is a way of being present to both the obvious and the subtle aspects of a situation, analyzing options, and responding in a deeply musical way. Music-thanatologists do not use sheet music in the vigil setting, as the music is embodied and offered uniquely in the moment.

It is the job of the music-thanatologist to be a calm and professional, kind, yet anonymous presence at the bedside of the dying. The role is often to serve as a peaceful and clear center in the turbulent waters of end-of-life care, as patients, families, and caregivers strive to understand, to accept, to make meaning, and to help. While music-thanatologists may be present as death occurs, this is not typical.[2] Many patients receive more than one music vigil. This multi-vigil approach, over days, weeks, or months, allows the patient to become at ease with this unique, arts-based healthcare intervention.

Upon receiving a referral from a social worker, nurse, physician, chaplain, family member, or even the patient, a music-thanatologist will assess the patient need and determine if a music vigil is appropriate and desired by the patient/family. If so, a 20–32 string, levered harp will be brought to the patient's room. The music-thanatologist introduces herself to the patient, even if the person is unconscious, and explains the music vigil to everyone present. An understanding of the patient's clinical background and medical history helps the music-thanatologist decide how to allow musical prescriptions to emerge. The music-thanatologist assesses the patient's pulse at the wrist (if it is appropriate to touch the patient), visually observes the respiration rate, and notes the intensity of any agitation, the warmth or coolness of the skin, and the level of consciousness. It is also important to notice the emotional state of the patient and anyone present.

This information leads to decisions regarding which musical elements to use and how they might be delivered to best meet the needs of the patient and others present for the vigil. In this way, the music is able to "be with" the listener even as it responds to them in a deeply thoughtful way. Adaptability, flexibility, and the capacity to follow what they observe, with the prescriptive delivery of music, are unique skills that are carefully honed by music-thanatologists.

Silence is an important part of the music vigil. It allows the music to sink in more deeply and for processing to take place on inner levels. After a few initial moments of silence, the music-thanatologist begins to play or sing, while constantly observing the patient for any outward responses, anything that may indicate how they are receiving the music in that moment. There is silence in between the musical offerings as the music-thanatologist observes the patient, deciding what musical elements to bring in next, based on the patient's responses to what has been offered. Each piece played or sung is thoughtfully chosen to create an atmosphere in which agitation may lessen and relaxation and sleep are welcome. The music also creates a space for the expression of grief. Observable changes in the patient may or may not occur. After twenty- to forty-five minutes, the music vigil will end and the music-thanatologist will thank everyone and quietly leave.

Music-thanatologists write about the vigils they provide in the form of "clinical narratives" and chart notes. They communicate about clinical, spiritual, and musical observations they make during the music vigil and about the responses of patients and loved ones. The vigil narratives teach us about the dying process. Sometimes the narratives are simple: a person is able to drift into a deep sleep, or an issue is resolved and the person is able to let go. Sometimes the narratives are more profound. Anxiety dissolves and agitation decreases, all without drugs. Pain that is not touched by morphine is gone. Sometimes the music creates a space where family members can move beyond their own grief to be able to share words of acceptance with their loved one: "It's okay to go now. We will be all right." This may help the person step over the threshold into death more easily.

An example of an actual vigil narrative is provided below in Box 14.1. Pseudonyms are used to protect identities.

BOX 14.1   SAMPLE MUSIC-THANATOLOGY VIGIL NARRATIVE

Vigil narrative

Jay is fifteen years old. His grandfather is dying. Jay stands in the corner farthest from his grandfather's hospital bed, seemingly disinterested in the harps and the people who have entered the room to offer a gift of music. Jay gives a brief shrug of his shoulders then looks away when we greet him. His mother, Sally, sits in a chair near the window. She gets up to welcome us and thanks us for coming. A woman in her mid-forties, Sally seems tired beyond her years. Her clothes are wrinkled and I wonder how long she has been here. Her eyes are red and puffy and she holds a handkerchief tightly in one hand. She appears tense and struggles not to cry. She apologizes for Jay's lack of cordiality, saying that he has never been around anyone who is dying before and is really quite upset. This comment earns a quick, angry glance from Jay who attempts to shrink even further into the corner, stuffing his hands into his pockets and looking studiously at the floor.

Sally then introduces us to Marion, her mother, who is seated next to the bed. Marion is stroking her husband's arm. She looks up, surprised by our presence, then smiles and nods her head in greeting before turning her attention back to her husband. Sally says that her mother is quite hard of hearing and doesn't really understand who we are, only that we will play harp music for Jack.

Jack is seventy-five years old. Looking at his tan face beneath short-cropped silver hair and at his well-muscled arms I guess that Jack is a man who is accustomed to the out-of-doors and to physical activity. His appearance is in sharp contrast to the stillness with which he is lying in this hospital bed, a ventilator tube down his throat and various other tubes and wires running from beneath the bed sheets to monitors and bags. Jack has been in the hospital's Intensive Care Unit since yesterday morning. He suffered a massive stroke while playing golf. He is reported as unconscious, maybe comatose. We are told that his family has made the decision to have Jack taken off of the ventilator (extubated). The doctor is doubtful that Jack will be able to breathe on his own.

I greet Jack's still form with gentle touch and quiet words. I glance at the monitor for information about his respiration and pulse rates then place my fingertips over his radial pulse, finding it quite weak. I also count Jack's respirations by watching his chest and abdomen. This will tell me if Jack is breathing more than what the ventilator is providing. I count an even, consistent ten breaths per minute, just what the monitor shows. Jack's skin feels a bit warmer than my own, but not hot and not overly moist as I rest my hand briefly on his arm and then on his forehead. We sit quietly for a few moments with the family.

Music is introduced into the room, first with one harp playing single tones for some time before accompanying chords are added. The melody that emerges is a blessing, with short, simple phrases that are repeated, bringing easy familiarity. The minor tonality creates an atmosphere which invites reflection and lends itself to the interior processing that Jack may be doing as he lays quietly on his back with eyes closed. The music is offered so that phrases begin as Jack's inhalations roll over into exhalations.

Following the breath in this way provides a framework, a steady rhythmic place in which Jack and his family may rest and process the experience.

There is a slight scraping sound in the corner of the room as Jay pushes a chair out of his way and begins to move toward the door. His chin is tucked far into his chest, and one hand makes a furtive swipe at tears welling in his eyes. He makes a muffled comment in our direction about having something in his eye as he leaves the room.

We continue to play as Jay leaves the room. His mother watches after him, but does not follow. A musical field is beginning to build, and sound reverberates in a subtle manner throughout the room. Voices are added and text is sung. With each repetition of the simple melody a verse ends with the words "In thine own way."

This is a time outside of the usual temporal boundaries for Jack and for his family. It will unfold in its own way within each of them. There is no controlling it. It will not be hurried nor prolonged by the needs or desires of any of us.

Sally moves to stand behind her mother, and with her hands on Marion's shoulders begins to cry. "I know he's going to die," she says through her tears, "and I don't know how to let him go yet. What will I do without him? I wish there was something I could do for him – no one ever taught me how to do this. I can't sleep or eat. All I do is cry." Her words are choked off by sobs that cause a rhythmic motion in her shoulders. Her mother reaches up, placing her hands over her daughter's. As tears stream silently down her own face she tells Sally to go ahead and let it all out, that she'll feel better for it.

The texture of the music is unlayered until one harp sings single tones, never quite coming to rest in the final tonic note. This creates a sense of incompleteness that reflects the emotional texture that is present in the room. We sit quietly, listening to Jack's machine driven respirations and to Sally's sobs, which slowly mellow into a low moaning sound that blends with the sounds of the harp and of the machinery, creating a kind of musical language all its own. The respiratory therapist enters quietly and goes to Sally and Marion to ask if they are ready for the extubation to take place. Sally looks at her mother who slowly nods her consent. The two women rise and Marion bends down close and whispers something into Jack's ear. Then, touching his lips with kissed fingertips she straightens and turns to leave the room. The family has decided not to be present for the actual extubation. They will wait in the hall and return as soon as the procedure has taken place. Sally asks the therapist what to expect. Will Jack die as soon as the tube is out? The therapist says that Jack may breathe on his own, but that it is impossible to know. Sally asks if we will play during the procedure and we say yes. She bends over her father, putting her arms around him as best she can, her tears falling from her cheeks onto his. She says: "It's okay Dad, you can go, we're right here. I love you so much, and so does Jay. It's just so hard for him to say good-bye. I love you Daddy. I hope you can hear me." She straightens up and stands looking *at her father, tears streaming down her face. At the doorway she turns and thanks us before joining her mother. Both women stand in the hallway, looking back into the room at Jack.*

A Gregorian chant emerges from the harp. The unmetered melody rises upward where it lingers before moving in single steps back down, coming to rest, again and again on the strong steady C tonic. This lends grounding to the atmosphere in the room. Major chords accompany the melody with judicious insertion of minor chords. This creates a balance between the major and the minor, between the inward nature of Jack's physical state and the outward motion that surrounds him as the medical team prepares.

The music moves in a wave, riding on all that is present, lifting and expanding, then descending and returning. The text speaks of the mother as intercessor, and I think of Marion and Sally like steady pillars, holding some greater space of safe harbor for Jack even as they lament in their own valley of tears, as in the unsung text of this chant.

The nurse has joined the therapist and their hands work swiftly and gently, turning off the ventilator and removing the tubing from Jack's throat. The doctor talks Jack through it just as he might with a conscious patient, letting him know just what they are doing. "There, that's got to feel better," he says as they finish removing the tube. Jack makes a gurgling sound that seems to come from deep in his chest. He coughs as they suction the fluid from his mouth and throat. Then with a rattling pull of air Jack breathes, haltingly, on his own. The strings of the harps sound with some force, so that the music encompasses the sounds of the machines, the talking, and then the sudden silence as the machines are turned off.

The musical prescription has changed and the unmetered phrasing now fol-lows Jack's irregular breaths, offering a framework for this new breathing pat-tern. Hopefully, the rhythmic flexibility within the stable, consistent structure of the musical melody will communicate to Jack on some level, acknowledging his process and allowing him to sense the support that surrounds him.

Marion and Sally are ushered back in by the nurse. Jay is with them now. He is very pale and moves stiffly as he follows the women into the room. He reminds me of a very small child, peeking out from behind his mother and grandmother. The two women go to Jack. They stroke his hair and face from either side of the bed. Jay inches closer until he touches the bed with his legs. Sally moves aside so that Jay can move nearer. Hesitant at first, he moves closer to his grandfather. Looking at his grandmother across the bed Jay says: "See Gramma, he's still breathing. Maybe he can still hear us." With this Jay places his hand on his grandfather's chest and says: "Grammpa it's me, Jay. I love you Grammpa. I just want to say good-bye, and thank you for being such a great Grammpa." Jay's cheeks are wet with tears, but he doesn't seem to notice. Relinquishing all his former control he sits down on the edge of the bed and lays his head on his grandfather's chest as sobs wrack his body.

The music has not stopped. It remains throughout, providing a blanket, enfold-ing Jack, his family, and the medical team.

> As Jay's tears subside he wipes his face on his sleeve and leans back against his mother. There is beauty and comfort in the tears of this family as they join together in their final vigil for their beloved Jack, who continues to breathe in irregular, ragged breaths that rattle with phlegm.
>
> Harps and voices have settled into stillness as we all wait, resting and watching in these timeless moments. The only sounds are those of Jack's labored breathing and the muffled sounds outside the room.
>
> It is hard to know how many minutes have passed as music emerges into the velvet silence. A simple prayer: "Protect us Lord, as we stay awake. Watch over us as we sleep . . ." The minor tonality weaves deeply into the reflective atmosphere that now surrounds Jack. Each loved one is alone even as they are together here. They are moving into yet another phase of this cycle of life and death with Jack. They have used words to express their love and sorrow, and where words could not express their hearts they sat in silence and they cried. They have invited us to share this difficult time with them and allowed us to aid their journey with the compound medicine of music.
>
> The lights are low and the room is peaceful as we say our good-byes and take our leave. The music will remain with Jack and his family in the silence of waiting. There is openness and possibility.
>
> Jack died peacefully the next day, in the presence of his loving family.

Responses to music-thanatology

Many people around the world have already experienced the peace, comfort, and beauty that music-thanatology provides. A survey of the members of the Music-Thanatology Association International (MTAI) indicates that, in 2013, over 230,000 patients, family members, and friends had received more than 91,000 vigils. These numbers continue to grow every day.

The most common responses to a music vigil that music-thanatologists observe are relaxation, lessening of anxiety and agitation, and the tendency of patients (and sometimes loved ones) to rest and to sleep. It is well known that lack of rest can exacerbate pain, anxiety, and restlessness, decreasing the quality of life for the patient and family caregivers. Music-thanatology vigils consistently result in the reduction of these undesired symptoms of the stress of illness at the end of life.

A statistical study lead by the Veterans Affairs Medical Center in Portland, Oregon, suggests more extensive investigation, "as our study supports that this intervention has benefits, almost no risk, minimal cost, and may improve patient-family experience of the dying process" (Ganzini, Rakoski, Cohn, & Mularski, 2015).

Another statistical study at the University of Utah, with sixty-five patients receiving vigils from two different music-thanatologists, showed that patients became significantly less agitated after a music vigil ($p = <.05$). Patients' respirations changed significantly, becoming slower, requiring less effort ($p = <.01$), and becoming deeper (p = <.05). Patients also became significantly less wakeful (p = <.05). Changes in pulse rates were not significant (Freeman et al., 2006).

Anecdotal evidence of these outcomes is supported by research findings. For example, a 2005 study at Deakin University in Australia demonstrated that music-thanatology vigils for terminal patients diminished agitation. The investigators (Cox & Roberts, 2005) also observed that respiration rates slowed and breathing became deeper after music vigils.

The authors, through long experience as professional music-thanatologists, can attest to the ways in which music is able to become part of end-of-life healthcare for all involved. The experience of the music can remain with families long after the death of their loved one. The music-thanatologist is trained to take in the total environment and respond to it musically in a way that can expand beyond what is present into a place of peace and beauty. This can help to create a memory that contains two very different states of being. On the one hand, a person may remember the sadness, grief, and negative emotions. They may recall the difficult sights and sounds that were present as they made life-altering decisions and then stood by as those decisions were carried out. In addition, and on the other side of that experiential coin, they may remember the beauty, peaceful atmosphere, and the comfort they derived from the music that was present. They may remember thoughts and feelings that arose as they listened to the music. Sadness and grief need not walk alone.

Initiating a music-thanatology program in a hospital or hospice setting is relatively straightforward. First, key staff members and institutional leadership need to support the idea of introducing music-thanatology alongside other palliative care and hospice services. Then, financial support needs to be identified and secured. Philanthropy should be part of the long- term plan. Music-thanatology will naturally interest donors, especially once a program is in place. Next, a certified music-thanatologist needs to be hired or contracted. Initial introductory sessions that involve verbal presentation and experiential exposure to the music helps build a shared culture of support for the work among clinical and other hospital caregivers and volunteers. Such sessions can also be held among potential donors. Actual implementation of a program mainly involves administrative coordination, coordination with clinical caregivers, rounding for developing a case-finding model, and scheduling. Integration of the program into the care setting also includes alignment with the use of the electronic medical record for both referrals and documentation of care. It must be understood that music-thanatology is not simply music at the bedside of the dying, but a dimension of the clinical care being provided in support of the shared treatment plan for patients at the end of life.

Music-thanatology as a palliative care and end-of-life arts program enhances the work of the healthcare team by providing an overarching and universal theme. It is timeless. The gentle resonance of harp and voice – following, waiting, responding, and offering compassion, beauty, and unconditional love – is understood at the level of the heart. It whispers to the soul while comforting the mind and body.

Notes

1 See Hollis (2010) for detailed insight into the work of the music-thanatologist.
2 Analysis of records of tens of thousands of music vigils at SHMC reveal a music-thanatology presence in the final moments of life at only around twenty percent of cases. This number would be higher if more music-thanatologists were on call during evening and night shifts.

References and further readings

Byock, I. (1997). *Dying well: Peace and possibilities at the end of life.* New York: Riverhead Books.

Byock, I. (2012). *The best care possible.* New York: Penguin Group.

Chiplasky, L. M. (2013). End-of-life-care: Are nurses educationally prepared? *RNJournal.* Retrieved from http://rnjournal.com/journal-of-nursing/end-of-life-care-are-nurses-educationally-prepared

Connor, S. R. (2009). *Hospice and palliative care: The essential guide* (2nd ed). New York: Routledge.

Cox, H., & Roberts, P. (2005). *Relief of suffering at end of life: Report from an Australian project to implement and evaluate a live harp music-thanatology program.* Geelong, Australia: Deakin University.

Freeman, L., Caserta, M., Lund, D., Rossa, S., Dowdy, S., & Partenheimer, A. (2006). Music-thanatology: Prescriptive harp music as palliative care for the dying patient. *American Journal of Hospice & Palliative Medicine, 23*(2), 100–104.

Ganzini, L., Rakoski, A., Cohn, S., & Mularski, R. A. (2015). Family members' views on the benefits of harp music vigils for terminally-ill or dying loved ones. *Palliative Supportive Care, 13*(1), 41–44.

Groves, R. F. (2005). *The American book of dying.* Berkeley, CA: Celestial Arts.

Hollis, J. L. (2010). *Music at the end of life: Easing the pain and preparing the passage.* Santa Barbara, CA: ABC-CLIO, LLC.

Music Thanatology Association International. Retrieved from http://www.mtai.org

15

EVOKING SPIRIT

Utilizing the arts with adults with cancer

Shanti Norris

The relationship between art and healing can be traced back to the earliest form of medicine – which is shamanism. Shamans incorporated drumming, music, imagery, drama, and ritual to evoke spirit and to promote healing. Anthropologists tell us that shamanism is found in every culture in the world. Shamans taught that in order to heal, you must treat the spirit first, and they employed the arts to do so. When a person fell ill, the shaman asked three questions: When did you stop telling your story? When did you stop going into the silence? And, when did you stop singing?

The arts are a powerful tool for healing. Utilizing well-chosen techniques in a small group setting, any person can successfully find ways to represent their feelings and emotions, hopes, and dreams. Sharing these words and images in a safe environment can help patients regain a sense of wholeness and hope in the face of a life-threatening illness, and can transform frustration, pain, and victimization into renewal and rebirth. Over time, medicine and the arts became separated. Fortunately, there is a re-emergent understanding that the arts can again be utilized as tools for healing.

Since 1996, Smith Center for Healing and the Arts, a Washington, DC based nonprofit, has integrated the arts into supportive programs for people with cancer, their caregivers, and medical professionals, including hospital artist-in-residence programs, retreats, and creativity programs. One of Smith Center's primary goals is to engage individuals in a creative process that will contribute positively to their healing. Adult cancer survivors and their caregivers engage with poetry and writing, music, mask-making, and painting in an urban cancer support center and during weeklong residential retreats. Professional artists work with cancer survivors, family members, and clinical staff in Washington, DC hospitals.

Curing versus healing

In biomedicine there is an important dialogue about the distinction between curing and healing. Curing occurs through an intervention – such as medicine or surgery – with absence of illness as the intended outcome. Healing is something larger that aims for a return to wholeness and includes the physical, mental, emotional, and spiritual dimensions of life. Ideally, curing and healing will take place in unison, but even when cure is not possible, healing always is. While guiding cancer retreats, Smith Center and Commonweal co-founder MacArthur Fellow Michael Lerner often says, "Whether or not we can affect the course of disease is in question, and sometimes you can, but there is *definitely* the ability to alter the *experience* of the illness, and there is a possibility *that itself* will alter the course of the disease" (M. Lerner, personal communication, September 20, 1996). In this realm of healing, the arts have great power.

Cancer as a turning point

Psychiatrist Larry LeShan began working with cancer patients in the 1950s in New York City. He concluded that the traditional psychotherapeutic technique of asking what is wrong, what caused it, and how it can be fixed might not be the best approach for people facing life-threatening illness. Instead he asked his patients, what is *right* with you? What makes you feel most fully alive?

Dr. Le Shan (1994) asks, "What is your song? What do you want to do with your remaining time?" For many people, the answers often lie in the creative realm: "I have always wanted to be a musician, to dance, to paint, to write" (p. 23). We may not be able to become a professional ballerina while undergoing cancer treatment in our forties, but we *can* dance, or write, or sing, or paint.

At Smith Center retreats, we often quote a verse from W. H. Auden. In the poem, a country doctor ruminates on cancer:

> *Childless women get it*
> *And men when they retire–*
> *It's as though they needed some outlet*
> *For that foiled creative fire.*

Of course we do not wish to suggest, as the country doctor, that repressed creativity causes cancer, but the verse suggests a great insight: for those facing cancer, engaging creativity often kindles a spark, engages the immune system, and enlivens the life force.

Professional artists often speak about the creative process as a reenactment of the creation story – of suddenly becoming alive and feeling a new sense of vitality. You can often see and sense this happening while working with patients as they engage in simple creative processes, sometimes for the first time since they were children.

This chapter begins with a general overview of an integrative arts and health program for oncology patients, followed by a description of the Smith Center's experiences in implementing its own programs. The chapter ends with practical considerations for working with professional artists and implementing programs for people affected by cancer.

Considerations when developing a new program

It is not possible to deliver good-quality cancer care without addressing patients' psychosocial health needs. A 2012 American College of Surgeons Commission on Cancer report states: "Psychosocial services are essential components of comprehensive cancer care and are provided to patients with cancer and their caregivers throughout the continuum of care." Implementation of an arts program for cancer patients is a dynamic component to address psychosocial care.

An integrated healing arts program can also increase a cancer center's visibility and reinforce a reputation as a "patient first" facility within the community. An integrated healing arts program can be a vital part of expansion planning and can focus on one or more of four major areas: patients, staff, hospital environment, and community.

Patients: bring trained artists to work with patients bedside and in the waiting room and expand to include performances, workshops, and exhibits
Staff: develop programs for staff, including lunch time sessions, in-services, performances, and regular staff retreats
Hospital environment: healing gardens and sacred spaces inside and outside the facility, new artwork for the community spaces, use of electronic media
Community: festivals, concerts, community projects, and collaborations with local schools, communities, and media outlets

Whether a program is created from within the cancer center administration or brought into a hospital by an outside entity, the essential components are the same. When beginning or introducing an arts program into a new hospital cancer center there are four key phases, each with several practical considerations.

Phase 1: Articulation of mission and goals

- Define art and healing
- Define the mission of the program relative to the healthcare institution's mission, culture, and patient population
- Develop specific goals for patient, staff, healing environment, and community programs
- Define health outcomes associated with a healing arts program
- Establish an interdisciplinary program planning team, including expertise in grant writing, arts, program planning, statistics, and human resources
- Obtain input from internal stakeholders, such as administrative staff, nurses, physicians, and artists through multiple focus groups and individual interviews
- Obtain input from external stakeholders, such as other area hospitals and existing healing arts programs through site visits and interviews
- Enlist an outside consulting service or art and medicine organization with experience

Phase 2: Development of action plan/budget

- Identify partnerships and collaborations, including establishing a formal contract for collaboration between your organization and the hospital (note that it takes an extended time to get contracts passed by a hospital's legal team)
- Identify healing arts coordinator (onsite or offsite)
- Identify specific goals and objectives of the overall program and its components
- Hold monthly planning meetings to work on program plan, marketing plan, and fundraising plan for the healing arts program
- Develop evaluation models for each program component
- Identify funding sources
- Develop a budget
- If part of a hospital expansion, meet with the architect if possible

Phase 3: Implementation

- Begin implementing specific program components
- Continue to expand existing artist-in-residence program

Phase 4: Evaluation

- Implement process evaluations of ongoing program activities
- Identify potential areas of research

The Smith Center story

Smith Center for Healing and the Arts was founded in 1996 as an arts, education, and health nonprofit with a primary focus on serving adults with cancer. Located in a two-story building in an active arts and restaurant district of Washington, DC, it offers ongoing supportive programs in a renovated street level space, which includes a healing arts gallery, courtyard, and light-filled program space. Programs include support groups, nutrition classes, yoga, creativity classes, and retreats. It also offers a national training program on Integrative Oncology Navigation to train "navigators" to help people navigate the experience of cancer. Over the course of fifteen years, it has brought professional artists to work with cancer patients at three area hospitals, as well as with Wounded Warriors at Walter Reed National Military Medical Center. The Smith Center also hosts the *Joan Hisaoka Healing Arts Gallery*, dedicated to exhibiting fine art that explores the innate connection between healing and creativity.

Smith Center's Hospital Based Artist-in-Residence Program has three primary goals: (1) Engage patients in creative arts activities as part of the healing process; (2) Educate and support artists to work in the healthcare community; and (3) Create awareness and support for the arts in healthcare.

Organizational history

Smith Center for Healing and the Arts, like most arts and health programs, started small. Smith Center initially approached two hospitals and suggested a collaborative artist-in-residence program in the cancer centers. Funding was initially provided from general operating expenses and through fundraising events and grants. Hospitals provided the bulk of art supplies and some office/art supply storage space. By year three, participating hospitals provided funding to cover nearly all costs, including stipends for eight artists, gallery exhibitions, art supplies, and administration. A third hospital approached Smith Center and funded the project. A fourth hospital was added to replicate the successful program with a different patient population (Wounded Warriors).

Smith Center's model trains and oversees professional artists to work with patients in clinical settings to bring the healing power of the arts bedside and in waiting rooms. An art therapy model is a different approach and utilizes clinically trained and licensed art therapists who utilize the arts to both diagnose and treat illness. While both are innately healing and can bring much to bear on a patient's wellbeing, artists-in-residence are *not* clinicians.

Smith Center identifies potential artists-in-residence and uses questionnaires and interviews to screen them for qualities such as "a genuine interest in people, a caring attitude, sensitivity to cultural and ethnic values, knowledge and experience in a chosen art form, respect for the creative process and products, understanding of

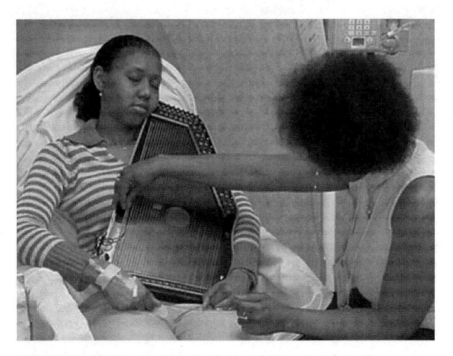

FIGURE 15.1 Smith Center Artist-in-Residence with Patient in Infusion Center

personal limitations, flexibility, and a sense of humor" (Rollins & Riccio, 2002, pp. 9–10). Cancer survivors should be a minimum of one year past treatment end before they can apply to work with people with cancer, as experience has shown the Smith Center that those who have recently undergone treatment may find it too difficult to work in this environment. A two-day intensive training is followed by hospital based training on protocol, HIPPA compliance, and other related matters. That is followed by several weeks of "shadowing" existing artists-in-residence onsite, whenever possible. After an initial probationary period, artists are contracted on an annual basis and usually work half-day sessions weekly (some work at more than one hospital). Artists meet monthly for supervision, to share techniques and stories, for community, and to process loss and grief when patients die.

Smith Center artists have included visual artists, storytellers, poets, dancers, musicians, and even a comedian. Artists represent different cultures, including those from Liberia and Cameroon. Over time, they share techniques and grow in craft. Artists learn to stop and quiet themselves each time before entering a patient's room. It takes courage and presence to walk into a hospital room and offer an arts activity, not knowing what you will find. They spend time with individuals and family members, and often they represent the only time a patient can make a choice about what is happening to them. They enter the room to visit with a person – not a patient – and train themselves to "see" the whole and perfect human being.

Gaining acceptance in hospitals is often a challenge. When Smith Center began working in urban cancer centers, hospital staff often expressed the sentiment, "I don't know who you are, but please stay out of my way." Nurses would tell artists *not* to see a patient who was angry or upset. Once the clinical staff got to know the artists-in-residence, they would *request* artists to visit patients who were angry or upset. Initially, doctors would interrupt the artists when they came into a room, but over time doctors would often wait for artists to finish with a patient. Smith Center learned that it is important to offer quarterly in-service trainings to educate clinicians, and to offer lunchtime experiential sessions for clinicians as well. Medical staff appreciate the stress reduction and gain firsthand familiarity with arts-based programs, which prompts them to refer patients. Well-trained artists become part of the treatment team, and doctors, nurses, and social workers begin to see them as partners.

BOX 15.1   SUCCESSFUL ARTS IN HEALTHCARE ACTIVITIES

Here are a few examples of activities for patients, staff, and for the general public in community settings, many of which Smith Center has incorporated in their healing arts programs.

Patients

- Interactive CD ROM's for patients: touch screens for visual art, poetry
- Writing projects: journaling, workshops

- Healing Images Group (visual arts group) meeting 1.5 hours 2x/month to promote creative process; foster sacred, ritual space with a closing session where art is exhibited
- Guided imagery for patients, for example before surgery, and individual tape players secured in patient rooms
- Cameras for patients so they can communicate the cancer experience and showcase photos in a gallery space
- "Tape Art": like tape but it does not pull off paint: for patient rooms
- Stress/relaxation channel
- Card making activities
- Collection of writings in waiting areas
- Art cart with donated pictures that patients can choose to put up in their rooms

Staff

- Days of Renewal: paid day retreat for nurses and other staff
- "Stress busters" program once a month with staff including an art activity
- Watercolor painting at nurses stations which are made into laminated bookmarks for them
- Employee art show every year throughout institute starting with the paintings from the recent staff retreat
- Writing projects: journaling, workshops
- Development of a Caring for the Caregiver program
- Card making activities
- Staff concerts

Community

- Arts Festivals in the community
- Regional art from local artists/galleries displayed throughout the cancer institute
- Partnership with local schools to display work

Healing environment

- Development of healing gardens both inside and outside the cancer institute
- Inspiration Fountain focal point
- Labyrinth
- Patient art displays throughout the cancer institute
- Painted ceiling tiles in patient rooms
- Tiling walls or spaces throughout the institution with ceramic tiles painted by patients

- Promotion of the art programs in each room through flyers painted by staff
- Chamber music by University music department
- Creation of art by staff for the patient rooms
- Performance troupes in community spaces
- Creation of murals by artists for patients and staff to paint
- Storytelling and art kits in waiting rooms to decrease frustration of wait time
- Art for wayfinding

Evaluate to demonstrate value

One of the challenges facing arts and health programs is how to determine whether specific programs make enough of a difference in the care and treatment of patients to justify spending limited resources on them. As referenced throughout the chapters of this book, the benefits of the arts and health are well documented in the literature. In 2003, the Smith Center conducted a study to investigate how creative arts activities (such as those offered by artists-in-residence) are perceived by patients, including their effects on their healing process. The evaluation sought answers to the following questions:

1 Why do patients and caregivers choose to participate in creative arts activities?
2 How does engagement in creative arts activities affect patients and caregivers?
3 How is engagement in creative arts activities perceived as a contributing factor to the healing process of patients and caregivers?

Findings from the evaluation were used to improve the program. The evaluation report contained detailed results, but key findings that were of particular interest to decision-makers were: one hundred percent of patients and caregivers said that participation in an arts activity was beneficial to their healing process. Most patients and caregivers felt calm (eighty-two percent) and cheerful (sixty-three percent) after participation in an arts activity. Structured interviews with patients about the effects they experienced as a result of participating in creative activity included testimonials about pain, anxiety, and stress reduction, hope or spiritual renewal, coping or regaining control, motivation or inspiration, pleasure or humor, and overcoming personal limitations.

In addition to periodic formal evaluation, the Smith Center collects anecdotal information from artists and hospital staff about program strengths, weaknesses, and effectiveness. Indeed, anecdotal records provide compelling and poignant evidence of the healing value of creative arts activity for individuals facing a life-threatening illness such as cancer. Through processes of ongoing evaluation and continual improvement, the Smith Center's administrative staff members have identified a number of valuable lessons in managing arts programs in healthcare settings, which are provided in Box 15.2.

BOX 15.2 ARTS IN HEALTHCARE MANAGEMENT LESSONS LEARNED BY THE SMITH CENTER

- Work with professional artists.
- Train artists in clinical issues, hospital protocol, HIPPA, etc.
- Contract with and pay artists. This results in a more professional relationship, sense of responsibility, and commitment.
- Conduct regular supervision meetings with artists to create community and share experiences, tools, and techniques and to process challenging cases and losses.
- Provide regular in-service trainings for clinical staff.
- Provide artists with identification name badge and explanatory literature.
- Secure "real estate" in the hospital/cancer center for an office so artists can keep supplies, record patient logs, and refer patients to each other.
- Create a rolling "art cart" for art supplies that might include drawing, painting, modeling, craft, and writing supplies, and musical instruments, etc.
- Provide lunchtime creativity sessions with clinical staff.
- Keep an open communication line with administrative and clinical staff.
- Designate a representative to attend tumor board meetings (if possible) and be part of the integrated patient approach.
- Schedule at least three artists per week, each working a half-day in the cancer center. Fewer artists have a lesser impact upon the atmosphere and fail to become part of the healing environment.
- Arrange for artists to get patient referrals from the charge nurse.

Techniques and tools for working with groups

A significant component of Smith Center's community program is working in a small group setting at retreats or workshops. Group size is usually no larger than ten. Through facilitated movement, writing, drawing, and painting, people are empowered to draw or write what they cannot or dare not speak. There are hundreds of creative tools that can be utilized. A few strategies and foci for group-based activities utilized are summarized below, and additional information about group-based arts can be found in the reference list provided at the end of this chapter.

Focus on process rather than product

There are two primary categories of creative techniques to use with people with cancer or other illness – those that emphasize product and those that emphasize process. In product work, the aim is to create a beautiful finished piece of art.

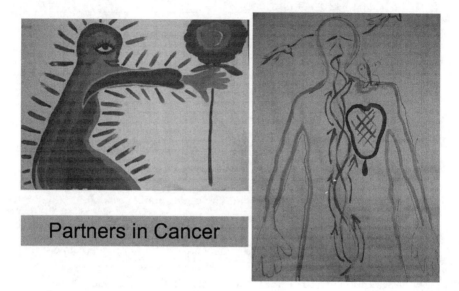

FIGURE 15.2 Husband and Wife Healing Paintings

In process work, the "act" of creating is a goal in itself, with great therapeutic potential.

In general, the Smith Center emphasizes process over product by seeking to utilize the arts to gain insight into feelings and emotions and to steer away from competition and judgments about value. A skillful facilitator, whether working one-on-one or in a group, can inspire even a fearful or doubtful individual to be bold, trust the process, and be surprised. This kind of exploration can be a rewarding experience in the midst of painful, depressing, or isolating medical treatment. Patients are delighted to learn something new while in the hospital and often feel renewed in the process.

Engage the life force

There is something fundamentally enlivening about art-making. People often reflect that they feel more alive after working on a creative project, even a simple one, even after viewing art or listening to music. Art-making engages the life force and increases vitality while potentially supporting the immune system.

Evoke the power of symbolic imagery

Symbols, imagery, and metaphor are the language of the unconscious. A basic tenet of psychological healing is to bring the unconscious into the conscious mind, through a myriad of ways. What becomes conscious can be integrated and dealt with – can be healed. Through imagery we can access the tremendous wisdom potential of our unconscious mind. Artists/facilitators can refrain from "interpreting" symbolic imagery for patients, but can sometimes be helpful in evoking self-knowledge by asking patients what the symbols might mean to them.

Celebrate the community of peers

Sharing a creative process in a group of people going through cancer can be powerful. The creative process often brings up personal stories and people learn from each other. In a well run group, each individual feels seen and heard and feels that they are contributing to another's healing. It is useful to ask people to state their **Intention** as they begin. It focuses individuals on why they are there, and evokes a shared intention of healing. When we experience an insight, or share a meaningful experience, it is profoundly useful to have a **Witness**. We no longer feel alone in our suffering. The group provides that for each other. Each person gives the **Gift of Presence**. For many people one of the characteristic experiences of cancer is a sense of isolation – of being alone, or of not being understood. In a community of peers, we are seen and heard: **We Are Not Alone**.

Select the artist facilitator mindfully

Selecting a facilitator (or artist-in-residence) is the single most important choice in developing a program. The wounded healer archetype is universal because people who have suffered deeply and have not only survived but prevailed tend to be compassionate and understanding. They are often kind and accepting. They know the importance of a friend.

Facilitators must be comfortable with deep places. The wounded healer has been in dark and difficult places and knows that one can return healed, though changed. Whatever blame, shame, fear, or anger they might feel in working with patients, they see as their own response and do not project that onto the patient.

One or two facilitators must be responsible for ensuring that it is psychically safe for individuals to process thoughts and emotions. They create a "safe space" or "hold the space." They respond authentically and wisely to what is going on in the moment and are in service of the wellbeing of each person in the room. They know when to share their own experience and when to hold back. They respect each person's experience and ability to find their own truth and answers. They have a profound ability to listen.

Encourage honesty

In almost every group session with people with cancer, someone says, "If one more person tells me to be positive, I'm going to scream!" While it is important to have a positive orientation, it is psychologically healthy to be able to first experience, and then express, whatever emotion one is feeling. In this work it is more important to be authentic in thoughts and feelings than to try to be positive. There is often an almost universal sigh of relief when artists articulate this to the group.

Set the stage for listening

One of the most underestimated gifts we can give each other is the gift of our presence, the gift of listening. It's important that facilitators as well as co-participants know that we are not there to fix each other, but to "attend," to be with, and to give the gift of listening and witnessing.

It is important to set guidelines for each session in order to promote speaking and listening in a safe atmosphere. Ask people not to interrupt each other. Ask people not to comment on others' artwork unless asked. Remind people not to jump in to try and help or fix someone when they talk about difficult or challenging circumstances.

Think about physical space and confidentiality

Creating a safe space when working with small groups is important. People need to feel safe to explore, confront, and share deep and potentially vulnerable feelings. In order to do this you need to have a **Quiet Room**. If you don't have this in the hospital, then you need to keep the work at a more superficial level. Promise **Confidentiality**. In a hospital setting, HIPPA regulations are designed to guarantee this. In a community setting, by verbalizing this at the beginning of each session, facilitators and patients can agree they are free to share their experiences with friends, but in a way that does NOT identify co-participants. This is essential.

Use multiple modalities

In a small group setting where there is a shared experience of illness and an intent to heal, there are many techniques that can be used by thoughtful facilitators. It can be very effective to incorporate multiple modalities in a single session, for example moving from writing into drawing or from visualization into painting. Examples of simple drawing, painting, and writing exercises that have proven useful in the Smith Center programs and retreats are described in Box 15.3 below.

BOX 15.3 EXAMPLES OF USING DRAWING AND WRITING IN ARTS IN HEALTHCARE GROUPS

Using drawing and writing in arts in healthcare groups

Drawing example 1

1) Have participants draw the inner critic, that voice that keeps us from doing things. That voice from childhood, parents, teachers that tells us we

are not good enough. 2) Draw self portraits – begin with how you see yourself. Do a second portrait, this time draw how the world sees you. 3) Using childlike stick figures draw your home and family as it was when you were a child. Next draw your home and family as it is now.

Each exercise can by drawn in ten minutes or so. Following the exercise go around and ask each person to say a few words about the experience as they hold up their drawing.

It's important to set a few guidelines first: ask others not to comment. People are free to pass if they prefer not to speak. This is an important part of the exercise and can be somewhat cathartic.

Drawing example 2

Start by asking participants to simply play with the colored chalk or oil pastels and paper that are available on the tables for four or five minutes. As they play remind them how we made art as children without waiting for instructions or permission. Assure everyone that there is no right or wrong, but to have fun with the materials.

Next do a five-minute exercise where participants are asked to draw an emotion. Start with pain. Let participants know they have just a few minutes for a short sketch, which can be a feeling, a thought, a current or past experience, physical or emotional. Go around the room and ask each person to briefly say something about his or her drawing or the experience it evoked, as described above.

Taking a fresh sheet of paper, next draw anger. After five or six minutes, let participants know to finish up their drawing. Have each person share. It is helpful to end this session by drawing love or contentment (a "positive" emotion). I often ask people how they feel when we are done. Many people feel relaxed or relieved. One note of caution: I recommend against drawing fear. It often brings up a lot of emotion – more than can be comfortably held and shared in a short one-time session. This is best left to professional art therapists.

This simple technique works well with most groups. It allows people to talk about difficult emotions in a way that can be comfortably managed. Time permitting, you can move on to other projects, such as a longer drawing or painting of a healing visualization or a writing exercise.

Drawing example 3

It is effective to create a simple healing visualization after which participants can draw or paint what they "saw" or felt during the brief visualization. There are many available resources for creating or using visualization techniques. Barbara Ganin (1999) offers a particularly relevant one wherein she gently guides participants to enter into a relaxed state and then asks them to imagine or visualize, "What needs to be healed?" followed by, "What would that healing look like?" A visualization loosely based on her model has been used with great success in Smith Center retreats for many years.

Saving My Life

FIGURE 15.3: *Saving My Life*: Cancer Retreat Participant Drawings of his Internal Experience at the Beginning and End of Retreat

Poetry and writing example

Smith Center uses poetry in cancer retreats as inspiration to encourage participants to write about their experience. Reading selected poems aloud (taking turns) is a great prompt. Selected poems should resonate with the facilitator and be appropriate to the group setting. They may or may not refer to cancer or illness specifically, but address pain and loss as well as hope and meaning.

After reading poetry together use specific prompts to write. Give a time limit. At the end of each exercise, offer each participant the opportunity to read what they wrote (or pass) in a safe environment, without interruption and without feedback from the group. Have them read the piece slowly and twice. If the facilitator is a writer, they can choose to emphasize the strengths of each piece and make suggestions for follow up on further writing. At the end of the retreat, with permission, we give participants copies of all the poems written on their retreat.

Conclusion

"*Creativity is a premier form of psychological adaptation. It involves the ability to change and improve all features of the environment.*"

— Albert Rothenberg, M. D.

A poet asks a patient a few questions about himself, and writes down some phrases. A little later he reads them back as a poem. His own words have been transformed into a poem. Suddenly the patient sees himself differently, in a new way. He feels seen and heard and knows that he is not alone. His life outside this hospital room matters and the room suddenly feels larger. He senses that he will be okay, that he will continue his life as before.

A woman in her fifties undergoing chemotherapy and radiation for stage four colon cancer slowly walks the hospital hallways. She wonders which is worse – the illness or the treatment that she feels may kill her. From far away she hears a piece of classical music being played on the piano in the lobby. Holding the railing, she stops and listens. For years to come she will say, "In that moment I knew that I could do this, I knew I would be all right."

Some of life's most important moments involve beautiful music, language, and imagery. The arts have the power to help us transform suffering into meaning.

References and further readings

American College of Surgeons Commission on Cancer. (2012). *Cancer Program Standards 2012: Ensuring Patient-Centered Care V1.2.1.* Chicago: American College of Surgeons.

Archer, S., Buxton, S., & Sheffield, D. (2015). The effect of creative psychological interventions on psychological outcomes for adult cancer patients: a systematic review of randomized controlled trials. *Psycho-Oncology 24,* 1–10.

Borgmann, E. (2002). Art therapy with three women diagnosed with cancer. *Art Psychotherapy, 29*(5), 245–251.

Bray, S. (2006). *When words heal: Writing through cancer.* Berkeley, CA: Frog, Ltd.

Carey, J. (2006). *What good are the arts?* New York: Oxford University Press.

Cepeda, M.S., Chapman, C.R., Miranda, N., Sanchez, R., Rodriguez, C.H., Restrepo, A.E., Ferrer, L.M., Linares, R.A., & Carr, D.B. (2008). Emotional disclosure through patient narrative may improve pain and well being: Results of a randomized controlled trial in patients with cancer pain. *Journal of Pain and Symptom Management, 35*(6), 623–631.

Cleveland, W. (2008). *Art and upheaval: Artists on the world's frontlines.* New York: New Village Press.

Cohen, B., Barnes, M., & Rankin, A. (1995). *Managing traumatic stress through art.* Baltimore, MD: The Sidran Press.

de Botton, A., & Armstrong, J. (2013). *Art as therapy.* New York: Phaidon Press.

Deschner, J.W. (2007). *Arts in Healthcare Programs and Practitioners: Sampling the Spectrum in the US and Canada* (Arts in Healthcare Advocates white paper #1/update).

Egnew, T.R. (2005). The meaning of healing: Transcending suffering. *Annals of Family Medicine 3(3),* 255–262.

Ferszt, G., Massotti, E., Williams, J., & Miller, J. (2000). The impact of an art program on an inpatient oncology unit. *Illness, Crisis, & Loss, 8*(2), 189–199.

Firestone, S.P. (2013). *Art as a catalyst for resilience: Women artists with life-threatening illness* (Unpublished doctoral dissertation). Lesley University, Cambridge, MA.

Ganin, B. (1999) *Art and healing: Using expressive art to heal your body, mind, and spirit.* New York: Three Rivers Press.

Homicki, B., & Joyce, E.K. (2004). Art illuminates patients' experience at the Massachusetts General Hospital Cancer Center. *The Oncologist, 9,* 111–114.

Institute of Medicine (IOM). (2008). *Cancer care for the whole patient: Meeting psychosocial health needs.* Washington, DC: The National Academies Press.

Kaltsatou, A., Mameletzi, D., & Douka, S. (2011). Physical and psychological benefits of a 24-week traditional dance program in breast cancer survivors. *Journal of Bodywork and Movement Therapies, 15*(2), 162–167.

Lerner, M. (1996). *Choices in healing: Integrating the best of conventional and complementary approaches to cancer.* Boston: MIT Press.

LeShan, L. (1994). *Cancer as a turning point: A handbook for people with cancer, their families, and health professionals.* New York: Plume.

May, R. (1994). *The courage to create.* New York: W. W. Norton & Company.

Monti, D., Peterson, C., Kunkel, E., Hauck, W., Peawuignot, E., Rhodes, L., & Brainard, G. (2006). A randomized, controlled trial of mindfulness-based art therapy (MBAT) for women with cancer. *Psychooncology, 15*(5), 363–373.

Morgan, N., Graves, K., Poggi, E., & Cheson, B. (2008). Implementing an expressive writing study in a cancer clinic. *The Oncologist, 13*(2), 196–204.

Pennebaker, J. (2004). *Writing to heal: A guided journal for recovering from trauma and emotional upheaval.* Wheat Ridge, CO: Center for Journal Therapy, Inc.

Pennebaker, J., & Evans, J. (2014). *Expressive writing: Words that heal.* Enumclaw, WA: Idyll Arbor.

Puig, A., Lee, S. M., Goodwin, L., & Sherrard, P. A. D. (2006). The efficacy of creative arts therapies to enhance emotional expression, spirituality and psychological well-being of newly diagnosed stage I and stage II breast cancer patients: a preliminary study: *Arts Psychotherapy, 33*(3), 218–228.

Richardson, M. M., Babiak-Vazquez, A. E., & Frenkel, M. A. (2008). Music therapy in a comprehensive cancer center. *Journal of the Society for Integrative Oncology, 6*(2), 76–81.

Rockwood-Lane, M. (2005). Spirit body healing – A hermeneutic, phenomenological study examining the lived experience of art and healing. *Cancer Nursing, 28*(4), 285–291.

Rollins, J., & Riccio, L. (2002). *Art is the heART: An arts-in-healthcare program for children and families in home and hospice care.* Washington, DC: WVSA Arts Connection.

Skeath, P., & Norris, S. (2013). The nature of life transforming changes among cancer survivors. *Qualitative Health Research 23,* 1155. Retrieved from http://qhr.sagepub.com/content/23/9/1155

Smith, G. J. W., Lilja, Å., & Salford, L. G. (2002). Creativity and breast cancer. *Creativity Research Journal, 14*(2), 157–162.

PART 5

Managing arts in healthcare programs for caregivers

16

USING THE ARTS TO CARE FOR PARAPROFESSIONAL AND FAMILY CAREGIVERS

Lynn Kable

Caregivers – people who care for others – contribute greatly to our society. Paid professional and paraprofessional caregivers are few compared to the large number of unpaid, informal caregivers to be found among families and friends of people requiring care. This chapter provides an overview of what is involved in paraprofessional and informal caregiving, discusses the pressures facing these groups of caregivers, and advocates for the importance of providing arts-based caring for caregiver programs. It is argued that artists helping caregivers learn to use music, story, dance, writing, or visual art to lessen their stress and enjoy life more provide a valuable service not only to the caregivers themselves, but also to our society as a whole.

After introducing and defining the field of caregiving, this chapter discusses how arts programs can contribute to the wellbeing of paraprofessional and family caregivers through educational and instrumental support; health screening, monitoring, and support; social support; and stress reduction activities. The chapter concludes with four examples of programs in the United States that effectively care for the caregiver.

Who are caregivers?

While no single definition exists for *caregivers* (or *carers* in the UK) or *caregiving*, the website of the Family Caregiver Alliance's National Center on Caregiving (2015) (see caregiver.org) defines an *informal caregiver* as "an unpaid individual (a spouse, partner, family member, friend, or neighbor) involved in assisting others with activities of daily living and/or medical tasks." In contrast, this organization defines *formal caregivers* as "paid care providers providing care in one's home or in a care setting (daycare, residential, care facility, etc.)." Researchers refer to *caregiving* as "the act of providing unpaid assistance and support to family members or acquaintances who have physical, psychological, or developmental needs. Caring for others generally takes on three forms: instrumental, emotional, and informational caring" (Caregiving, n.d.). The website www.caregivertoolkit.ca (*Caregiver toolkit*, n.d.) explains that the caregiving is associated with the responsibility for providing care in areas such as the following:

- Practical assistance with basic activities of daily living (e.g., housekeeping, shopping, meal preparation)
- Personal care (e.g., help with monitoring medication, bathing)
- Physical help (e.g., assistance with movement, supervision, direct medical care)
- Emotional and social support (e.g., visiting, transportation, talking about emotions)
- Finding and accessing services (e.g., housing, medical support)
- Behavioral support (e.g., communicating effectively, managing challenging behaviors)
- Financial help (e.g., financial support, managing finances)

Unpaid family, friends, and neighbors provide by far the most amount of caregiving in the United States. Hospice, religious groups, and civic programs also train and supervise volunteers to be caregivers. However, two formal groups of caregivers are also active in healthcare settings: professional caregivers, and paraprofessional caregivers. Highly trained professional caregivers, such as physicians and nurses, are key members of a caregiving team, but many less highly trained but paid paraprofessional caregivers are also instrumental to the provision of healthcare. Paraprofessional caregivers serve in such positions as home health aides, nursing assistants, and "sitters."

Common to all three groups of caregivers is that they provide continuous care over a long period of time to individuals with physical or mental illnesses or disabling conditions, who require assistance to conduct Activities of Daily Living (ADL). ADLs are basic self-care tasks that include feeding, toileting, selecting proper attire, grooming, maintaining continence, putting on clothes, bathing, walking, and transferring (such as moving from bed to wheelchair). Geriatric-care professionals often discuss ADLs in connection with Instrumental Activities of Daily Living (IADL), which are more complex skills needed to successfully live independently. IADLs include activities such as managing finances, handling transportation, shopping, preparing meals, using the telephone and other communication devices, managing medications, housework, and basic home maintenance (Kernisan & Scott, n.d.).

Informal Caregivers are unpaid family, neighbors, and friends who care for a chronically ill, disabled, or frail family member or friend. The US National Alliance for Family Caregiving and the American Association of Retired Persons (AARP) reported in 2009 that, in the past year, 65.7 million individuals had reported being informal caregivers. According to this study, caregivers spent an average of 20.4 hours per week providing care. In 2009, the typical family caregiver in the US was profiled as "a 49-year-old woman caring for her widowed 69-year-old mother who does not live with her. She is married and employed. Approximately 66% of family caregivers are women. More than 37% have children or grandchildren under 18 years old living with them" (Caregiving statistics, 2015). It is noteworthy that a 2010 MetLife study oft-cited on websites related to this topic found that twenty percent of employed female caregivers over fifty years old report symptoms of depression, compared to eight percent of their non-caregiving peers (National Alliance for Caregiving and MetLife, 2010).

Formal Caregivers with highly professional training include physicians, nurses, therapists, psychologists, and social workers. Hospitals, hospices, medical schools, and long-term care facilities have experienced loss of professional staff that they as employers attribute to caregiving issues, especially caregiver stress, burnout, and compassion fatigue. In this book, Chapter 17 discusses in detail these medical staff issues and ways in which arts programs may help healthcare institutions address these challenges.

Formal Paraprofessional Caregivers are paid individuals who provide hands-on assistance to dependent, frail, or disabled adults. The professional titles of these caregivers include certified nursing assistants, home care aides, companions, elder assistants, universal worker, home health aides, nurses aides, orderlies, carers, and "sitters." These individuals may work full-time or part-time, and may be hired privately or through an agency. They may also work in long-term care facilities, such as adult daycare centers, assisted living, or skilled nursing units. "The typical paraprofessional or formal caregiver is a middle-aged, single mother with a low educational level, who lives below or near poverty. The wages of nursing assistants and home health aides are among the lowest of any occupation in the U.S. They have few benefits. . . . There is a completely erroneous perception that their work is unskilled – that to do this work, you do not need a lot of skill" (Barbara Hogan, cited in Society for the Arts in Healthcare, 2003, p. 14).

Employers of paraprofessional caregivers note that further exacerbating caregiver stress on these individuals is the fact that many of these caregivers work for hire during the day and then go home and care for a frail family member the rest of the day, all night, and on weekends. In the United States, many paraprofessional caregivers are foreign-born or undereducated, with low English language skills. These caregivers are trained to do specific, highly repetitive tasks – which are often stressful – with patients who may be difficult and uncooperative. And, these caregivers often have two jobs to make ends meet for their family (Beverly Craft and Denise Scruggs, personal communication, summer 2014).

With the aging "baby boomer" population in the United States and the ever-increasing ability of clinical medicine to extend life, demand for all types of caregiving will certainly rise. An array of helpful websites for caregivers, as referenced above and in the references list of this chapter, as well as research reports, articles, and book publications (such as Baily, 1985; Renzenbrink, 2011) seek to attend to the self-care needs of caregivers. In 2003, the Society for the Arts in Healthcare together with the Society for the Arts in Healthcare Japan and Tanpopo-No-Yet Foundation published *Caring for Caregivers: A Grassroots USA-Japan Initiative*. Drawing on this publication and on current information provided in interviews by renowned arts in healthcare leaders,[1] this chapter focuses on the needs for self-care that exist among informal caregivers and paraprofessional caregivers, and discusses strategies for art program design and implementation to address these needs.

The importance of caring for caregiver programs

As with professional caregivers, discussed in Chapter 17, paraprofessional and family caregivers experience significant stress and burnout. Factors for burnout in these two groups of caregivers include demanding schedules, high physical and cognitive workload, inadequate preparation, varying work shifts, low social recognition, lack of financial resources, lack of support, role ambiguity, difficult client/patient behaviors, and coping with death and dying (Alkema, Linton & Davies, 2008; Hilliard, 2006). Informal, unpaid caregivers provide the most patient care in the United States, typically in addition to other full-time, demanding workloads and other family responsibilities. According to the *Evercare Survey of the Economic Downturn and Its Impact on Family Caregiving* (National Alliance for Caregiving and Evercare, 2009), "The value of the services family caregivers provide for 'free,' when caring for older adults, is estimated to be $375 billion a year. That is almost twice as much as is actually spent on homecare and nursing home services combined ($158 billion)." The financial impact of caregiving is significant on employers. "Using the average additional cost of a series of major health conditions (such as depression, hypertension, and diabetes) reported by employees with eldercare responsibilities and non-caregiving employees, the estimated average additional health cost to employers is 8% more for those with eldercare responsibilities. . . . When extrapolated to the business sector generally, this 8% differential in healthcare for caregiving employees is estimated conservatively as costing U.S. employers $13.4 billion per year" (National Alliance for Caregiving and MetLife, 2010).

Numerous studies show that self-care programs and activities are crucial for caregivers to be able to reduce stress and proactively address burnout. Sherman (2004) contends that self-care is a form of insulation against burnout and stress, and that maintaining the mind–body–spirit connection is important. Alkema, Linton, and Davies (2008) suggest specific self-care strategies: eating regularly (physical care), making time for self-reflection (psychological care), allowing oneself to cry (emotional care), being open to inspiration (spiritual care), taking time to form positive relationships with coworkers (workplace care), and striving for balance among work, family, relationships, play, and rest (balance). Keidel (2002, p. 204) similarly suggests that practical strategies for dealing with burnout include "feed[ing] your spiritual side," eating healthily and exercising, and maintaining a good work/personal life balance.

Arts programs designed to care for the caregiver can be very supportive of formal and informal caregivers alike. As Naj Wikoff stated in an interview with the author in summer 2014, "Because of the high cost of staff turnover, both in financial terms coupled with the loss of institutional memory, and the time required to train new personnel and for them to become fully familiarized with the institution, its culture and clients, a growing value of the arts to a hospital is in their ability to enhance job satisfaction, reduce job-related stress, and strengthen a sense of community. Programs credited with retaining even one nurse or doctor are often said to have paid their own way."

How can arts programs contribute to the wellbeing of caregivers?

Arts-based programs, initiatives, and activities can provide positive and cost-effective solutions to the caregiving challenges discussed above. These solutions tend to fall into four major categories: educational and instrumental support, health screening and monitoring, social support, and stress reduction activities.

Educational and instrumental support

Arts programs can provide opportunities for caregivers to learn new skills and techniques to support patients in ADLs and IADLs, and caregivers in requirements of their employment.

Many arts-based programs are now training caregivers in computer use to help in-home informal, volunteer, and paraprofessional caregivers combat feelings of isolation, to increase opportunities for education by professionals online, and for peer support. As a further expansion of technology in caregiver settings, an intriguing example is provided by Pauline Daniels: the Goodwin House in Alexandria, Virginia is currently having a young staff member develop and regularly integrate into patient care a particular "app" for an activity that staff and volunteers at any level can do with a resident.

Health screening, monitoring, and support

Respite and renewal programs can provide opportunities for informal and paraprofessional caregivers to attend to their own appointments and health needs, and to learn self-care skills.

Numerous arts-based respite programs provide a dual service to caregivers and the individuals for whom they provide care. These combine a regularly scheduled arts group for the individual in care with an opportunity for the caregiver to attend to appointments, run errands, exercise, or enjoy a social engagement. For example, Healing Arts Initiative (HAI) in New York City provides the opportunity for children with developmental disabilities to participate in visual and participatory performing arts experiences while their parents do needed chores (see hainyc.org for detailed program information).

Caregiver programs can take place at the same time in different parts of the same building for both caregivers and for older frail individuals in care. These programs can provide health-promoting arts activities, such as a dance or movement class or a storytelling workshop for the caregiver, while the person for whom they care takes part in less strenuous arts programs from collage-making to music. New York's Museum of Modern Art Department of Education established "Meet me at MoMA" (see www.moma.org/meetme/) as a special initiative to make museum visits enjoyable to both people with Alzheimer's and dementia and their care partners from private homes and from care facility settings. Between 2007 and 2014, MoMA's education staff ran and replicated in other museums access programs, including gallery visits and discussions for individuals with Alzheimer's and caregivers visiting together.

Retreat locations can be integrated into healthcare design as an important venue for respite and renewal. A retreat can be a room within a hospital or long-term care facility set aside for solitary thinking, and can be accessed by both formal and informal caregivers. It can be a healing garden (see Chapter 5) where caregivers sit, relax, and "de-stress" alone or with a friend. Retreats can also be an organized weekend or work-week session with peers to discuss difficult issues. For example, Aesthetics Inc. in San Diego, California designed and developed a twelve–step garden with artistically designed and built "steps" surrounding a central labyrinth for use of drug and alcohol patients and caregivers at McDonald Center at Scripps Hospital. The Smith Center for Healing and the Arts in Washington, DC, designed weekend physician retreats for oncologists. The retreats included meditation, sandtray (based on the work of Carl Jung), and writing, and encouraged physicians to give themselves permission to grieve for their own patients who had died (Society for the Arts in Healthcare, 2003, pp. 28, 34–37).

Recognizing that spiritual care is a crucial aspect of caring for caregivers, aesthetically designed retreat locations also provide environments in which family caregivers and professional and paraprofessional caregivers can engage in prayer or meditation. Another example from Scripps Mercy Hospital in San Diego is a prayer bowl outside of Holy Family Chapel. Staff, family, and patients are encouraged to write a request for prayer and drop it into the specially designed, large, beautiful glass prayer bowl (Kable, 2008, slide 24).

Social support

Recreational arts and retreat programs can provide opportunities to participate in social arts events, and to share feelings and experiences with peers.

Rage and anger are emotions that many caregivers feel, but many do not give themselves permission to express. An interesting example of an arts-based channel for expressing rage comes from the Koubou Shoubu long-term care facility in Kagoshima, Japan. Koubou Shoubu, a residence and shelter workshop, has extremely high standards for beautiful furniture that is created by caregiving carpenters, then "distressed" by residents with intellectual challenges. The facility also has a caregiver's "shout" group, which is a performance group similar to a chorus, but which uses syllables shouted aggressively instead of tuneful music (Society for the Arts in Healthcare, 2003, pp. 130–132).

Stress reduction activities

A wide array of arts activities can contribute to stress reduction and work-life balance. Such activities include arts projects, gardening, choral singing, instrumental music, visiting museums, and participating in memorial ceremonies. Opportunities for caregivers to express their feelings in art, sandtray, poetry, prose, and storytelling can also provide significant emotional support. Excellent examples of well-organized arts-based programs focused on providing recreational outlets to caregivers abound, of which a few are profiled below.

Duke University Medical Center's (DUMC) Cultural Services Program established its first major, ongoing "Caring for Caregivers Projects" in the 1990s with a four-pronged effort celebrating the arts. First, an annual staff musical, featuring DUMC staff members from all departments and all levels of staff performed with a professional director, a full orchestra, and a conductor. Second, a sculpture garden for viewing and personal retreat was created outside the staff cafeteria. Major sculpture pieces were commissioned or purchased by the Medical Center. Third, an annual DUMC staff art show took place in a hospital parking lot, with prizes in numerous categories from oil and watercolor painting to drawing and jewelry making. Fourth, a biannual staff and community poetry contest was established, supervised by a part-time hospital staff poet, who also conducted a lunchtime poet's round table (Society for the Arts in Healthcare, 2003, pp. 98–100).

The University of Michigan Hospitals Gifts of Art Program received funding from the state's Arts Council to hold a series of caring for caregivers activities for all staff and all family caregivers on all three shifts in the hospital over a period of about one week. Activities included art created on each shift and on each ward by having staff and family caregivers paint on "canvases" of old hospital laundry, which were then displayed by hanging each piece on a clothesline in each hallway. Drum circles led by musicians and hospital music therapists were held on each shift – during the day and evening shifts in the courtyards, and at night in the soundproofed cafeteria (Kable, 2008, slides 33–34).

On a smaller institutional scale, the Goodwin House in Alexandria, Virginia, provides many levels of geriatric care, from residential and assisted living to memory support and twenty-four-hour nursing care. Goodwin House capitalizes on the diverse and international nature of its professional and non-professional staff and its residents in its activities. Goodwin House sponsors a day to wear one's own ethnic clothes, and a day to share international foods, days in which people can take pride in their own culture. Goodwin House also sponsors several annual staff and patient talent shows in which everyone is encouraged to display their abilities (Pauline Daniels, personal communication, summer 2014).

With these preliminary examples of how arts-based programs can contribute to formal and informal caregiver wellbeing, the remainder of the chapter now profiles a few specific caregiver support ideas and programs as provided through interviews with several leaders in arts in healthcare management.

Example 1: Encouraging paraprofessional caregivers to bring creativity to their work

The Goodwin House, introduced above, encourages paraprofessionals to creatively engage with each resident or patient at the time of delivering care. Pauline Daniels, the facility's director of life enrichment, suggests, "Encourage paraprofessionals to be more creative in their job activities, and to talk less and listen more. If words aren't working, sing! You will get the resident's attention. Put on music and sing to the resident, or tell a story while the individual is getting dressed. Try to use physical gestures instead of words if it seems you are not communicating effectively verbally. Also – a different kind of touch, such as less direct and more intimate touch – rubbing of the resident's hand or brushing hair out of their face and looking at them in the eye instead of repositioning their body by simply lifting them. Take a moment to engage them."

Daniels continues by explaining that "the training that CNAs [certified nursing assistants] receive now is extremely task oriented – the very antithesis of creative personal choices. Sometimes adding creative activities makes paraprofessionals feel that there is one more thing they have to do, when they feel they don't have the time to complete all their tasks now. By helping them to accomplish their required tasks in a more creative way they can also be more efficient because they get less resistance from patients. Stress-reducing creative play has to be re-introduced. I try to speak about creative activities as positive engagement, such as you might have with your own family."

Daniels says that she tends to start with an activity that uses the senses, and encourages caregivers to appeal to each individual patient's strengths, be they sight, sound, smell, hearing, or touch. She likes "short-term activities lasting fifteen minutes, such as reaching into a bag to touch something and trying to guess what it is. Something anyone can do."

Example 2: Supporting informal caregivers for individuals living with cancer

In a summer 2014 interview, Shanti Norris, who runs a cancer support program as executive director of Smith Center for Healing and the Arts in Washington, DC, stated that she has found that caregivers in the cancer community can be equally or more stressed than the cancer survivor for whom they are caring. She asserts that caregivers are in great need of relaxing arts activities, but that it is "harder to get caregivers in the door of the program than cancer survivors." Caregivers, she says, are often asked about the condition of someone for whom they are caring, but they are less often asked about themselves. Norris suggests: "It is particularly important to give opportunities for caregivers to tell their stories. Writing is near the top of my list of arts activities, and also storytelling."

The Smith Center also sponsors activities and retreats in which cancer survivors and their caregivers are encouraged to participate together. Norris sometimes leads a visual arts exercise, in which a group separates into a cancer survivor and their caregiver/partner working together. One person lies down on a large piece of paper and the other person traces an outline of their body from about hip height, up around the head and back down on the other side. Then the partners switch, and the process is repeated. Norris leads the entire group in a guided visualization, asking, "What do you each need for your healing? What in your body needs to be healed? What might your own healing look like?" Norris points out that "cancer is not the only thing that needs to be healed. There can be relationship issues or childhood trauma that is unresolved." Finally, in this exercise, each person is asked to do a self-portrait within the tracing of their body drawn by their partner, based on what they saw and felt during the guided visualization.

Example 3: Supporting formal caregivers in creative music performance

The University of Michigan Hospitals' Gifts of Art Program coordinates a Life Sciences Orchestra, comprised of seventy-five to eighty orchestra members who are employees of the hospital or faculty in Life Sciences at the University of Michigan. Musicians include physicians, fellows, post docs, medical students, nursing students, and many different categories of healthcare professionals. According to Gifts of Art director Elaine Sims, the Life Sciences Orchestra held its first concert in 2001 and now performs two concerts a year for an audience of about 2,000 people per concert, without charge to the audience. In order to keep the highest quality music possible, a conductor is brought in from the university's prestigious doctoral program in Orchestral Conducting, and the assistant conductor is recruited from the master's program. The conductor is paid a salary, and the assistant receives an honorarium. Orchestra members must audition for the conductor annually. Music for each concert is selected by the conductor, assistant conductor, and the executive committee of the orchestra. Each year, the orchestra chooses an individual from university leadership to introduce each concert. Gifts of Art commissions professional original art for the poster and program graphics.

Doctors who are members of the orchestra have told Sims and others that "it is very special to be among our own community making music." Students say that they enjoy playing side by side with world-famous professors and physicians. The orchestra is multi-generational, ranging in age from pre-med undergraduates to emeritus professors in their eighties. According to Sims, "The orchestra is now used as a recruiting tool for the University, the Medical School, and the Medical

FIGURE 16.1 Life Sciences Orchestra of University of Michigan Health Systems in Performance

Center. An evaluation psychiatrist did an impact study on feelings of connectedness and stress reduction that showed positive results."

Example 4: Caring for caregivers of people who are dying, or who are grieving for those who have recently died

According to consultant and thanatologist Sandra Bertman (personal communication, 2014), building on her published work of 2015, 1999, and 1991, "Engaging in the arts, as participant or observer, is in itself a creative act. This is often catalyst enough not only to arouse our senses, but to stimulate our imaginations, causing us to wonder, to analyze, to feel connected (or disconnected), to be inspired. The engagement with art, whether through reading or writing, viewing or drawing, listening or enacting, involves attention, analysis, identification, catharsis, and insight. The beauty of the process is its openness to interpretations, to the way any of us – therapist, nurse, patient, client, colleague – takes it in and uses it for oneself, in personal and professional contexts."

Bertman (2011; 2015) suggests that, in our western culture, traditionally, therapy's goal was to resolve the patient's problems. Consistent with the medical model, even art therapy focuses on diagnosis, analysis, and interpretation. Helping the patient or client to gain insight through the imagery they drew was the goal. This has evolved to a fundamental belief of the arts and healthcare movement: that an artist can be with another person just to make art, and that the process in itself is

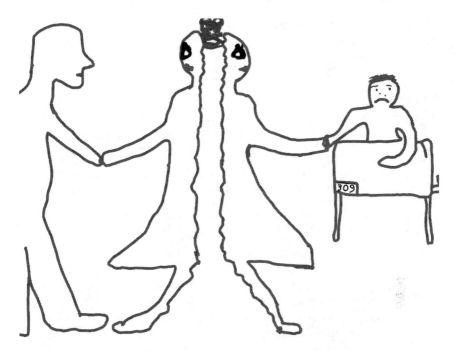

FIGURE 16.2 Divided Allegiances of an Oncology Nurse

healing. No outcome measurement other than the client's experience of the process as being meaningful is necessary.

A Chinese proverb cited by Bertman (1991) says, "You cannot prevent the birds of sorrow from flying overhead; but you can prevent them from building nests in your hair" (p. 88). The subtle implication made by Bertman (1991, pp. 101–166) is that creative healing is accessible to everyone, and that it is less a question of treatment than about freeing the creative spirit within. We, too – doctors, nurses, social workers, chaplains, volunteers – have no immunity to the birds of sorrow. In fact, our ability to care is in direct proportion to our vulnerability and for us to stay authentic in our caregiving roles, we need periodic booster shots.

While Bertman's scholarship is focused on the use of arts and humanities in support of caregivers in end-of-life settings, her work emphasizes the importance of caregiver wellbeing throughout the full spectrum of healthcare settings.

Conclusion

This chapter has provided an introduction to the types of formal and informal caregivers active in the United States. Professional, paraprofessional, and family caregivers alike have significant needs for self-care that can be addressed through arts-based initiatives and programming. This chapter has profiled examples of several excellent arts programs that meet the needs of caregivers, and offers in the reference list below some key sources for further introductory reading on this topic.

Note

1 The author thanks Sandra Bertman, www.sandrabertman.com; Beverly Craft, owner and geriatric care manager at Care OPTIONS Plus, LLC in Lynchburg, VA; Pauline Daniels, director of Life Enrichment, Goodwin House in Alexandria, VA; Shanti Norris, co-founder and Executive Director/CEO, Smith Center for Healing and the Arts in Washington, DC; Judy Rollins, www.rollinsandassoc.com; Denise Scruggs, director, Beard Center on Aging at Lynchburg College in Lynchburg, Virginia, www.lynchburg.edu/beard-center-aging; Elaine Sims, director, Gifts of Art Program at the University of Michigan Health System in Ann Arbor, Michigan; and Naj Wikoff, founder and President of Creative Healing, in Keene Valley, New York, for participating in interviews in summer 2014 and for generously providing information on current exemplary practices in caring for caregivers.

References

Alkema, K., Linton, J., & Davies, R. (2008). A study of the relationship between self-care, compassion satisfaction, compassion fatigue, and burnout among hospice professionals. *Journal of Social Work in End-of-Life & Palliative Care, 4*(2), 101–119.

Bailey, R. (1985). *Coping with stress in caring.* Boston, MA: Blackwell Scientific Publications.

Bertman, S. L. (1991). *Facing death: Images, insights and interventions.* New York: Taylor & Francis.

Bertman, S. (1999). *Grief and the healing arts: Creativity as therapy.* New York: Baywood.

Bertman, S. (2011). Expressive arts and thanatology: An image a day. *In ADEC Forum, 37*(1), 1–7.

Bertman, S. (2015). Using the arts and humanities with the dying, bereaved, . . . and ourselves. In J. Stillion & T. Attig (Eds.), *Death, dying and bereavement: Contemporary perspectives, institutions, and practices* (pp. 245–260). New York: Springer.

Caregiver toolkit. (n.d.) Retrieved from www.caregivertoolkit.ca

Caregiving, definition(s) of. (n.d.) *Work and family researchers network.* Retrieved from https://workfamily.sas.upenn.edu/glossary/c/caregiving-definitions

Caregiving statistics. (2015). *Caregiver Action Network.* Retrieved from www.caregiveraction.org/statistics

Family Caregiver Alliance, National Center on Caregiving. (2015). Retrieved from https://caregiver.org

Kable, L. (2008). *Caring for caregivers, professional, formal and informal through use of the arts, humanities, design, exercise, education, and peer support* [Webinar]. Washington, DC: Society for the Arts and Healthcare Consulting Service.

Keidel, G. C. (2002). Burnout and compassion fatigue among hospice caregivers. *American Journal of Hospice and Palliative Medicine, 19,* 200–205.

National Alliance for Caregiving and Evercare. (2009). *Evercare survey of the economic downturn and its impact on family caregiving.* Retrieved from www.caregiving.org/data/EVC_Caregivers_Economy_Report%20FINAL_4–28–09.pdf

National Alliance for Caregiving and MetLife Mature Market Institute. (2010). *MetLife study of working caregivers and employer health costs.* Retrieved from www.metlife.com/

assets/cao/mmi/publications/studies/2010/mmi-working-caregivers-employers-health-care-costs.pdf

National Alliance for Caregiving in collaboration with AARP (2009). *Caregiving in the United States.* Retrieved from www.caregiving.org/data/Caregiving_in_the_US_2009_full_report.pdf

Renzenbrink, I. (2011). *Caregiver stress and staff support in illness, dying, and bereavement.* New York: Oxford University Press.

RN turnover costs hospitals an estimated $9.75 billion annually [Blog post]. (2010). *INSPIRE by Alter+Care.* Retrieved from www.altergroup.com/alter-care-blog/index.php/healthcare/rn-turnover-costs/

Sherman, D. W. (2004). Nurses' stress and burnout. *The American Journal of Nursing, 104*(5), 48–57.

Society for the Arts in Healthcare and Society for the Arts in Healthcare Japan, Tanpopo-No-Ye Foundation. (2003). *Caring for caregivers: A grassroots USA-Japan initiative.* Washington, DC: Society for the Arts in Healthcare.

17

ARTS PROGRAMS FOR MEDICAL STAFF

Nancy Morgan

Twenty-first century healthcare imposes new burdens on medical staff that impact the wellbeing of patients, organizations, and the professionals themselves. The ongoing challenge of caring for very sick people is exacerbated by corporate and government-driven demand for greater efficiency and cost savings. Fewer staff must accomplish more in less time. Staff must be all things to all people: patients, management, and government regulators. This squeeze produces inordinate amounts of stress that manifest as burnout, turnover, and medical error.

Studies referenced throughout this chapter suggest that wellness programs may alleviate stress and provide ongoing self-care training. Arts programs for staff have been implemented at major hospitals to alleviate all forms of stress. Georgetown University Hospital offers one of the most comprehensive, system-wide arts programs for medical and support staff. Georgetown Arts and Humanities Programs will serve as exemplars in this chapter that identifies primary medical staff issues, their scope and significance, and arts programs that address these issues by helping staff manage the physical and emotional demands unique to today's healthcare environment. The Georgetown model will serve as a template for crafting recommendations to establish staff arts programs in healthcare settings.

Medical staff issues

Burnout, high turnover rates and medical error are serious problems facing all medical institutions. According to research, these interrelated issues may be caused by long hours in intense work environments, poor management, and lack of collaborative support (McHugh, 2011). Additional causes cited by Hilliard (2006) are dealing with "difficult" or "demanding" patients, unfavorable environmental conditions, and coping with death and dying. When working with healthcare administrators to develop arts programs for medical staff, all of these should be considered.

Burnout

Burnout is a term used to describe the physical and emotional effects of extremely demanding work with very sick people, coupled with inadequate training to manage cumulative levels of stress. Burnout manifests as emotional exhaustion, loss of compassion, and feelings of reduced competence (Khamisa, Peltzer, & Oldenburg, 2013). A unique form of burnout, called *compassion fatigue*, is defined as "a deep physical, emotional, and spiritual exhaustion accompanied by acute emotional pain" (Alkema, Linton, & Davies, 2008, p. 103). Burnout and compassion fatigue can negatively affect a professional caregiver's ability to "provide services, maintain personal and professional relationships, leading to high turnover rates, loss of productivity, and diminished capacity to enjoy life" (Showalter, 2010, p. 240).

Nurses may be more vulnerable to burnout and compassion fatigue due to prolonged personal contact of an emotional nature with patients (Coetzee & Klopper, 2010; Khamisa et al., 2013). Negative health outcomes include anxiety, depression, somatic symptoms, and social dysfunction (Khamisa et al., 2013), which can result in low productivity, high turnover rates, adverse patient events, job-related errors, poor service, and lower patient satisfaction ratings (Hilliard, 2006; Khamisa et al., 2013). Pressure to meet rigorous efficiency and cost-saving standards can tie the hands of even the best managers and practitioners, creating emotionally unsustainable conditions that impact quality of care. Mhyren, Ekeberg, and Stokland (2013) suggest in a study of job satisfaction and burnout that the problem is insufficient time to recover from stressful events. Studies of significant factors associated with burnout suggest participation in wellness and stress management programs may lower incidence of burnout (Alkema, Linton, & Davies, 2008; Amoufo, Hanballi, Patel, & Singh, 2015; Potter, Deshields, & Rodriguez, 2013; Romani & Askar, 2014; Showalter, 2010).

Staff turnover

The correlation between burnout and staff turnover is significant. Laporta's, Burns's, and Doig's (2005) report on turnover in ICU units suggests lack of positive team culture, good working relationships, and supportive resources, including stress management programs, are responsible for high turnover rates, recruitment challenges, and crippling costs of replacing highly trained staff. When staff reach the breaking point and management fails to address concerns, leaving seems to be the only solution.

Emotional exhaustion is associated with a higher intention to quit among nurses (Myhren et al., 2013). Studies of nurse turnover indicate the cost of advertising, recruiting, training, and compensating for lost productivity can add up to roughly $60,000.00 per nurse and significantly impact patient mortality (Hayes, 2006). "Nationally, it is estimated that 1.3 million RNs are employed by hospitals. With an average turnover rate of approximately 15 percent, that translates to 195,000 nurse positions turning over every year at an estimated total cost of $9.75 billion" (RN, 2010).

Researchers Stichler (2009) and Applebaum, Fowler, Fiedler, Osinubi, and Robson (2010) point to the physical work environment as a factor in turnover and other work performance issues. "There is mounting evidence that the physical work environment affects job performance, job satisfaction, employee injuries, worker behaviors, communication patterns, employee fatigue, employee error rates, and physical and psychological stress" (Stichler, 2009, p. 181). According to Applebaum (2010), "The physical environment may influence a nurse's perceived level of stress and job satisfaction, which ultimately influences intention to turnover. Environmental factors such as noise, air quality, light, toxic exposures, temperature, humidity, and aesthetics have been examined for their effects on both patients and workers" (p. 324).

High turnover rates have great implications not only for the quality, consistency, and stability of services provided to people in need, but also for the working conditions of the remaining staff, in such outcomes as increased workloads, disrupted team cohesion, and decreased morale (Hayes, 2006). Providing and taking part in a variety of self-care activities appears to be key to prevention of medical staff burnout and turnover (Alkema et al., 2008; Coetzee & Klopper, 2010; Sherman, 2004; Showalter, 2010).

Medical error

Preventable medical errors are the scourge of the healthcare culture. Identified as systemic in the report, *To Err is Human: Building a Safer Health System* (2000), estimates suggest that 98,000 people die annually as a result of medical error. Medical errors manifest most often as inaccuracies in medication dosage and surgical procedure, according to the Minnesota Hospital Association's *Time Out Guide*. Grober and Bohnen (2005) define medical error as "an act of omission or commission in planning or execution that contributes or could contribute to an unintended result" (p. 42). Although the original report suggests system failures are primarily to blame rather than human wrongdoing, subsequent studies point to poor communication, exhaustion, and inadequate protocol that may impact a patient's health. In other words, stressful working conditions that lead to burnout and turnover also endanger patient lives. In a study of the causes of medical error among medical residents, the three manifestations of burnout – emotional exhaustion, depersonalization, and lower feelings of personal accomplishment – were associated with medical error (Kang, Lihm, & Kong, 2013).

In addition to the impact of medical error on patients and their families, studies have shown that doctors accused of the error suffer as secondary victims. A study by Stangierski et al. (2012) reports that symptoms of burnout that frequently cause medical error intensify after the incident. "Having made an error a doctor may react with distress, self-doubt, a sense of loss of self, fear or depression and shame that linger for a long time, predisposing a doctor to professional burnout that in turn, following a vicious circle, promotes the foregoing" (p. 572). Burnout appears to be the nucleus of a network of problems plaguing the healthcare community that demands attention at the education, prevention, and treatment levels for the optimum functioning of entire healthcare systems. From the causes of burnout to the symptoms and consequences, a trail of evidence suggests possible solutions.

The arts as antidotes: strategies for improving wellbeing and job performance

The arts play a significant role in reducing burnout, turnover, and medical error by addressing their causes (Aycock & Boyle, 2009; O'Callaghan, 2009; Popkin et al., 2011; Repar, 2007). Introducing creative breaks before, during, and after the work day that provide physical and emotional outlets may alleviate work pressures, creating a humane, collaborative, and aesthetically appealing environment where medical staff can be at and do their best. All programs in dance, music, visual art, theater, and writing provide multiple enhancements to wellbeing. Three program examples from Georgetown University Hospital's Arts and Humanities Program demonstrate how the arts effectively address these systemic problems.

Painting to prevent burnout

The manager of a busy oncology inpatient wing was approached about hosting a visiting artist who would spend two hours each week in the nurses' station, teaching painting. The manager's response was polite but firm. She did not want to waste the artist's time. "Our nurses are too busy." With consent to do a trial run, the artist set up canvases, paints, and brushes around the table. One by one, nurses sat down during breaks, painted a few petals on a sunflower and returned to their patients, smiling, relaxed.

"Your patient called for you, let me find out what she needs while you finish that flower." Teamwork and collegiality were improved, according to the nurse manager. Pride in the colorful murals that beautified the hallways and patient

FIGURE 17.1 Nevin Bossart Leads Painting Class in Oncology Nurses' Station, Georgetown University Hospital

rooms was significant. "That's the panel I painted," a nurse points out, beaming. Nurses arrange their shifts to be sure they are scheduled to work on art day.

Partnering with management to reduce turnover

Expressive writing, or recording thoughts and feelings about life events, may produce health benefits like improved memory, better sleep quality, help processing traumatic events, or fewer intrusive thoughts that may impact focus on patient care (Frisina, Borod, & Lepore, 2004). Several decades of research on writing and health reveal a multitude of benefits and few negative outcomes (Lepore & Smyth, 2002). The nurse educator requested journals for all new nurses and instruction for nurse managers on how to facilitate expressive writing sessions throughout the year as part of the nurses' training. Each education session ended with reflection time, thirty minutes to record thoughts and feelings about the new instruction, as well as personal topics. Establishing a habit of writing to address work and personal issues serves as an accessible and cost-efficient coping tool that can relieve stress and improve mental clarity.

Further efforts to help nurses cope with the stressors that lead to turnover were carried out in partnership with the Josie King Foundation, an organization dedicated to reducing medical error with evidence-based education programs for doctors and nurses. Sorrel King initiated a number of projects, including *The Nurse's Journal Project* (King, Wesol, & Sexton, 2007). As an adjunct to the Georgetown Lombardi expressive writing program, a series of workshops that engage nurses in the practice of writing was designed and tested using the nurses' journals distributed to hospitals by the Josie King Foundation. Many nurses initially resisted writing and were reluctant to participate. They soon discovered that writing thoughts and feelings was cathartic, helping them address and process distracting personal and professional issues and clear their minds. Nurses commented in post-writing evaluations: "I felt stressed at the beginning of writing and relaxed at the end;" and "I feel like I understand things better after I write them down."

The nurse manager of one group reported that she "noticed a marked difference in staff interactions and morale" after completing the writing workshop series. The Foundation produced a *Guide to Nurse's Journal Facilitation*, a step-by-step guide to enable nurse managers to lead writing groups. Teaming up with nurse educators, nurse managers, and the Josie King Foundation, tools for self-expression and self-care became part of nurses' orientation and ongoing training at Georgetown University Hospital.

Stretch breaks enhance US time out strategies for reducing medical error

US hospitals have introduced a *Time Out* procedure to reduce incidents of medical error. Staff are required to pause and take a moment to review a checklist of information related to the patient awaiting a procedure to insure they are focused, alert, and ready to administer the correct treatment. More than a checklist, it is behavior modification, a re-scripting of pre-surgery events that counteracts system inadequacies and pressures to fit more procedures in each day to improve efficiency and cut costs (Minnesota Hospital Association).

The pre-surgery "time out," as described by the Minnesota Safe Surgery Coalition, requires that all activity cease. The surgeon engages the team, and each member of the team in turn describes their role in the procedure. Anyone may call a safety time out. Eye contact is required at all times. Active listening eliminates multitasking. The time out takes one minute.

Georgetown University Hospital takes the *Time Out* practice to a new level with *Ready to Move*. This five-minute stretch activity led by a dance instructor engages both body and mind, alleviates exhaustion and distraction, and encourages teamwork and full staff participation, all hallmarks of improved patient safety initiatives. Plus, it is fun and therefore mood-enhancing, cathartic, community building, and regularly repeatable to assist in reducing medical error as needed. *Ready to Move* ensures a thorough physical and emotional respite between patient interactions. The dance instructor assumes the role of team leader, requiring complete attention and disengagement from all other stimuli. Could the stretch program reduce medical error and save lives? Parallels between the objectives and procedures associated with *Ready to Move* and *Time Out* suggest that this possibility merits investigation.

FIGURE 17.2 Daniel Burkholder Leads Staff Stretch Break in Intensive Care Unit, Georgetown University Hospital

Implementing staff arts programs in a healthcare setting

Arts and Humanities Programs for staff at Georgetown University Hospital serve as a model for similar program design and implementation in other healthcare institutions. In the remainder of this chapter, a number of elements are presented that have contributed to the success and sustainability of these programs.

Administrative support

Many hospital arts programs are initiated and supported by a CEO or other high-level manager who experiences firsthand the benefits of staff arts programs and serves as the program's leading advocate. Strong allies in key departments like human resources, nursing, and physician administration are vital to the implementation and ongoing support and participation in staff arts programs. Hospital managers need to understand how programs meet their primary objectives. CEOs and presidents must be armed with facts, figures, and photographs to make the case for staff arts programs to shareholders and the greater community. Present clear goals that mirror the goals of the organization. Engage management in hands-on activities and invite them to observe events and talk with staff about their impressions.

Scale

Start small with a visible event that demonstrates the value to staff, board, and patients. Show how this activity leads to improvements in mood, team spirit, attitude toward work, and fewer sick leave requests over time.

Funding

Most programs begin with outside funding, a grant, foundation gift, fundraiser, or donation from a family with a history of support for the hospital. Any of these sources can help jumpstart a program, providing evidence to attract additional benefactors. Local arts councils and hospital charities can provide modest seed grants.

Management

A full-time director of arts in healthcare onsite ensures program quality, inclusiveness, and equitable program distribution. Telling the story through photographs, testimony, attendance figures, behavior, and statistical changes helps establish arts programs as essential to staff wellbeing and the smooth and efficient running of the organization. Networking with colleagues at other institutions promotes cost sharing and an exchange of ideas, contributing to excellence in the field of arts in healthcare.

Program design

Arts activities should have universal appeal and not require any prior knowledge of an art form. Care must be taken to avoid exclusivity in the form of language or instruction that may inhibit full staff engagement. Programs should fit comfortably in the space with sufficient materials provided for the number of expected participants. Program length should reflect the amount of time designated for staff break. Provisions should be made for staff unable to attend. Extra supplies and individual art kits containing materials and instructions can be distributed to absent members.

Program location: meet them where they are

How can busy medical staff in high-pressure work environments find time to engage in the arts? The answer is to meet them where they are – during meetings, at lunch, before or after work, and in the heart of the workplace. Performances can be located to benefit the entire community. Writing and yoga may require some degree of privacy, although visibility raises awareness and helps increase participation.

Everyone has to eat

Arts events that center around mealtime may generate interest. Caring for the Caregiver: The Art of Self Care is a monthly event offering cancer center staff a nutritious lunch and workshops in creative forms of self-care by guest artists. Painting, singing, gentle yoga, cooking, writing, therapeutic music, or mask-making fill an hour's time between bites of food and light-hearted conversation. "I'm not talented!" excuses disappear as the joy of the art-making process takes over. Program objectives like work respite, stress reduction, and socialization are easily met while participants acquire an arsenal of skills for ongoing self-care.

Retreat

Many nurses simply cannot take time to engage in arts programs during the workday. Whether due to personal work ethic, unsupportive management, or the nature of their work schedule, a work-time respite isn't feasible. A nurses' retreat day offers a variety of art forms that nurture the spirit, promote creative expression, and restore vitality. The event is announced several months in advance to provide sufficient lead-time for leave requests. Retreats take place in pleasant non-work settings, infused with nature. A nutritious lunch, time for socializing, and artist-led activities help nurses focus on personal needs, affirm a sense of self, express emotions, and recalibrate priorities to reflect better personal care. Retreats can be the most valuable arts in healthcare program with long-term impact on participants. "My nurses were smiling and chatting about the retreat for weeks after the retreat. They are more cooperative and collaborative in their work."

Screening, training, and supporting artists

Artists who work with staff in healthcare settings must be able to function with limited space, interruptions, and distractions. A chorus of beepers ring as participants rush in and out. Artists must understand they are part of a complex care team. Priorities may require a program be moved, shortened, delayed, or canceled. In other words, artists must thrive in unpredictable circumstances, understand when a health crisis takes precedence over art-making, and not take any of these disruptions personally.

Artists should excel in their discipline as practitioners and teachers, helping participants over the "I'm not talented" threshold toward relaxation and enjoyment of the art-making process. Care must be taken to be positive and avoid any sense of competition or unattainable standards. Everyone is presumed a beginner and treated with patience and good humor.

Few artists have medical training and may find work in healthcare settings stressful. Regular check-ins, individually with the program director and in group settings with other artists, encourages the open expression of thoughts and feelings about hospital sights and sounds that may be unsettling. Going beyond words, artists can take turns facilitating art-making for fellow artists to prevent burnout and turnover in their own community.

Program promotion

All internal and external communication channels should be utilized to promote arts programs and enable participation. Establish clear objectives. Is the primary program goal creative expression? Stress relief? Improved aesthetics? Reduced turnover? Use organization websites, electronic calendars, list serves, and department bulletin boards to announce and update programs. Photographs of staff engaged in art-making entice other departments to sign up for a program.

Organize an annual staff morale program orientation: a splashy, visible, accessible event that allows the staff to interact with artists, sign up for programs, and take brochures back to their departments to share with colleagues.

Celebrate the leaders

Not all department managers appreciate or take time for arts programs for their staff. Those who do are rewarded with improved mood, greater cooperation, and increased teamwork. They serve as a model for the entire facility and should be recognized. Their engagement assures staff that arts activities are an accepted part of the workday that is approved by institutional leadership.

When the dance instructor visits the pediatric clinic or the food service department, the managers of both programs immediately come out of their offices, announce to staff that it is time to stretch, and make sure everyone shows up. Those managers participate fully and their staff engage in stretching with confidence, knowing their managers approve of and support staff efforts to be at their best for themselves and for the people in their care.

Evaluation

How can staff programs be measured? Numbers of participants can be recorded to note changes over time. Staff complete evaluations, grading aspects of the program like quality of the presenter, level of enjoyment, likelihood of pursuing the activity on their own, and changes in mood during or after the program. Continued research assessing the impact of staff arts programs on burnout, medical error, and turnover will strengthen the case for arts programs for healthcare staff and contribute to sustainability.

Conclusion

Medical staff face many challenges when engaging in patient care, impeding the ability to provide optimum care. The rigors of modern healthcare produce burnout, turnover, and medical error, three problems that threaten the quality of healthcare. As demonstrated by the Georgetown University Hospital's Arts and Humanities Programs, arts programs for staff can enhance morale, generate team spirit, and improve physical and emotional wellbeing through creative expression and environmental aesthetics. These programs provide an antidote to medical staff issues and contribute to the overall quality of life of the healthcare community. Georgetown University's experience with arts in healthcare programs suggest that the arts can help hospitals meet key objectives related to efficiency, cost savings, staff morale, and patient safety. Arts programs for medical staff are essential to the optimum functioning of staff in all healthcare facilities, and provide a competitive edge when recruiting new staff.

References

Alkema, K., Linton, J., & Davies, R. (2008). A study of the relationship between self-care, compassion satisfaction, compassion fatigue and burnout among hospice professionals. *Journal of Social Work in End-of-Life & Palliative Care, 4*(2), 101–119.

Amoufo, E., Hanballi, N., Patel, A., & Singh, P. (2015, March). What are the significant factors associated with burnout in doctors? *Occupational Medicine, 65*(2), 117–121.

Applebaum, D., Fowler, S., Fiedler, N., Osinubi, O., & Robson, M. (2010). The impact of environmental factors on nursing stress, job satisfaction, and turnover intention. *Journal of Nursing Administration, 40*, 323–328.

Aycock, N., & Boyle, D. (2009). Interventions to manage compassion fatigue in oncology nursing. *Clinical Journal of Oncology Nursing, 13*(2), 183–191.

Coetzee, S.K., & Klopper, H.C. (2010). Compassion fatigue within nursing practice: A concept analysis. *Nursing and Health Sciences, 12*, 235–243.

Frisina, P.G., Borod, J.C., & Lepore, S.J. (2004). A meta-analysis of the effects of written emotional disclosure on the health outcomes of clinical populations. *The Journal of Nervous and Mental Disease, 192*, 629–634.

Grober, E. D., & Bohnen, J. (2005). Defining medical error. *Canadian Journal of Surgery, 48*(1), 39–44.

Hayes, L. (2006). Nurse turnover, a literature review. *International Journal of Nursing Studies, 43*(2).

Hilliard, R. E. (2006). The effect of music therapy sessions on compassion fatigue and team building of professional hospice caregivers. *The Arts in Psychotherapy, 33*, 395–401.

Kang, E. K., Lihm, H. S., & Kong, E. H. (2013). Association of intern and resident burnout with self-reported medical errors. *Korean Journal of Family Medicine, 34*(1), 36–42.

Khamisa, N., Peltzer, K., & Oldenburg, B. (2013). Burnout in relation to specific contributing factors and health outcomes among nurses: A systematic review. *International Journal of Environmental Research, 10*(6), 2214–2240.

King, S., Wesol, A., & Sexton, J. (2007). *Nurse's Journal.* Josie King Foundation. Retrieved from http://www.josieking.org/nursesjournal#sthash.ZKimEwyl.dpuf

Laporta, D., Burns, J., & Doig, C. J. (2005). Bench-to-bedside review: Dealing with increased intensive care unit staff turnover: a leadership challenge. *Critical Care, 9*(5), 454–458.

Lepore, S., & Smyth, J. (Eds.). (2002). *The writing cure: How expressive writing promotes health and emotional well-being.* Washington, DC: American Psychological Association.

McHugh, M. D., Kutney-Lee, A., Cimiotti, J. P., Sloane, D. M., & Aiken, L. H. (2011). Nurses' widespread job dissatisfaction, burnout and frustration with health benefits signals problems for patient care. *Health Affairs, 2*, 202–221.

Minnesota Hospital Association. *Time Out* [Physician peer-peer DVD]. Retrieved from http://www.mnhospitals.org/Portals/0/documents/ptsafety/site/time-out-guide.doc

Myhren H., Ekeberg, O., & Stokland, O. (2013). Job satisfaction and burnout among intensive care unit nurses and physicians. *Critical Care Research and Practice, 2013*, 1–6.

O'Callaghan, C. (2009). Objectivist and constructivist music therapy research in oncology and palliative care: An overview and reflection. *Music and Medicine, 1*(1), 41–60.

Popkin, K., Levin, T., Lichtenthal, W. G., Redl, N., Roghstein, H. D., Siegel, D., & Coyle, N. (2011). A pilot music therapy-centered grief intervention for nurses and ancillary staff working in cancer settings. *Music and Medicine, 3*(1), 40–46.

Potter, P., Deshields, T., & Rodriguez, S. (2013). Developing a systemic program for compassion fatigue. *Nursing Administration Quarterly, 37*(4), 326–332.

Repar, P. A., & Patton, D. (2007, July/August). Stress reduction for nurses through Arts-in-Medicine at the University of New Mexico hospitals. *Holistic Nursing Practices,* 182–186.

RN turnover costs hospitals an estimated $9.75 billion annually [Blog post]. (2010). *INSPIRE by Alter+Care.* Retrieved from www.altergroup.com/alter-care-blog/index.php/healthcare/rn-turnover-costs/

Romani, M., & Askar, K. (2014). Burnout among physicians. *Libyan Journal of Medicine, 9*, 23556. Retrieved from http://www.libyanjournalofmedicine.net/index.php/ljm/article/view/23556

Sherman, D. W. (2004). Nurses' stress and burnout. *The American Journal of Nursing, 104*(5), 48–57.

Showalter, S. E. (2010). Compassion fatigue: What is it? Why does it matter? *American Journal of Hospice & Palliative Medicine, 27*(4), 239–242.

Stangierski, A., Warmuz-Stangierska, I., Ruchała, M., Zdanowska, J., Głowacka, M. D., Sowiński, J., & Ruchała, P. (2012). Medical errors – not only patients' problem. *Archives of Medical Science, 8*(3), 569–574.

Stichler J. F. (2009). Healthy, healthful, and healing environments: A nursing perspective. *Critical Care Nursing Quarterly, 32*(3), 176–188.

18

PREPARING THE MIND AND LEARNING TO SEE

Art museums as training grounds for medical students and residents

Lisa Abia-Smith

The work of an art museum educator is to forge connections between an object and the visitor in order to find meaning and create engagement. The process of helping the viewer to see is a collaborative process and it often elicits discussion, debate, and new perspectives about what a person sees after further investigation of art. Whether within a museum gallery or an undergraduate studio course, a formal training in art is really a training in observation. Art students are taught how to look carefully and how to interpret works by scanning and discussing visual images to find meaning. Similarly, the most successful doctors are those who are well-versed in perception and hold superior observation skills. Both practices rely upon interpreting nonverbal and visual cues to draw conclusions, and the two fields, art and medicine, are not mutually exclusive. Gaining skills in observation and critical thinking start at an early age as children when we try to make sense of the world around us. We use our visual skills to make meaning and decode ideas and problems.

As the K–12 education system in the United States currently faces another education reform such as adopting Common Core Curriculum Standards, there is a heavy focus on providing students with experiences where they can achieve "21st Century Learning Skills" (Azzam, 2009). Part of these 21st Century Learning Skills include "the Learning and Innovation Skills," known as the 4Cs: critical thinking, communication, collaboration, and creativity (Trilling & Fadel, 2009, p. 176). In order to succeed in the rigors of a university and be ready to compete in the workforce, skills in synthesizing data, drawing conclusions, and collaborating on ideas are essential for success. These skills also apply to the practice of medicine. The arts are perfectly positioned to integrate with clinical training by providing medical students with these skills. The outcome of such efforts among physicians is improved reasoning and observation skills, and also enhanced interpersonal skills to improve patient relations (Yenawine, 2013).

How can the arts strengthen the medical profession?

Exposure to the arts beginning at an early age, including visiting art museums and participation on field trips, contributes to the development of visual literacy, communication skills, critical thinking, and flexible thinking. A study conducted in 2011 investigated the impact of guided art inquiry sessions using Visual Thinking Strategies questions at the Crystal Bridges Museum in Arkansas with students from rural and high-poverty schools. Outcomes such as critical thinking, empathy, and tolerance were measured after students viewed the works of art. As depicted in Figure 18.1, the results illustrated an increase in observing, interpreting, evaluating, associating, problem finding, comparing, and flexible thinking, particularly for students from rural communities (Green, Kisda, & Bowen, 2014).

Skill sets in critical thinking, empathy, and tolerance are not only important for child development; indeed, they are also considered important skill sets for successful physicians. At the same time as K–12 education is being reformed to develop these twenty-first century skills, medical schools across the country are also encountering systematic change and reevaluating levels and standards of care and restructuring medical school preparation. In 2010, the Carnegie Foundation for the Advancement of Teaching published *Educating Physicians: A Call for Reform of Medical School and Residency*. The 2010 report called for medical education reform, emphasizing the need to develop a holistic structure that takes into account a community of innovative teaching. The primary message of the report

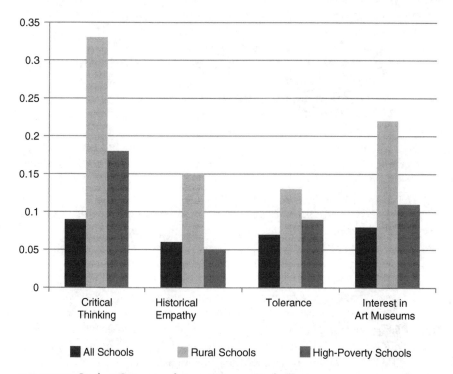

FIGURE 18.1 Student Outcomes from a Museum Study Tour

was that a new vision was needed to drive medical education to the next level of excellence. "The future demands new approaches to shaping the minds, hands and hearts of physicians" (Cooke, Irby, & O'Brien, 2010, p. 15). The authors called for a much-needed dialogue to strengthen medical education and, ultimately, provide better patient care. The report concludes with the recommendation that medical school personnel "drive medical education to a new field of excellence" (p. 15).

This report challenged medical schools to choose whether to "continue in the direction established over a hundred years ago or take a fundamentally different course, guided by contemporary innovation and new understanding about how people learn" (Cooke et al., 2010, p. 221). One of the areas addressed in the study was to "offer elective programs to support the development of skills for inquiry and improvement" (p. 221). This call to action has been embraced by medical schools across the globe, and significant reform underway includes the use of humanities, art museums, and art education strategies to improve the profession.

During the past decade, at least three studies have been conducted throughout the United States examining the impact that the arts has on honing physicians' observation skills and improving communication skills. Each study concluded that medical students who participated in a formal training (workshops and classes) for as few as ten hours demonstrated better visual diagnostic skills when viewing photographs of dermatological lesions than students who only received conventional training. The workshops included a range of lessons, including drawing live models, group discussions around a painting in a museum, focused observation exercises with authentic works of art on display in museum and gallery settings, and didactics that integrate fine arts concepts with physical diagnosis topics (Braverman et al., 2001). These studies clearly demonstrate the impact arts-based workshops have on training and improving skills in observation, listening, critical thinking, and empathy for patients. The next section presents two well-developed educational approaches that embody these ideas.

Visual thinking strategies

One of the most effective techniques used in museum-based courses for medical students and staff is a method called Visual Thinking Strategies (VTS). Museum educators have been using this method since its inception in the 1990s as a teaching approach proven to improve critical thinking, visual literacy, and communication skills. VTS is an inquiry-based method of looking at art that was developed by cognitive psychologist Abigail Housen and museum educator Philip Yenawine (2013). Housen's research on aesthetic development started in the 1970s and followed Piaget's assessment that perception and cognition develop in stages and that each stage is characterized by a discrete bundle of strategies (Kennedy, Fisher, & Ennis, 1991). VTS aims to improve critical thinking and reasoning skills through the process of investigating works of art. Housen tried to determine how these stages also applied to aesthetic thought and how it develops. Housen and Yenawine (2004) began to test this approach with school children visiting the Museum of Modern Art in New York, where Yenawine was the director of education. At that time, Yenawine was facing questions by his museum board members and funders asking how the process of looking at art was benefiting the K–12 students who were participating in museum tours. The two embarked on creating the curriculum that has now expanded to over 175 schools throughout the US, as well as in 11 other countries. Housen's studies of the use of VTS over the past two decades documents growth in aesthetic thinking, and that other cognitive operations such as speculation, observation, and reasoning on the basis of evidence also develop in a relatively short time (DeSantis & Housen, 1996). These skills have been documented as transferring from art viewing to examining other phenomena, as well as to reading and writing (Yenawine, 2013).

VTS is successful because it provides an arena for investigating works of art and interpreting them to find meaning. It is not a traditional approach to looking at art, wherein a facilitator provides facts and figures about the object and lectures about content. VTS is a conversation-based approach that also requires the viewer to justify what he or she sees and back up theories with reason and evidence. VTS provides a series of questions and prompts the viewer to clearly state their reasons for their interpretation. By using the prompts, students are asked to think carefully about what they see in carefully selected works of art, describe what is happening, and then document their statements with evidence from the image or artifact. The teacher's role is one of facilitator (see the facilitator script chart provided in Figure 18.2) – asking key open-ended questions, acknowledging student responses, paraphrasing their answers, pointing to parts of an image being referred to, probing student input to encourage more in-depth visual analysis, and making connections across responses to surface commonalities and differences in students' interpretations.

Using a carefully chosen representation of paintings and photographs, VTS focuses on developing visual literacy through open-ended questions such as, "What do we see in this picture?" The most effective works of art when using VTS are those that have a strong narrative or story. Paintings and drawings that are rich in detail and have images of people present opportunities for viewers to discuss, theorize, and find meaning. When using VTS, at first it is best to avoid abstract images until viewers become comfortable with the looking process.

Visual Thinking Strategies (VTS) Sequence Model:

1) Take 60–90 seconds to look at each work of art in silence.
2) The facilitator always starts with the question "What do you see?"
3) Paraphrase the viewer's response.
4) Then ask "What do you see that makes you say that?" (Ask your viewer to describe their observation.)
5) Repeat what the viewer says.
6) Follow up with the question "What more can we find?"

FIGURE 18.2 Visual Thinking Strategies (VTS) Sequence Model

Pointing and paraphrasing, the facilitator seeks evidence by asking: "What do you see that makes you say that?" Participants learn that multiple perspectives, respectful listening, and collaboration lead to broader understandings. The method creates an environment where using unobtrusive strategies enables the viewer to speak freely, candidly, and naturally when viewing a work of art, with minimal influence from the facilitator.

The method is so effective that twenty medical schools across the US and Ireland use some form of VTS in the training of medical students. The formula consistently engages medical students in critical observation of art and encourages them to find evidence-based meaning for themselves. VTS is proven to teach the skills of observation, critical thinking, and language development when used over a period of time (personal communication with Philip Yenawine, April 5, 2014).

Museums Uniting with Schools in Education (MUSE)

Howard Gardner, although known for his research on Multiple Intelligences (1983), developed another visual arts inquiry approach used in museums called MUSE: Museums Uniting with Schools in Education. Over a three-year period, a selection of museum educators, K–12 teachers, administrators, and curators representing eleven countries collaborated to develop specific education strategies to enhance the art education of young children (Davis, 1996). The collaborators explored the potential of art museums to serve as integral elements of education, with the aim of turning the focus of teaching art away from the subject or theme toward the learner. The program, which was developed to accommodate a range of intelligences defined by Howard Gardner, came up with five entry points that children could engage to explore a work of art: Aesthetic (What colors do you see?); Narratives (What stories are going on in this picture?); Logical/Linear (What lines and shapes do you see?); Foundational (Is this art?); and Experiential (Could you turn this sculpture into another form of art?) (Davis, 1996).

Although MUSE was originally intended for use in museums and K–12 settings, one medical school faculty member has found a way to apply MUSE to teaching medical students when assessing patients. Dr. Tony Ryan is a Consultant Neonatologist at the Department of Neonatology, Cork University Maternity Hospital, and a Professor in Pediatrics and Child Health at University College Cork, Ireland. He uses two art strategies (VTS and MUSE) in his professional practice, and these two strategies are also the basis for teaching medical students and residents on his floor. The strengths of MUSE's approaches transcends the traditional K–12 audience for which it was intended and provides training for medical students to improve their clinician skills. The three foci of MUSE when investigating a work of art are: 1) Inquiry: posing open-ended questions without right or wrong answers; 2) Access: appealing to a wide range of learners; and 3) Reflection: providing opportunities for thinking about one's own thinking (Davis, 1996).

Application of VTS, MUSE, and inquiry-based techniques in medical education

The expansion of VTS and MUSE to medical schools is further supported by Owen Slozberg, former executive director of a nonprofit research group that expanded the VTS curriculum nationwide. Slozberg (2008) believes VTS helps hone the skills doctors need to carefully assess symptoms while considering different hypotheses. He is currently the program director at Commonweal in Bolinas, California, and still uses VTS when presenting on ideas ranging from social justice to global climate change. Because VTS prompts students to back up their suppositions with evidence, he attests to the alignment with patient examination. "By doing so, there is a translation to enhancing diagnostic skills" (Owen Slozberg, personal communication, March 23, 2014).

The VTS and MUSE approaches have also been supported by a number of studies conducted by the University of Texas San Antonio, Yale, and Cornell's Weill School of Medicine. Each of these studies investigated the direct relationship engagement in the arts has on strengthening skills in medical students and physicians, focusing on skills such as diagnostic skills, doctor-patient relationships, coordination in surgery, interpersonal skills, and patient satisfaction. For a study conducted by faculty at Harvard Medical and Dental School, in 2004–2005, Katz selected 24 pre-clinical first- and second-year medical students to determine how, if at all, looking at works of art made an impact on visual acuity and observation skills. Students enrolled in a course titled, "Training the Eye: Improving the Art of Physical Diagnosis," attended class sessions held at the Isabella Stewart Gardner Museum and Boston Museum of Fine Arts. After ten weeks of course participation, the study revealed the direct correlation between VTS and improved observation skills (Naghshineh et al., 2008). In this study, researchers compared twenty-four Harvard medical and dental students who took a course offered with the Boston Museum of Fine Arts and thirty-four peers who did not. During a visual-skills exam, the VTS students on average made 18.3 accurate observations compared with an average of 13.3 in the other group. Evidence that the training improves clinical judgment was encouraging.

Similar studies have followed, and all have validated the value that visual arts experiences have on preparing medical professionals. One such study, called Art Rounds, was conducted at the University of Texas Health Science Center San Antonio (Klugman, Peel, & Beckmann-Mendez, 2011). The Art Rounds program uses VTS to teach visual observation skills to medical and nursing students. The goal of this study was to assess whether medical students' participation with VTS could improve skills such as observation, "increase tolerance for ambiguity, and increase interest in learning communication skills" (Klugman et al., 2011, p. 1). During this study, thirty-two medical students participated in three sessions for an hour and a half where they observed and interpreted three works of art. The small groups of medical students were led by art museum educators and focused on interpreting works of art to find meaning. Assessment measures, such as pre- and post-workshop evaluations measuring the quality and quantity of the medical students' responses and the Communication Skills Attitude Scale Statistical analyses, compared pre- and post-test time looking at images, number of words used to describe images, and number of observations made according to gender and discipline. The results supported the contention that training in appreciating art is a valuable and transferable skill that can be learned by medical students. The study found that "the students significantly increased the amount of time they spent looking at art and patient images . . . , the number of words they used to describe art, . . . and the number of observations made of art and patient images." The study also found that "students significantly increased their tolerance for ambiguity and positive views toward healthcare professional communication skills" (Klugman et al., 2011, p. 1266). The authors of this study concluded that these improved observation skills may help with patient care and assist with building collaborative medical team relationships and group dynamics. The results of these studies have inspired dozens of medical school–art museum partnerships, which recognize and build on the value that the visual arts contribute to improving medical education. Visual arts-based training can create better doctors, both in terms of expertise in diagnosing ability, and also in communicating with patients.

Alexa Miller, founder of a medical education consultancy titled ArtsPractica, provides further support for these findings. Her firm's mission is committed to improving healthcare quality, reducing misdiagnosis, and increasing arts engagement in medical training. Miller's organization provides education and training for medical professionals in how to use the arts to create better communication and observation skills. VTS is the educational strategy used by Miller and her staff. In an interview with the author, Miller offered insight into the design of a course she offers medical students at Harvard University. She noted that in the Harvard class, one of the most important things medical students find helpful is to put the lessons learned in the museum into practice in the clinic. After engaging in looking sessions held at the museums, medical students go on rounds with the primary purpose of learning to observe patients. Students examine everything from a rash on a leg to chipped fingernail polish, or pictures of the patient's family on their hospital room wall. Miller has found that exercises such as this are imperative to helping the students develop their observation skills. She commented that medical students are trained to become obsessed with numbers and words as sources of information, and that they often neglect what is most visible and in front of them. The VTS process assists with developing "looking skills" and discussion to retrieve information.

After participating in a ninety-minute webinar on VTS sponsored by the American Medical School Association and led by Alexa Miller (2014), medical students commented on the benefits of just one session of engaging in VTS. Two of the students stated that the VTS process taught them to slow down and look further at a work of art, and that they learned they could apply that same contemplative process to examining a patient. During one investigation of a painting, a student commented that she knew the arts had a place in healing and coping with illness, but she hadn't considered how engagement in the practice of art could make her a better physician until now.

Miller uses her experience as an artist and museum educator to train medical professionals through inquiry-based discussions with visual art. She finds that medical professionals are trained to live in a world of clarity – eschewing ambiguity – and that the process of looking at a painting without any prior knowledge and discussing what the viewer sees can contribute to enhanced comfort with ambiguity and, resultingly, skills needed to be a better doctor (Miller, Grohe, Khoshbin, & Katz, 2013). Because ambiguity implies not having the right answer, or correct diagnosis, the process of interpreting works of art assists in learning to feel comfortable in an ambiguous situation, and the capacity to adjust one's ideas to find a new solution or nuance.

In 2014, Miller was invited by Dr. Neal Fleisher, Clinical Associate Professor in the Department of General Dentistry and Director of Pre-doctoral Periodontology, and Dr. Judith Jones, Professor and Chair in the Department of General Dentistry, both at Harvard, to lead a professional development workshop for Harvard Medical and Dental School. After the sessions, Fleisher noted, "At a time when the world and clinics are going at breakneck pace, the Visual Thinking Strategy approach uses art to train students and faculty to slow down, take the time to make sure they connect with their patients, collect all the pertinent information about their patients and record it" (Boston University newsletter, 2014). Through the process of analyzing a work of art with no information given, medical students become comfortable with the unknown and are able to pursue new approaches and shifts in perceptions. There are over forty collaborative programs between art museums and medical schools across the United States and in Ireland, six of which are highlighted in the next section of this chapter.

Medical school and art museum collaboration program examples

Yale University program

Dr. Irwin Braverman (2000) began the first documented arts integration program for medical students in the US. His workshop, is still taught today at Yale's Center for British Art with co-founder Linda Friedlaender, curator of education at the museum. His preliminary hypothesis, which has now been proven through studies such as Harvard's, was that engagement in the arts and visual arts interpretation would enhance medical students' observation skills. Braverman refers to the art as "surrogates for the patients" during these workshops. Museum educators assist Braverman and Friedlaender in selecting art works that have a strong narrative and story in order to foster a rich dialogue for the medical students. Yale's program became mandatory for first-year students after a 2001 study showed that scores on observation tests increased by nine percent among students who participated in the one-day session in the Yale Center for

British Art Museum in front of authentic works of art (Linda Friedlaender, personal communication, July 2014).

Rather than a traditional art museum tour, where visitors are lectured to and receive information about a work of art, these workshops focus on a facilitation process. Students provide a visual inventory by scanning a painting or photograph and following a set of guided questions. The process involves teamwork, providing a climate where students communicate together about an issue or aspect observed in the work of art. Friedlaender describes this approach as a way to "slow down the students." Their training encourages them "to arrive with a diagnosis immediately and find the right answer." Indeed, Friedlaender refers to this integration of visual arts training for medical students and professionals as a "museum intervention" (personal communication, July 2, 2014). Yale's program will soon expand in response to a restructuring and rethinking of pedagogy at the Yale Medical School. Because medical students are trained to come to a diagnosis as quickly as possible, this process of slowing down and pausing to reflect upon a work of art conditions them to take the time for that same reflection when scanning an MRI or conducting a visual intake of a patient.

Friedlaender, a museum educator, and the medical staff at Yale are not concerned with teaching the medical students aesthetic development. The time spent in the art museum looking at works of art is purely about the process of looking at a work of art to enhance observation skills. When describing her workshop for medical students, she stated that their workshop has an "interdisciplinary approach to decrease silo effects on campus and contribute to a more holistic education for medical students." The workshops at the Yale Center for British Art use a contemplative approach to slow down the students' urge to jump to a quick conclusion. "By taking students to the art museum to look at paintings that none of them have encountered, they are all at the same starting point" (Linda Friedlaender, personal communication, July 2014).

Although the workshops at Yale are not viewed explicitly as using VTS teaching methods, the formula is similar. Medical students are asked to conduct a visual inventory of a work describing details about what they see. Rather than pointing out facts and figures about a piece, medical students are asked to come up with hypotheses and theories about what they see and then discuss, as a group, reasons for their statements. This process can take up to ten–twelve minutes, as all students in the group are asked to provide insight about what wasn't mentioned. After spending time in the galleries, the students participate in a follow-up activity where they are given a photograph of a skin lesion. In this exercise, the obvious elements are quickly discussed, and the medical students are prompted to see things that were previously unnoticed. Dr. Braverman tells his students "to recognize signs and symptoms that we have taught you about, but take it further and find signs we haven't taught" (personal communication, July 2014). In summary, the art-based training at Yale University's Medical School represents the notion that art can be used as a surrogate for patients to develop foundational skills in visual examination and acuity.

University of Michigan Program

The Medical Arts Program at the University of Michigan (UM) offers an extensive and multidisciplinary program for medical students. An average of eight performing and visual arts programs are offered each year, including visits by performing artists. Each event draws attendance from thirty-five medical students. Past program examples include a performance of the opera *Einstein on the Beach* followed by a workshop, discussion, and dinner with a member of the Phillip Glass Ensemble, and integrated workshops with students from the MFA in Creative Writing program. UM also offers a program called *Patient-Centered Experience*, where first- and second-year medical students take a required two-year course focused on the arts, with a culminating exhibition or performance at the end of the course. UM's Medical Arts Program provides medical students with experiences where they can "better understand their own vulnerability and values and to be open and more comfortable discussing this with others" (Elaine Sims, personal communication, December 2014). In addition, these events have served as a catalyst for innovative thinking. They have stimulated cross-campus interactions and have helped to break down the artificial barriers that all too often separate the world of healthcare from the rest of the university in general, and the world of arts in particular. In addition they have raised awareness of the importance of the arts for healthcare, and of the importance of healthcare for scholarship throughout the university (Elaine Sims, personal communication, December 2014).

Weill Cornell Medical College Program

In 2001, medical faculty at Weill Cornell Medical College partnered with the museum staff from the Frick Collection, a private museum in New York City, and studied the impact of looking and analyzing paintings, specifically portraits, on medical students' observation skills. "Courses in physical diagnosis teach the students to recognize normal and abnormal findings . . . but do not emphasize the actual skill of careful looking in itself. Looking is often assumed" (Bardes, Gillers, & Herman, 2001, p. 1157). Courses such as those offered at Harvard and Yale give students the training to look and see beyond what is visible at first glance.

University of Washington School of Medicine Program

Dr. Andrea Kalus is the medical director of the UW Medical Dermatology Clinic in Seattle; she teaches a course for preclinical medical students using VTS at the Henry Art Gallery on campus. She cites being raised by a mother who was an art historian as a factor in how she has embraced works of art as part of her teaching at UW Medical School. Kalus collaborates with a museum educator from the Henry Art Gallery and has been teaching the course *Visual Thinking: How to Observe in Depth* for medical students since 2008. The course takes place over one term and uses contemporary and modern art on display in the museum for the weekly discussion and inquiry sessions. Since teaching this course, Kalus has witnessed the benefits of engagement with the visual arts as they translate to better observation skills, empathy, interpretation, critical thinking, and the ability to hone listening and communication skills (personal communication, August 13, 2014).

College of Medicine and Health Program, University College, Cork, Ireland

Dr. Tony Ryan integrates the use of VTS and MUSE to teach medical students in the Neonatal Intensive Care Unit (NICU). After using VTS and MUSE in his own practice, Ryan sought to enhance visual literacy and critical thinking in his students and "guide them into the multidisciplinary NICU community of practice, based on the theories of Multiple Intelligences, Situated Learning and the Cognitive Apprenticeship" (Tony Ryan, personal communication, June 23, 2014). Ryan takes his residents through the NICU and has them take a visual inventory with a slow, deliberative, reflective manner. Ryan uses the VTS questions and the MUSE five entry points and focuses the questions on patients just as he would do with a work of art. He uses the entry points and applies them to observations in the hospital.

Columbia University Program

The Program in Narrative Medicine at Columbia University's College of Physicians and Surgeons began a series of seminars in 2005 for first-year students using art to broaden their clinical experiences and deepen their insight into the practice of medicine. Their Arts in Medicine Project expanded the Narrative Medicine Seminars into the use of the visual arts, adding three museum-based courses and a life drawing class. Each of the museum classes (situated at the Museum of Modern Art, the Metropolitan Museum of Art, and the Frick Collection) is taught by a museum educator, and each class focuses on improving observation and communication skills.

Additional medical schools using art museums for courses and workshops can be found across the country. A listing of fourteen major medical school/art museum collaborations is provided in Table 18.1 below.

TABLE 18.1 Selection of Medical School/Art Museum and Gallery Collaboration

University	Medical School	Program/Museum
Boston University Boston, MA	Boston University School of Medicine	Museum Fine Arts, Boston
Cork University Cork, Ireland	University College Cork School of Medicine	MUSE/VTS with medical students of Dr. Tony Ryan, Professor in Pediatrics & Child Health, Department of Neonatology, Cork University Maternity Hospital

(Continued)

TABLE 18.1 (Continued)

University	Medical School	Program/Museum
Cornell University New York, NY	Weill Cornell Medical College	Frick Collection
Harvard University Boston, MA	Harvard Medical School Harvard School of Dental Medicine	Isabella Stewart Gardner Museum
Rutgers University Rutgers, NJ	Robert Wood Johnson Medical School	"Art and the Body Course" taught by faculty in Art History, Genetics, and English Departments
Stanford University Palo Alto, CA	Stanford University School of Medicine	The Arts, Medicine and Humanities Program and the Iris & B. Gerald Cantor Center for Visual Arts
University of Chicago Chicago, IL	Pritzker School of Medicine	Art and Medicine: Using Art to Explore the Practice of Medicine
University of Miami Coral Gables, FL	Miller School of Medicine	Lowe Art Museum
University of Michigan Detroit, MI	University of Michigan Medical School	The Art of Observation: Enhancing Clinical Skills Through Analysis
University of Minnesota Minnesota, MN	University of Minnesota Medical School	Minneapolis Institute of Arts
University of Southern California Los Angeles, CA	Keck School of Medicine	LA Museum of Contemporary Art
University of Texas San Antonio San Antonio, TX	University of Texas Health Science Center	Art Rounds
University of Washington Seattle, WA	University of Washington School of Medicine	Henry Art Gallery, "Visual Thinking: How to Observe in Depth"
Yale University New Haven, CT	Yale School of Medicine	Yale Center for British Art

Art museums as laboratories

Art museums, particularly academic art museums, have a mission to use their collection to teach across disciplines and educate beyond art history and natural alliances. Museums in the twenty-first century are more responsive to their audiences and are more than organizations that collect and preserve objects.

Many museums in the United States were founded with a purpose of educating their visitors through object-based learning opportunities. The responsiveness to community was embraced early in the twentieth century when John Cotton Dana, (1999/1935) founder of the Newark Museum and museum historian wrote, "Museums need to find what aid the community needed and find ways to accommodate those needs and find solutions" (p. 28). His philosophy resonates today, and the recent republishing of his early writings echoes the shift in museums to focus on relevance to the visitor and helping visitors make meaning out of objects.

According to Stephen Weil, noted legal expert in the arts and a museum administrator long associated with the Smithsonian Institution, museums "use their very special competencies in dealing with objects to improve the quality of individual human lives and to enhance the well-being of human communities" (Weil, 1999, p. 231). In his chapter titled "From Being about Something to Being for Somebody," Weil discusses the shift in museums to expand their teaching mission beyond traditional audiences such as patrons. Weil and Dana contend that museums should find ways to connect their collections and exhibitions for not only teaching about culture, but for using the objects to transform meaning and create dialogues.

These dialogues sometimes stem from museums using their collections and exhibitions to aid in memory and reminiscence. Museums such at the Frye Museum in Seattle, the Museum of Modern Art in New York (MOMA), and the Minneapolis Institute of Arts (MIA) each have education programs for adults with dementia and Alzheimer's disease that use inquiry-based techniques such as VTS to recover memories. These museums also occasionally use medical students to provide tours and conversations with patients. The MIA's "Discover Your Story" program provides tours for small groups of visitors who have been diagnosed with early- to mid-stage Alzheimer's and related dementias. Specially trained docents and medical students lead conversation-based tours of the collection to facilitate conversations about works of art on display and connections to personal life stories.

Programs at the Jordan Schnitzer Museum of Art at the University of Oregon, for which the author of this chapter serves as Director of Education, include VTS workshops for children who have been diagnosed on the spectrum of autism. For these children, who have trouble expressing themselves verbally, the museum workshops utilizing VTS have been instrumental in assisting them with finding a language that communicates their ideas clearly. Undergraduate students in special education work alongside occupational therapists during the facilitation to learn how art production is used for therapeutic improvement and social integration. For the past two years, the museum has expanded its Arts and Health outreach program to local healthcare sites, such as Holly Residential, an assisted living center for patients who have experienced traumatic brain or spinal injuries. Each week the museum education staff and trained undergraduate students from the university lead art workshops and inquiry-based lessons for patients to assist with mobility, improving fine and gross motor skills, and creative expression.

Summary

Training medical students to become excellent doctors includes helping them to develop skills to elicit useful information from a patient and to understand how "to translate nonverbal information into actionable data" (Christenson, 2011). Before medical students become physicians, it is essential that they master a cadre of clinical skills in addition to an increasingly complex knowledge base. The programs highlighted in this chapter draw upon the resources of authentic works of art and provide students with encounters that build toward honing observation skills. The process of spending time contemplating a painting, analyzing what is happening, and then providing a visual inventory with detail assists medical students with the skills necessary to be successful in patient care.

Visual literacy and programs such as VTS and MUSE are effective in building these physicians' skill sets because they expand medical students' and medical personnel's observation skills, thus leading to better diagnostic capabilities. Medical educators and physicians such as Dr. Tony Ryan have found that these two interpretive programs can also help doctors connect to their patients on a deeper level. By improving observation and inspection skills, medical staff can play an integral role in delivering accurate medical assessment and evaluation. These programs combine systematic observation exercises in investigating works of art with inquiry-based discussions. The techniques link artistic concepts to physical examination skills that lead to increases in frequency of participants' observations and sophistication of responses on a structured post-course evaluation.

Through the VTS and inquiry-based approaches, medical students have learned to be more patient, listen actively, paraphrase, reflect, and appraise diagnostic connections and possibilities based upon observation, and to ask others for their interpretation of the evidence presented. Physicians such as Ryan contend that by using these art methods, doctors are better communicators with their patients and their caregivers. Using art museums as laboratories in training future physicians is more than a novelty. The impact is significant not only in refining observation, reasoning, and communication skills for medical students, but also in providing them with the training of not jumping to conclusions quickly or making interpretations before careful observation. As illustrated in this chapter, each of these programs uses the investigation of art as a catalyst for improving patient care and preparing medical students to become more observant.

Professional development resources for health practitioners

Visual Understanding through Education (VUE) offers one-day practicums for medical personnel on Visual Thinking Strategies, and organizations such as ArtsPractica and ArtMedSight provide consultancy and workshops for medical staff and students across the country.

ArtMedInsight
Anna Willieme

Director
info@artmedsighnt.org
http://artmedinsight.org/

ArtsPractica
Alexa Miller
Principal and Founder
617–903–0984
alexa@artspractica.com
artspractica.com

Visual Thinking Strategies
Yoon Kang O'Higgins
Senior VTS Trainer
718–302–0232
vtshome.org

References and further readings

Azzam, A. M. (2009, September). Why creativity now? A conversation with Sir Ken Robinson. *Education Leadership, 67*(1), 22–26.

Bardes, C., Gillers, D., & Herman, A. (2001). Learning to look: developing clinical observational skills at an art museum. *Museum Education, 35,* 1157–1161.

Boston University, Henry M. Goldman School of Dental Medicine. (2014, January 28). Faculty development program explores art and dentistry (Newsletter). Retrieved from http://www. bu.edu/dental/2014/01/28/faculty-development-program-explores-art-and-dentistry/

Braverman, I. (2001). *Jacqueline C. Dolev MD, Linda Krohner Friedlaender MS, Irwin M Braverman MD, Use of Fine Art to Enhance Diagnostic Skills. JAMA 286:* 1020–1, 2001.

Christenson, G. (2011, July). Why we need the arts in medicine. *Minnesota Medicine.* Retrieved from http://www.minnesotamedicine.com/Past-Issues/Past-Issues-2011/July-2011/ Why-We-Need-the-Arts-in-Medicine

Cooke, M., Irby, D., & O'Brien, B. (2010). *Educating physicians: A call for reform of medical school and residency.* San Francisco, CA: Jossey-Bass.

Dana, J., & Peniston, W. (1999/1935). *The new museum: Selected writings.* Newark, NJ: Newark Museum Association.

Davis, J., & Gardner, H. (1992). *The arts, education, and aesthetic knowing: Ninety-first yearbook of the National Society for the Study of Education, Part II.* Chicago, IL: University of Chicago Press.

Davis, J. (1996). *The MUSE book (Museums Uniting with Schools in Education; Building on our knowledge).* Cambridge, MA: Project Zero, Harvard Graduate School of Education Strategies.

de la Croix, A., Rose, C., Wildig, E., & Willson, S. (2011, November). Arts-based learning in medical education: the students' perspective. *Medical Education, 45*(11), 1090–1100.

Dempsey, E., McCarthy, M., & Ryan, T. (2014, June 29). Arts education programmes as catalysts for situated learning among medical students (Submitted for publication. Journal of Medical Education).

DeSantis, K., & Housen A. (1996). *A brief guide to developmental theory and aesthetic development.* Brooklyn, NY: Visual Thinking Strategies. Retrieved from http://vtshome.org/ research/articles-other-readings. Last accessed, March 3, 2015.

Duke, L., Grohe, M., Miller, A., & Williams, R. (2011). Art museums as places of learning and reflection for the medical field. *Journal of Museum Education, 36*(1).

Friedlaender, G., & Friedlaender, L. (2013). Art in science: Enhancing observational skills. *Clinical Orthopaedics and Related Research, 471*(7), 2065–2067.

Gardner, H. (1983). Frames of mind: The theory of multiple intelligences. New York: Basic Books.

Green, J., Kisda, B., & Bowen, D. (2014). The Educational Value of Field Trips. *Education Next, 14*(1). Retrieved from http://edexcellence.net/the-educational-value-of-field-trips

Housen, A. (1992). Validating a measure of aesthetic development for museums and schools. *ILVS Review, 2*(2), 215–216. Retrieved March 1, 2015.

Housen, A., & DeSantis, K. (1999). Report on the Pilot Assessment Project Thinking Through Art 1997–98. Prepared for the Museum of Fine Arts, Boston.

Kennedy, M., Fisher, M. B., & Ennis, R. H. (1991). *Critical thinking: Literature review and needed research.* Hillsdale, NJ: Lawrence Erlbaum & Associates.

Klugman, C., Peel, J., & Beckmann-Mendez, D. (2011). Art rounds: Teaching interprofessional students visual thinking strategies at one school. *Academic Medicine, 86*(10), 1266–1271.

Melwani, L. (2011). *Lassi with lavina.* Retrieved from http://www.lassiwithlavina.com/books/abraham-verghese-the-healing-touchstone/html

Miller, A., Grohe, M., Khoshbin, S., & Katz, J. (2013). From the galleries to the clinic: Applying art museum lessons to patient care. *Journal of Medical Humanities, 34,* 433–438.

Miller, A. (2014 Personal communication). Webinar participant, February 21, 2014. American Medical Student Association. Session lead by Alexa Miller, Principal, ArtsPractica. "Aesthetic Attention".

Naghshineh, S., Hafler, J. P., Miller, A. R., Blanco, M. A., Lipsitz, S., Dubroff, R., Shahram, K, & Katz, J. T. (2008, July). Formal art observation training improves medical students' visual diagnostic skills. *Journal of Internal Medicine, 23*(7), 991–997. Retrieved from: http://www.ncbi.nlm.nih.gov/pmc/articles/PMC2517949/

Rees, C., Sheard, C., & Davies, S. (2002). The development of a scale to measure medical students' attitudes towards communication skills learning: the Communication Skills Attitude Scale (CSAS). *Association for the Study of Medical Education, 36*(2), 141–147.

Song, Kyung M. (2008). *UW Uses artwork to help sharpen the visual skills of future doctors.* Kyung M. Song, Seattle Times. December 1, 2008 http://www.seattletimes.com/seattle-news/uw-uses-artwork-to-help-sharpen-visual-skills-of-future-doctors/ Retrieved October 29, 2014.

Trilling, B., & Fadel, C. (2009). *21st century skills: Learning for life in our times.* San Francisco, CA: Jossey-Bass.

Veon, R. (2004). Visual Thinking Strategies Model Education 2004. Retrieved from: http://igniteart.weebly.com/uploads/6/8/0/0/680012/aesthetic_stages_3_visual_thinking_strategies.pdf Last retrieved August 1, 2015.

Weil, S. E. (1999). Being about something to being for somebody: The ongoing transformation of the American museum. *America's Museums, 128*(3), 229–258. Retrieved from http://www.jstor.org/stable/20027573

Yenawine, P. (2013). *Visual thinking strategies: Using art to deepen learning across school disciplines.* Cambridge, MA: Harvard.

ABOUT THE EDITOR
AND CONTRIBUTORS

Patricia Dewey Lambert, Editor

Patricia Dewey Lambert, PhD, is associate professor and director of the Arts and Administration Program at the University of Oregon, where she also directs the UO Center for Community Arts and Cultural Policy. Patricia's professional experience in Europe and the United States includes positions as a professional musician, arts administrator, artist manager, foundation programs administrator, English teacher, marketing communications consultant, research fellow, and professor. Her main research areas are international cultural policy, cultural development, arts in healthcare, and arts administration education. She has published articles in *Higher Education*, the *International Journal of Arts Management*, the *International Journal of Cultural Policy*, the *Journal of Arts Management, Law, and Society*, and *Studies in Art Education*. Patricia holds a bachelor's degree in vocal performance from Indiana University, master's degrees in international business and arts management, and a PhD in arts education/arts policy and administration. Patricia currently serves as principal investigator for an interdisciplinary Arts in Healthcare Research Consortium based at the University of Oregon, and she oversees a new master's degree concentration area of study in Arts in Healthcare Management, launched in fall 2012 by the UO Arts and Administration Program. She is also currently training to become a certified therapeutic musician as a student in the International Harp Therapy Program.

Lisa Abia-Smith

Lisa Abia-Smith is the director of education at the University of Oregon's Jordan Schnitzer Museum of Art and instructor of Arts Management at the UO, teaching courses in museum education and accessible arts curriculum development. Before her hire at the UO, she was a visiting assistant professor of Art Education at SUNY Buffalo State College from 1995 to 1997, where she taught courses in art and museum education. She was hired at Buffalo State to create the nation's first concentration program in Museum Education for Special Needs for the master's degree of Art Education. She has also held positions as the Assistant Education Curator at the Jewish Museum in San Francisco, natural science teacher at the Oakland Museum of California, and was an art educator at the Rose Resnick Lighthouse for the Blind in San Francisco. Lisa has served on the Oregon Task Force developing and updating Oregon's Core Content Standards for the Arts and has served as a reviewer and contributor for the art teacher PRAXIS tests for Oregon. Lisa earned a master's degree in Museum Studies from John F. Kennedy University, a bachelor's degree in art from St. Mary's College of California, and studied art history and painting at Leo Marschutz Art School in France. She presents nationally at conferences on arts and healthcare programs, including Therapy in Education Settings, sponsored by Regional and Statewide Services for Students with Orthopedic Impairments Office of Learning/Student Services, Oregon Department of Education.

Misty Chambers

As Clinical Operations/Design Specialist with Earl Swensson Associates, Inc. (ESa), Misty Chambers serves in a healthcare planning and research capacity. She is a licensed Registered Nurse with over 30 years of experience in clinical and administrative roles, in addition to healthcare planning and design. Misty was President of the Board of Directors and a Distinguished Fellow of the Arts & Health Alliance. She is an EDAC (evidence-based design) Accredited Individual, a founding member of the Nursing Institute for Healthcare Design, and a leader in ESa's work with the Planetree Visionary Design network. Misty was named as one of the Women to Watch, Class of 2011, by Nashville Medical News, and she was an invited member of the Facility Guidelines Institute 2014 Revisions, Cost/Benefit Committee. She served as a member of the jury for the *HEALTHCAREDESIGN* Magazine/ Center for Health Design 2012 and 2013 Remodel/Renovation Showcases. She is involved in evidence-based design research, including a recently completed institutional review board-approved study. Misty is a published author and has presented at numerous conferences on healthcare planning and design-related topics, including the arts and architecture. Misty is a former member of both the Nashville Symphony Chorus and a professional hand bell ensemble. She is passionate about her role as a nurse in creating healthcare environments that support healing and incorporate the arts to have a positive impact on the wellbeing of individuals of all ages.

Randy Cohen

Randy Cohen is Vice President of Research and Policy at Americans for the Arts, the nation's advocacy organization for the arts. A member of the staff since 1991, Randy stands out as one of the most noted experts in the field of arts funding, research, policy, and using the arts to address community development issues. He published *The National Arts Index*, the annual measure of health and vitality of arts in the US, as well as the two premier economic studies of the arts industry – *Arts & Economic Prosperity*, the national impact study of nonprofit arts organizations and their audiences; and *Creative Industries*, an annual mapping study of the nation's 905,000 arts establishments and their employees. Randy led the development of the *National Arts Policy Roundtable*, an annual convening of leaders who focus on the advancement of American culture, launched in 2006 in partnership with Robert Redford and the Sundance Institute. A sought after speaker, Randy has given speeches in 49 states, and regularly appears in the news media – including the *Wall Street Journal*, *The New York Times*, and on CNN, CSPAN, CNBC, and NPR. His board work includes the Takoma Park Arts & Humanities Commission, a municipal agency he chaired for three years, and the League of Historic American Theaters.

Jane Franz

Jane Franz is an MTAI-certified music-thanatologist, involved in serving the physical, emotional, and spiritual needs of those with terminal illness, those who are dying, and their loved ones with prescriptively delivered harp and voice. She is a graduate of The Chalice of Repose Project in Missoula, Montana, and for many years served as the coordinator for Strings of Compassion, the music-thanatology practice for PeaceHealth Medical Centers and Hospices in Eugene, Springfield, Cottage Grove, and Florence, Oregon. She is also the Director of the Music-Thanatology Training Program offered through Lane Community College in Eugene, Oregon. Jane has served as the chair of the Code of Ethics Committee for the Music-Thanatology Association International since 2007. She has authored various articles and offers educational presentations for palliative caregiver populations in communities, hospitals, and hospices.

Donna Glassford

Donna Glassford's broad experience of connecting cultural arts organizations with healthcare venues and health initiatives spans over twenty-five years. She has served on the boards of Society for the Arts in Healthcare, the Nashville Arts Commission, and the Nashville Civic Design Center and produced arts in healthcare conferences in collaboration with MoMA, Sotheby's, the Society for the Arts in Healthcare and Vanderbilt University Medical Center. For fourteen years, Donna served as Executive Director of Cultural Enrichment at Vanderbilt University Medical Center, Nashville, Tennessee, where she built a world-renowned healing arts collection and oversaw programs such as exhibit galleries, therapeutic bedside art and music, the literary arts, healing gardens, and even a nurse musical. As an arts in healthcare consultant, Donna has collaborated with hospital administrators and planners, architects, and designers to ensure that art and art programming spaces are infused into the design of the building to improve healthcare environments. In 2011, Donna was awarded the honor of Distinguished Fellow by the Society for the Arts in Healthcare and was the recipient of the Nashville Arts and Business Council's Bowtie Award. An international speaker on the topic of art and health, Donna has spoken at conferences throughout the US and in England, Scotland, Australia, Lithuania, and Italy.

Gay Powell Hanna

Gay Powell Hanna, PhD, is an arts administrator, educator, and artist who has worked in the field of arts in healthcare for over twenty years. Currently, she directs the National Center for Creative Aging (NCCA), a national service organization dedicated to promoting creative engagement as vital to healthy aging. This organization is an umbrella organization to the field of the arts, aging, and health services, for which it provides a clearinghouse for information, technical assistance, and professional development across a wide spectrum of settings. Before her tenure at NCCA, Gay served as the executive director of the Society for the Arts in Healthcare (SAH), now the Global Alliance for Arts & Health. In this position, she produced the first state of the field report in partnership with the Joint Commission and Americans for the Arts, and established the first SAH national office in Washington, DC. Gay also served as the executive director of VSA Florida, an affiliate of the John F. Kennedy Center for the Performing Arts, where she developed arts in healthcare programs in partnership with the Florida Learning and Diagnostic Center at University of Florida. Gay is an associate professor in Health Science Programs at George Washington University. She has held faculty positions at Florida State University and University of South Florida. Gay is author of numerous publications, including *Art and Human Development* published by the National Endowment for the Arts. Her work is grounded in the arts; she has studied and practiced as a sculptor for over forty years.

Lynn Kable

Lynn Kable was named a Distinguished Fellow of the Society for Arts in Healthcare (SAH) in 2011. She was a founding member of the Society, representing HAI (Hospital Audiences, Inc., New York City). Lynn Kable was Director of On-Site Programs and later Program Development Director for HAI from 1976 to 1993. Lynn served on the SAH Board of Directors for twelve years, and was its President in 1995–1996. She was SAH's project director for the "Caring for Caregivers" exchange project between arts, humanities, and medical professionals and volunteers in Japan and the United States, which resulted in the SAH book, *Caring for Caregivers: A Grassroots USA-Japan Initiative*. For the SAH Consulting Service, she taught webinars on *Caring for Caregivers*; *Community Partnerships*; and *Uses of Theatre and Drama Therapy in Healthcare Settings*. She was development director for SAH's planning conference on using arts to educate people about diabetes type 2. From 1993–2002, with Seven Loaves, Inc./GOH Productions, she worked on international production and exchanges of artists, arts administrators, and arts in healthcare professionals. Lynn moved to Virginia and in 2005 founded Amherst Glebe Arts Response, Inc. (AGAR), a rural arts and humanities organization that commissions and produces theatre and music and conducts digital media and oral history projects with elders in the Amherst County African American, Monacan Tribe, and White Communities. She is active in addressing caregiver issues with Central Virginia Alliance for Community Living (the Area Agency on Aging for Greater Lynchburg) and has served as a panelist for Virginia Commission for the Arts.

Sandy LaForge

Sandy LaForge holds a master's degree in development biology from Brown University and a master's degree in counseling psychology from Antioch University. Sandy completed her training in 1994 to become a certified music-thanatologist, which was a natural next step after her work in gerontology. Sandy worked for eleven years as research and personal assistant to Therese Schroeder-Sheker, the founder of music-thanatology and the Chalice of Repose Project School of Music-Thanatology. She worked at Providence St. Patrick Hospital in Missoula, Montana, and at the Hospice of Metro-Denver in Aurora, Colorado, as a music-thanatologist. Sandy has served as secretary, member-at-large, and has also developed special projects for the professional organization of music-thanatology, Music-Thanatology Association International. She is currently writing a book about music-thanatology with her co-author, Jane Franz.

Nancy Morgan

Nancy Morgan is the former director of Arts and Humanities and currently expressive writing clinician at the Lombardi Comprehensive Cancer Center at Georgetown University Hospital in Washington, DC. As director, Nancy managed visiting artist programs for patients, family, and medical caregivers, introducing the arts as tools for enhanced coping, self-expression, and communication. As writing clinician, she leads writing workshops for individuals and groups to manage the emotional impact of cancer. She is conducting research to assess the relationship between writing and emotional and physical wellbeing and is principle investigator of the study, *Implementing an Expressive Writing Study in a Cancer Clinic*, published in *The Oncologist* (2008). Her articles are featured in publications including *Coping Magazine, The Oncology Nursing Society Newsletter, Caring for Caregivers: A Grassroots USA-Japan Initiative,* and *Radiated Voices: Poetic Response to Cancer.* Interviews have appeared in *Poets and Writers Magazine, The Washington Post, U.S. News and World Report, Oncology Issues,* and the *Gakken Nursing Magazine* of Japan. She has led workshops on writing and health and presented talks on arts in healthcare in the US and abroad. Her poetry is available in two chapbooks,

Writing from Life/Writing for Life, and *Last Lessons,* and also appears in *Radiated Voices: Poetic Response to Cancer,* by Ted Bowman.

Shanti Norris

Shanti Norris is co-founder and executive director of Smith Center for Healing and the Arts in Washington, DC. She founded the Joan Hisaoka Healing Arts Gallery and created a successful hospital-based artist-in-residence program currently serving Wounded Warriors at Walter Reed National Military Medical Center. She runs retreats for people with cancer, and co-created the Institute for Integrative Oncology Navigation at Smith Center, which offers national trainings in integrative patient navigation. She is a three-term member of CARRA, the patient advocacy program at the National Cancer Institute, and a graduate of Project LEAD from the National Breast Cancer Coalition. She is a graduate of the Georgetown University Nonprofit Leadership certificate course and the James P. Shannon Leadership Institute in Minneapolis/St. Paul. She is a former board member of the Society for the Arts in Healthcare and chaired their annual conference in 2004, and was named a Distinguished Fellow of the association in 2011. Shanti is a founding board member of The Art Connection in the Capital Region as well as Arts in Healthcare Advocates (AHA), and she is a frequent speaker on the healing power of the arts. Shanti's formal art training began at New York University and The Cooper Union in New York City and includes running the fine art studio of artist Peter Max. She is a member of ArtTable and remains an avid painter and sculptor.

Annette Ridenour

Annette Ridenour is the President and founder of Aesthetics, Inc., a thirty-five-year-old multidisciplinary healthcare design firm. The arts have always been at the center of her firm's many services, all devoted to improving the patient experience in healthcare. She has designed and facilitated visual arts, participative, and performing arts programs for hospitals throughout the United States. Annette is president emeritus of the Society for the Arts in Healthcare (Alliance for Arts in Health), and was a founding member. Annette is also a founding member of the Planetree Visionary Design Network, which promotes and provides guidelines for patient-centered design. She and her firm have received numerous awards, including the Society for Arts and Healthcare's Janice Palmer Award; the Symposium on Healthcare Design Founders award; The International Academy for Design and Health's 2012 first place award for Art in the Patient Environment; and a 2014 Generative Space Awards from The CARITAS Project. Annette is co-author of *Transforming the Healthcare Experience through the Arts,* a book that provides best practices and award-winning case studies for arts in healthcare, an overview of research and evaluation, and the business case for arts and healthcare. Annette and the work of Aesthetics have been published in numerous journals. She is a frequent lecturer on the field of arts and health both domestically and internationally.

Judy Rollins

Judy Rollins, PhD, brings over thirty years of arts and healthcare experience in research, consulting, program development, and education. She is a registered nurse with a BFA in the visual arts, an MS in child development and family studies, and a PhD in health and community studies. She holds a certificate in Evaluation Practice from George Washington University in Washington, DC. Judy has developed arts programming for patients, families, and healthcare staff in hospitals, hospice care, and the community, including military settings. She is adjunct assistant professor in the Department of Family Medicine with a secondary appointment in the Department of Pediatrics at Georgetown University School of Medicine in Washington, DC. She consults, writes, and researches on healthcare issues nationally and internationally, with a special interest in arts-informed research. Author of over one hundred publications, Judy is editor for *Pediatric Nursing* and North America regional editor for *Arts & Health: An International Journal for Research, Policy and Practice.* A two-time winner of the *American Journal of Nursing* book of the year award, Judy also is the recipient of the International Society of Nurses in Cancer Care Research Award, Johnson & Johnson/Society for the Arts in Healthcare Partnership to Promote Arts and Healing Award, National Science Foundation Scholarship, and The Japan Foundation Center for Global Partnership Travel Award. She was among the first group of recipients of the Society for the Arts in Healthcare's Distinguished Fellow awards.

Elaine Sims

Elaine Sims is director of the University of Michigan Health System Gifts of Art Program. Recognized as a best practices model program by the National Endowment of the Arts, Gifts of Art brings the worlds of art and music to the University of Michigan Health System. Known as a pioneer in the field, Sims began working in the field of arts and health in 1990. Her areas of expertise include the visual and performing arts, healing gardens, caring for the caregiver initiatives, as well as a full spectrum of arts in healthcare offerings. These include art cart programs, bedside music, bedside art, storytelling and writing programs, medical school arts curriculum, and running a full medical center orchestra. Gifts of Art is one of the first and most comprehensive arts in healthcare programs in the country. It is one of the founding members of the Global Alliance for Arts & Health (formerly the Society for the Arts in Healthcare), and Elaine is a past president of the Global Alliance, and has been recognized as a Distinguished Fellow as well as a recipient of the Janice Palmer Award for her contributions to the field. She consults on behalf of the Global Alliance and has helped launch successful programs across the country. Sims is currently president of the board of The Arts in Healthcare Certification Commission (AIHCC). She was a charter member of the Commission for Art in Public Places in Ann Arbor, Michigan. As an "accidental artist," Elaine's work has appeared in the *New Yorker* magazine and museums around the world such as the State Tretyakov Gallery in Moscow.

Jana Kay Slater

Jana Kay Slater, PhD, is a research psychologist and independent program evaluator in Corvallis, Oregon, with more than thirty years' experience developing and evaluating arts, educational, and health programs. She was founding director of the Samaritan Health Services Center for Health Research and Quality (now Samaritan Research Institute), where she continues to consult, providing leadership and research support to Samaritan's Arts and Health Initiative. Jana Kay has served as an elected member of the Board to the American Evaluation Association. She was co-editor of *Advances in Survey Research* (1996, Jossey-Bass) and *Foundations and Evaluation: Contexts and Practices for Effective Philanthropy* (2004, John Wiley & Sons).

Jill Sonke

Jill Sonke is director of the Center for the Arts in Medicine at the University of Florida (UF) and assistant director of Shands Arts in Medicine at UF Health Shands Hospital. She serves on the faculty of the University of Florida Center for Arts in Medicine, and as an affiliated faculty member in the School of Theatre & Dance, the Center for African Studies, and the Center for Movement Disorders and Neurorestoration. With over twenty years of experience and leadership in arts in medicine, Jill is active in research, curriculum and program development, and international cultural exchange. Her current research focuses on dance and Parkinson's disease, use of the arts in public health and health messaging, and the effects of live preferential music on quality and cost of care in emergency medicine. Jill is the recipient of a New Forms Florida Fellowship Award, an Individual Artist Fellowship Award from the State of Florida, an Excellence in Teaching Award from the National Institute for Staff and Organizational Development, a UF Internationalizing the Curriculum Award, a UF Most Outstanding Service Learning Faculty Award, and over one hundred grant awards for her programs and research at the University of Florida.

Katie White

Katie White, DMA, recently completed a doctoral degree in Viola Performance from the University of Oregon with a supporting area in Arts Administration and a Graduate Certificate in Nonprofit Management. She earned performance degrees from Baylor University in Waco, Texas, and has performed internationally with chamber and orchestral ensembles such as the Waco Symphony, Baylor Chamber Orchestra, Opera of the Ozarks, Oregon Mozart Players, and the Eugene Symphony. She serves as the Development and Communications Director for the

Corvallis Youth Symphony Association in Corvallis, Oregon, is a member of the University of Oregon Arts in Healthcare Research Consortium, and performs and teaches throughout the Willamette Valley area. Her research interests include mapping the arts in healthcare field and creating community engagement training for classical musicians.

Naj Wikoff

Naj Wikoff, president emeritus of the Society for the Arts in Healthcare, has been a leading advocate for and pioneer in the field of arts and health for over thirty years. This former director of the Healing Arts Program of the C. Everett Koop Institute at the Dartmouth Medical School and director of Arts and Productions at the Cathedral St. John the Divine in New York City is a founding member of the National Initiative for the Arts in Health in the Military and Lesley University's Institute for Arts and Health. In 1999, Naj established Creative Healing Connections, which uses the arts and nature to support the healing of women living with cancer, military spouses, and veteran and active duty servicewomen living with PTSD and Military Sexual Trauma. The two-time Fulbright Senior Scholar regularly consults on arts and health and arts and trauma issues to health and arts institutions, and has worked with victims of war and terror in Palestine and Israel. Since 2006, Naj, as arts coordinator for Connecting Youth and Community, has been using the arts to reduce the use of tobacco, alcohol, and other drugs by teens.

INDEX

Page numbers in italic format indicate figures and tables.